Praise for *The Quiet Before*

"*The Quiet Before* is a splendid and singular history—great storytelling, elegant prose, spanning centuries but extremely timely, connecting dots in fresh and illuminating ways, surprising in its twists and turns, inspiring without trying too hard to inspire."

—KURT ANDERSEN, author of *Evil Geniuses*

"*The Quiet Before* is that rare book: arresting in its premise, supported by historical examples, and relevant to right now. Beckerman takes a close look at the media that led to the 'changed minds' of past revolutions, then challenges us to approach today's media with new eyes. How can we make it serve our urgent human purposes—among these the rethinking of human equality and the possibility of democracy? I loved it."

—SHERRY TURKLE, author of *The Empathy Diaries*

"All the myriad events fashioned by humans to create the world's history—be they wars or revolutions, artistic movements or responses to pandemics—have their points of origin in discussions, in discourses, in polemics, in simple statements nailed to church doors, in furtive comments uttered in basement bars, or in realizations made while waiting for traffic lights to change. In this wonderfully original and captivating book, Gal Beckerman reminds us that while natural events are so often announced with an unanticipated bang, human-made happenstances can more commonly trace their beginnings to little more than a cascade of gentle whispers."

—SIMON WINCHESTER, author of *The Professor and the Madman*

"Gal Beckerman's engrossing book only masquerades as a study of media and social change. It's really a series of irresistibly readable nonfiction novellas about unwitting revolutionaries who used new communications technologies to remake the world."

—JUDITH SHULEVITZ, author of *The Sabbath World*

"Nothing is more powerful than an idea whose time has come, but how do ideas ever get to the point where their time has come? Ideas have to be conceived, improved, and accepted by people, and we know little about how this happens. *The Quiet Before* is a fascinating and important exploration of how ideas that change the world incubate and spread."

—STEVEN PINKER, author of *Rationality*

"How does true social change occur? In this brilliant book filled with insightful analysis and colorful storytelling, Gal Beckerman shows that new ideas need to incubate through thoughtful discussions in order to create sustained movements. Today's social media hothouses, unfortunately, tend to produce flash mobs that flame out. We need to regain intimate forms of communication if we want to nurture real transformation. Rarely does a book give you a new way of looking at social change. This one does."

—WALTER ISAACSON, author of *The Code Breaker*

"In this penetrating feat of the intellect, Gal Beckerman explains the long and complicated relationship between the envisioning of new principles and the realization of such principles in the form of social transformation. Deploying a stunningly diverse set of narratives, he builds up evidence that the process is long and slow and nuanced. We tend to vest our admiration for—or dismay about—the work of activists who turn ideas into actions, but, in fact, it is those who conceive those ideas and those who gradually disseminate them who may be the greatest heroes. This book should be read by anyone interested in thinking."

—ANDREW SOLOMON, author of *Far from the Tree*

By Gal Beckerman

When They Come for Us, We'll Be Gone

The Quiet Before

The QUIET Before

The QUIET Before

On the Unexpected Origins
of Radical Ideas

Gal Beckerman

CROWN
NEW YORK

Published in the United States by Crown,
an imprint of Random House, a division of
Penguin Random House LLC, New York.

CROWN and the Crown colophon are registered trademarks of
Penguin Random House LLC.

Grateful acknowledgment is made to Alfred A. Knopf and Harold Ober Associates
for permission to reprint an excerpt of "Azikiwe in Jail" from *The Collected Poems
of Langston Hughes* by Langston Hughes, edited by Arnold Rampersad with
David Roessel, Associate Editor. Copyright © 1951 and 1994 by the
Estate of Langston Hughes. Reprinted by permission of Alfred A. Knopf,
an imprint of the Knopf Doubleday Publishing Group, a division of
Penguin Random House LLC and Harold Ober Associates.
All rights reserved.

Library of Congress Cataloging-in-Publication Data
Names: Beckerman, Gal, author.
Title: The quiet before / Gal Beckerman.
Description: First edition. | New York: Crown, [2022] |
Includes bibliographical references and index.
Identifiers: LCCN 2021044410 (print) | LCCN 2021044411 (ebook) |
ISBN 9781524759186 (hardcover) | ISBN 9781524759209 (ebook)
Subjects: LCSH: Protest movements. | Social change. | Civil society.
Classification: LCC HM883 .B43 2022 (print) | LCC HM883 (ebook) |
DDC 303.48/4—dc23/eng/20211102
LC record available at https://lccn.loc.gov/2021044410
LC ebook record available at https://lccn.loc.gov/2021044411

Printed in the United States of America on acid-free paper

crownpublishing.com

2 4 6 8 9 7 5 3 1

First Edition

Book design by Edwin Vazquez

To Debbie—

if not for you . . .

Whether we are experiencing the world through the lens of speech or the printed word or the television camera, our media-metaphors classify the world for us, sequence it, frame it, enlarge it, reduce it, color it, argue a case for what the world is like.

—Neil Postman

You can't just keep on yelling.

—Barack Obama

Contents

The QUIET Before

Introduction

_____

CHANGE—THE KIND THAT topples social norms and up-
roots orthodoxies—happens slowly at first. People don't just cut off the
king's head. For years and even decades they gossip about him, imagine him naked and ridiculous, demote him from deity to fallible mortal (with a head, which can be cut). This is true for revolutions of all
sorts. Slavery exists. And then a small group of people begin worrying
among themselves about the moral blight of humans owning other
humans, weighing what might be done. Their talking transforms them
into a group with a purpose, abolition, and discussion eventually bub-
bles up into action and then into the changing of minds and, eventually, laws.

   We are gripped by the moment when the crowd coalesces on the
street—the adrenaline, the tear gas, the deafening chants, a policeman
on horseback chasing down a lone protester or a man standing up to a
tank. But if we rewind to the instant when a solid block of shared reality is first cracked, it's usually a group of people talking. To be more
specific (and to reclaim a word that Silicon Valley has turned into
meaningless jargon), they are incubating. And the incubation of radical new ideas is a very distinct process with certain conditions: a tight

space, lots of heat, passionate whispering, and a degree of freedom to argue and work toward a common, focused aim.

Saul Alinsky, the community organizer whose *Rules for Radicals* became a bible for activists, wrote that successful revolutions follow the three-act structure of a play. "The first act introduces the characters and the plot, in the second act the plot and characters are developed as the play strives to hold the audience's attention. In the final act good and evil have their dramatic confrontation and resolution." The problem with the generation of revolutionaries that Alinsky was observing from his perch at the end of the 1960s was that they were impatient. They rushed to the third act, desiring the "revelation" that comes from good defeating evil. But this shortcut was not actually a shortcut; it was "confrontation for confrontation's sake—a flare-up and back to darkness."

It's in those first two acts where incubation occurs. Without the conjuring, the planning, the debating, the convincing, Alinsky knew, you might have a fantastic protest that leaves you slack-jawed but empty-handed.

Where does this kind of incubation happen today? Could it be on social media? On sites like Twitter and Facebook where a hashtag gone viral is still seen to possess subversive potential?

In our personal lives, we've become aware, mostly, that the platforms are good for some things and not for others. They are hyperactive. They are social in the way a loud cocktail party is, where you flit from conversation to conversation, drawn for a few minutes to someone's crazy story or funny joke, but leave drained by the end of the evening. These are spaces built, first, to make a profit. About this, we are no longer naïve. And as hosts of our conversations, the companies who created them have privileged a certain kind of talk and limited the potential of other kinds. This is by design. And though we still see these tools as a means for connection, we know—intuitively, at this point—what forms of expression attract the likes and thumbs-ups that are the dopamine reward for taking part. We need to produce the content that triggers big feelings (and "trigger" is the word): outrage, sadness, disgust.

If social media has made us distractible, dragging us through end-less streams of photos and bombastic comments, the implications for social movements shouldn't be too hard to grasp. From the Arab Spring uprising that began in 2010 to #MeToo at the end of the decade, movements that were made on social media also shaped themselves to fit the form of these amplifiers—full-throated blasts of information meant to grab attention and emotionally satisfy but hardly built to last. Our digital conversations often feel like they are happening through megaphones—a performance devoid of any true intimacy. Our move-ments, those crucibles of radical change, now have this same quality.

In the weeks after Donald Trump's inauguration, I found myself at protests nearly every weekend. Those were days when everyone I knew felt they wanted to *do* something, to channel the shock of his win—it wasn't even full-on indignation yet, just shock—into some kind of civic action. I've never been one for demonstrations, but I was out there with my wife and daughters (who made their own signs; one said in dripping red paint, "Love Not Hate Makes America Great"). It was good to be with other people, marching through midtown Manhattan. But it also occurred to me, in a moment of cynicism or clarity, that everyone around me was incessantly posing for their camera phones. I did it too; the photos were of course meant to be shared online. I didn't go to any more protests after those first few weeks, but the images of my daughters and their signs still live on Facebook. I had experienced Alinsky's third act.

For all the power social media has lent to movements, allowing them to mobilize with tremendous speed and unprecedented scale—getting everyone to the square or midtown Manhattan in a matter of hours—it has also stunted them. The paradox, as Zeynep Tufekci de-scribed it in her book, *Twitter and Tear Gas,* is that the megaphone can bring "a full-blown moment of attention" to activists "when they have little or no shared history of facing challenges together." The hard work of hammering out ideology and organizational structure, the building of a strong identity and the setting of goals, all of it can be leaped over, creating movements with all the depth and solidity of a raised-fist emoji.

What ends up getting lost—because a Twitter or Facebook really has no room for it—is incubation.

It's not that it can't happen on the internet. Donald Trump's election was proof, in part, of the successful brewing of the white supremacist and misogynist underworld of the alt-right. Their views were too toxic for the mainstream, so they created their own self-enclosed universes or were forced into them, first on sites like Reddit that preserved the old intense chat room structure of the early internet and then on 4chan or 8chan or more obscure platforms like Gab. They kept jumping into deeper holes where, among themselves, they could egg one another on, entertain conspiracy theories, argue about the best way to bring their perspectives to a wider public, try out memes, and vie for leadership. Many of the story lines that were nurtured there—about invasions across borders, nefarious forces controlling wealth and the media, grievances about the emasculating effects of feminism—would eventually find their way into the culture through the president's mouth.

This was incubation by necessity, when ideas are so noxious that we push them out of sight and then worry about how they might be fermenting unobserved. We've seen it with child pornography on the Dark Web and ISIS recruiting efforts, and these are the sorts of examples that jump to mind when we consider closed spaces these days. This is a shame, because in associating these secluded corners only with what is most destructive and abhorrent, we ignore their value, especially for those pro-social forces who badly need such places.

Consider Black Lives Matter, by all accounts one of the most successful movements of the past ten years. It started as a hashtag, literally, in 2013, and was followed by booms and busts—its visibility peaking after brutal (and often videotaped) instances of police violence, as it did, fiercely, in 2020.

Social media allowed activists to introduce and then reinforce for an enormous audience a narrative—the shockingly obvious one that the humanity of Black people should be taken seriously. The potential of a medium that yields such virality, that can set an agenda, cannot be overstated. It made inescapable the parts of our collective story that had been shunted away. In that summer of 2020, it was a fever, a good one, and it led people to demonstrate en masse, to put up lawn signs with the hashtag, to think and talk about race. Some symbols thought inviolable, like the stars and bars of the Confederate flag, came to be regarded as vile, almost instantaneously, by many more Americans. And then the summer ended.

There is narrative, and then there is the slow gathering of power. And Black Lives Matter activists themselves came to sense how social media hindered the latter. Where could they work out their common goals? Where could they formulate strategy and move from emotion to ideology (which in this movement spanned reform to revolution)? Where could they build to policy wins, organize to elect sympathetic lawmakers, or target protests to achieve specific, local, even wonky ends? Where could they meet for that harder task of reconfiguring and rearranging the structures that undergirded those torn-down symbols?

My first encounter with incubation came while I was researching the dissidents of the Soviet Union. Like the alt-right—and yet, of course, so unlike them—they were forced to create their own, more private spaces for communicating with one another. The state literally controlled all the means of publication, even down to registering every typewriter so a keystroke could be traced back to its owner. Samizdat was their solution. Composed on onionskin paper (sometimes up to ten or fifteen sheets typed at the same time) and passed from hand to hand, this became the dissidents' way of building and maintaining opposition to a totalitarian state. They wrote about what they were witnessing, compiling lists of human and civil rights violations. They produced essays about what they should do and then other essays countering those points. Writing from the West was translated and circulated as well. The network formed and strengthened around this writing. It was dangerous to produce—getting caught with samizdat could frequently get you sent somewhere far to the east—but this only increased the dissidents' level of commitment.

Out of samizdat they constructed a shadow civil society for debating and freethinking when their repressive environment made these activities impossible. For decades this continued. And when the Soviet

Union finally collapsed, an event precipitated by the country's unsustainable economic system more than anything else, an alternative idea of citizenship already existed, incubated, expressing a set of values that would soon become the norm (at least until a new authoritarianism arrived in the 2000s with Vladimir Putin). Samizdat and the ideals it kept stewing beneath the surface made it difficult for Soviet leaders, once their country was imploding, to let their people starve or run them over with tanks—the dissidents' vision was there, preserved, and could not be easily crushed.

At the archives, whenever I touched the nearly translucent sheets of paper, felt their fragility, and stared at the matter-of-fact black type, I was struck by the efficacy of samizdat. It demanded concentration. The high risk involved in creating it meant you had to think carefully about what you wanted to say. It also allowed for an exchange. The pages themselves contained multiple voices, multiple back-and-forths, all within the borders of their greater project. Samizdat produced a private world for the dissidents. No one could enter unless they had been handed a copy. This gave them the freedom to make mistakes, try out new concepts, and fantasize about a new, more humane order. And they controlled these pages. No one else dictated the form of samizdat or limited its content. If someone had a provocative poem about Brezhnev that they wanted to disseminate or an essay about the possible upsides of capitalism, they only had to find paper and a typewriter (usually on the black market), and the network would pick it up and spread their contribution.

The medium we use for conversation molds the kinds of conversations we can have, and even sets the boundaries of our thinking. This was Marshall McLuhan's great insight: the transition from oral to written to electronic culture brought along a shift in the way human beings processed reality, and it changed them. In the 1980s, Neil Postman, in his *Amusing Ourselves to Death*, picked up the baton from McLuhan and turned his ire on television, which he felt was adversely affecting the public discourse. "Its form excludes the content," was his way of phrasing it; in other words, a medium was a container that could hold certain kinds of thoughts and not others. For him the visual immediacy of television excluded rational argument, which print had done such a good job facilitating. What he would have made of something like TikTok, we can only guess.

When it comes to social media, what is excluded and what is elevated? If we approach these now ubiquitous modes of communication with this question, it becomes evident that they are not great for allowing radical ideas to stick, to slowly cohere. And the stakes are high. Even though we now raise an eyebrow when the Silicon Valley titans say their platforms exist to "change the world," we've stopped thinking of any other means through which the world can be changed. The platforms dominate. We mistakenly believe they are the equivalent of eighteenth-century coffeehouses (where democracy, fueled by caffeine and newspapers, was indeed incubated). But they are not good for that most essential first step in the process of making change; they only allow ideas to flare and return to darkness.

The history of revolutions is long, though, and full of other possibilities. How should we think about samizdat and all the other communal ways of interacting through writing that allowed oppositional opinions and identities to form—the lengthy underground stream, existing at least from the invention of movable type to the AOL chat room? What about letters and petitions and manifestos and small newspapers and zines? The great books by great men and women overshadow these subterranean outlets, but they stand just on the other side of our blurry memory of all that came before the internet, still there and still visible for the moment, an alternative way of understanding what it means for a medium to bring people together.

This book emerged out of an impulse to reclaim this untapped resource and see if it offered lessons for our frazzled twenty-first-century selves. "The marvels of communication technology in the present have produced a false consciousness about the past," wrote Robert Darnton, the Harvard historian, "a sense that communication has no history, or had nothing of importance to consider before the days of television and the Internet." Darnton himself has spent much of his career understanding how the French Revolution was incubated. In one book, he looked at how scraps of poetry deriding the monarch—passed hand to hand and pocket to pocket among students, clergymen, and clerks—helped bring about the vast changing of minds that led to the upheaval.

I wanted to return to such moments of inception, to the birth of the scientific revolution or the stirrings of anticolonialism or the genesis of third-wave feminism, and seek out the media that set up that first act. These stories may seem familiar on one level—known perhaps for their world-altering outcomes—but each contains an insight about what helps radical ideas come into being. We will bear down on this element in these histories, zoom in on the inkpot sitting on the writing desk of a seventeenth-century aristocrat, the steam drifting up from a printing press in 1930s Accra, the scissors and glue stick in a teenage girl's bedroom in the 1990s. The stories are particular, but layered on top of each other, they become a sort of palimpsest through which, peeking out, we can see patterns, and even something like truths, about what allowed the most threatening, liberating concepts to grow.

These pre-digital forms of communication demanded patience. Because they took time to produce and time to transmit from one person to another, they slowed things down, favoring an incremental accumulation of knowledge and connection. They also lent coherence, a way for scattered ideologies and feelings to be shaped into a single compellingly new perspective. Those who joined such conversations, ones that were deliberate and perhaps more labor-intensive to produce, gained a firmer sense of identity and solidarity, which in turn freed them up to imagine how they might order the world differently. Along with imagining came arguing, refining, and moving toward shared objectives. These were media that provided focus—that permitted people to take their dissatisfaction with a current set of rules and conventions and whittle it down into a spearhead. And, maybe most important, the activists and dissidents and thinkers who used these tools were in control of them. They created the platforms—and by creating them, they could set their parameters and make sure they served their ends.

Onto these histories, I'll add more layers from our very recent past, from the movements we've seen with our own eyes or scrolled past online, of young Egyptian revolutionaries and torch-wielding white supremacists. A medium that moves fast, reaching across vast networks, privileging the public and the performative, taking in constant and varied flows of information, and stringing us through emotional highs and lows, will always be good for spreading ideas quickly and widely. But the contrast with forms of communication that refine and actually allow for the emergence of those ideas will, I think, appear quite stark. Things should look different after we've walked all the way from the seventeenth century.

Once we're equipped with the knowledge of what *is* needed, the next question, naturally, is how we find it today within the confines of our online lives. There is no switching out the internet. But we can better appreciate those digital containers we use and acknowledge what they exclude. And where we do come upon the intense heat of incubation, we shouldn't assume it serves only dark purposes. History, as we'll see, tells us otherwise. Those first and second acts, in the quiet when revolutions are only impassioned conversations among the aggrieved and dreaming, are also where progressive change begins. We need to discover or create anew the stages on which those acts can unfold. Otherwise we risk a future in which the possibility of new realities, of alternative ways to live together in society, will remain just beyond our grasp.

Chapter 1

PATIENCE

———

Aɪx-ᴇɴ-Pʀᴏᴠᴇɴᴄᴇ, 1635

IT IS FOUR in the morning and the moon is full. Along with a
steady rain, a yellowish light falls on a handful of bustling men standing on the rooftop of an aristocrat's house, measuring and recording.
A local priest and a bookbinder are among them, taking turns looking
up at the night sky through a long brass telescope, while another group
is frantically working the lever of an enormous quadrant, gauging the
altitude of various stars. In one corner, a paragon of calm, sits an artist
with his sketchbook and charcoal, drawing the moon as a shadow begins to smudge it. The eclipse is finally starting.

The conductor of all this activity is late, but he's slowly making his
way up a stepladder, groaning. His stomach is burning, as it always
seems to be, and his eyesight is so poor he can see only a few feet in
front of him. Yet he refuses help. This is Nicolas-Claude Fabri de
Peiresc, master of this house, natural philosopher, and, most important, a connector of Europe's greatest minds. In this instant, he is also
a sickly old man who has been waiting for the past two decades for
this very moment.

He can't really enjoy it, though. Peiresc is not someone to relish a
realized dream. He is all self-discipline, even down to his food and

clothes. He never wears silk. If he drinks wine, it is white and heavily watered down. The only food he allows himself in excess are melons, and even these he argues have health benefits. He is filled with doubt about this ambitious experiment. It involves dozens of amateur participants, hundreds of miles apart, simultaneously observing a celestial phenomenon and accurately recording what they see. He has enlisted each one himself, corresponding with them over months, moving them past their apprehensions and insecurities, convincing them of the importance of their larger purpose: to collect data that, when gathered, will offer a correct measure of longitude. If it works, they'll be redrawing the map of the known world.

But failure seems likely, even to him. The proof comes through his spyglass. Peiresc had instructed three local men to climb a nearby hill outside Aix-en-Provence to log the night's events. They were to signal their arrival by lighting a fire. As the eclipse progresses, he looks over and sees not even the slightest flicker in the distance.

His mind goes to all the other observers. There is Father Michelange de Nantes on a rocky summit in Syria; a diplomat, François Galaup de Chasteuil, in Lebanon; another missionary, Agathange de Vendôme, in Egypt; Thomas d'Arcos, a former captive of Barbary pirates turned Muslim convert, in Tunis; and on the Continent, an array of scholarly friends in Italy, France, Germany, and the Netherlands. A Jesuit priest in Quebec is even taking part. What if they too fail to show up?

Later that morning in his overstuffed study, layered in crimson rugs and somber oil paintings, Peiresc turns to the activity that sustains him, even in dark moments: he writes a letter. As often in his solitary life, quill, ink, paper, and some quiet allow him to reenter an ongoing exchange with his dozens of friends, many of whom he has never met and will never meet in person. He enumerates his reasons for anxiety to Pierre Gassendi, the scholar-priest who is one of his main collaborators. The night was too cloudy. His team was not ready. Because of their "haste," his group on the roof had even "looked at the wrong side of the quadrant to take the numbers." And as for the men on the hill, he has since learned what happened: "The rain came, and frightened by thunder and lightning, they retreated to a hermitage without having the courage or inclination to return to indicate at least the setting of the moon." The venting continues, he dips his quill and scratches the words onto yellowed paper. "All the preparation was in vain."

THE PRINTING PRESS, not even two hundred years old then, is seen today as the revolutionary medium of Peiresc's era. The ability to reproduce pamphlets and books made it possible for a dissident priest like Martin Luther to broadcast his opinions and quickly gain a following, each printed text a whisper into the ear of a potential convert. But the post offered a quieter revolution. For hundreds of years, letters were an advanced technology. They were the first instance of thought traveling distance, disassociated bodily from thinker. But from Cicero until the early modern period, they moved from one place to another so slowly and so erratically that they often read more like alternating speeches than the volley of a conversation. This changed in Peiresc's time once the post became fast and relatively reliable. The possibility of regular correspondence now allowed for collaboration, for theories to be shared and disputed. For the slow accretion of knowledge that comes from the friction of two people trading ideas and observations.

For Peiresc, letters were units of intellectual exchange. Sitting in his study like a contented spider in the middle of an expansive web, he wrote and dictated about ten a day. They were also his only legacy, which is part of the reason his name is lost to us. He published no books, but when he died, two years after the eclipse, he left behind 100,000 pieces of paper in the form of dispatches, memoranda, and reading notes, which represented his life's work.

These were thoughts in process. Letters were good for teasing out concepts, which made them especially valuable to a man who spent his life testing established dogma. The seventeenth century was not a time to do that in one giant leap—not unless you wanted to end up like Giordano Bruno. Only three decades before, the Italian Dominican friar had been stripped, tied to a stake, and burned alive on the Campo de' Fiori in Rome for suggesting that our planet might not occupy the center of the universe. Others could take these risks, blast trumpets if they wanted. That wasn't Peiresc's approach. His ego wasn't immune to the desire to have a book to his name, and he had plans for many. But mostly out of caution, and also because he was so restless, letters became his mastered form.

This eclipse experiment, though elegant in his own mind, stretched the power of letters to its limit. He was attempting a group observation among scattered correspondents who had never so much as bothered to wonder about the moon before, or even what longitude meant. Peiresc had spent hundreds of hours writing to them—countless pages of instructions, sent along with diagrams and crude measuring instruments. He believed that the mechanics of the natural world would be grasped cumulatively, over generations, a process of verification and correction and further verification. "The brevity of human life does not allow that one person alone is sufficient; it is necessary to adopt the observations of a good number of others from the past centuries and future ones to clarify that which fits better," he once wrote. But still, when it came to the most far-flung of his collaborators, geographically and intellectually, it was an agonizing task just coaxing them to practice proper notation, let alone to trust the authority of their own eyes.

THE ECLIPSE ITSELF was not the point. It was only a marker of time—a giant clock in the sky, visible from everywhere. But Peiresc hoped this clock would help him complete at last one of his many, many lifelong projects, a partial list of which included an investigation of ancient weights and measures, a study of the Roman calendar of 354 (whose oldest surviving copy he had in his study), a catalog of gemstones that he and the Flemish painter Peter Paul Rubens had been compiling together, the publication of all the Samaritan versions of the Pentateuch in Hebrew, Aramaic, and Arabic, and an exhaustive history of Provence. But it was the longitude project that was perhaps his most idiosyncratic endeavor. For one thing, it was ambitious; there was no way he could do it alone. But also, his obsession with longitude had a particularly practical purpose: to calculate the length and width of the Mediterranean Sea.

He loved that body of water and anything to do with the people and cultures that encircled it. No detail was uninteresting to him. On the rare occasions when he left Aix, it was to visit the port of Marseille. There he would take in the salt air and all the humanity marching down the wooden docks. He was as curious about the customs of the Muslims, Samaritans, and Eastern Christians as he was about the ancient Greeks. He once heard the singing of galley slaves on a docked ship, and he found a musician to help him transcribe the tune into musical notation so he could capture the song of the "black Moor." But for Peiresc and everyone else, the sea's exact dimensions had remained elusive. For generations, sailors had been poorly navigating from the Strait of Gibraltar around the Cyclades and to the coast of the Ottoman Empire with little more than an inherited familiarity with the coastline, an astrolabe, and fifteen-hundred-year-old drawings.

For accuracy, longitude was needed, but calculating it had evaded astronomers and cartographers for so long that in 1598 Philip III of Spain even offered a perpetual pension to anyone who could figure it out. The problem was logistical. Though latitude could be gauged by measuring the height of the noonday sun, longitude required simultaneous observation—people in at least two different locations watching some fixed phenomenon in the sky and marking precisely when they had each seen it. The difference in time, Peiresc explained in one letter, "was equal to the difference in longitude."

Peiresc first imagined such an orchestra of observation in 1610 when he was thirty and had just finished reading Galileo Galilei's sensational *Sidereus nuncius,* in which the astronomer detailed his telescopic discoveries, including his sighting of the four moons of Jupiter. The book offered concrete proof that other forces were at work in the universe and that Earth might not be so central; after all, the moons orbited around Jupiter with little regard for us. Peiresc was as astonished as the rest of Europe's intellectual class, but what caught his attention was the usefulness of these distant moons. He began to record and chart their revolutions every night on homemade graph paper until he was able to predict their movements (the satellites, he soon wrote, were "exactly where our calculations placed them in completing their orbits"). The moons could serve as the celestial clock he needed for his longitude project. He hurriedly sent out his young assistant on a voyage across the Mediterranean, from Marseille to the Lebanese coastal town of Tripoli, stopping at the islands of Malta and Cyprus. In each location, he was to observe Jupiter and its moons, and Peiresc would do the same in Aix. In theory, comparing their data would give them the exact longitudinal location of each of his assistant's stops. But this first attempt failed miserably. Telescopes were then too new and imprecise to capture the necessary detail. That, and the young man was none too pleased to be on this trip. In his very first letter from "overseas," he wrote to Peiresc, "If God graces me to return to our house, the sea will never again have me as its subject."

A quarter century had passed, and Peiresc still dreamed of calculating longitude by having many people stare up at the sky at once on the same night. But over time he had switched to Earth's moon as a more visible reference point—and the notion of observing the phases of an eclipse through a telescope. Now, at fifty-five, he was finally in a position to make such a collective experiment happen.

Born to a family of magistrates and minor landowners in southeast France, Peiresc had spent his life collecting correspondents. First as a law student and in his travels to England, the Netherlands, and Italy (where he met Galileo after a mathematics lecture in Padua), and then even after he returned to Aix-en-Provence to take up a position in the parliament of Provence, he never stopped expanding his web of connections. He had linked up and become, over time, a leading citizen of the self-proclaimed Republic of Letters, the network of dozens and dozens of university scholars, learned aristocrats, and clergy spread throughout Europe. Together, they were exploring the era's newfound mysteries—astronomical, microscopic, and geographic.

The Republic was a collaborative venture that resembled the editorial board of a scientific journal (before such publications, and the notion of science as we know it, really existed) and was maintained through a patchwork of letters. The correspondents wrote to one another about their various tinkerings, floated theories, and sealed relationships by sharing fossils or anatomical drawings. Certain qualities of what would come to characterize the scientific community first took shape through these missives. It was "a laboratory in which ideas about civility were elaborated and lived," wrote Peter Miller, one of the few academics who has studied Peiresc's letters. And each individual letter, as another historian described it, was "a substitute for gentlemanly conversation," which enabled the writer "to produce intimacy and immediacy at a distance, without alienating the correspondent with argument." The letter writers embarked together on a project of seeking objective truth, and they acted as clearinghouses for one another, checking theories and exchanging information. The letter as a conveyor of voice, calibrated to express politeness and friendship, proved a particularly useful form for this joint research. And Peiresc always got the tone right. He was charming and generous, and he evinced a genuine curiosity about the discoveries of others.

A Republic of Letters had existed in some form since the Renaissance, a revival of a classical concept that originated with Cicero. But it really took off during the Reformation and the resulting religious wars that convulsed Europe from 1500 to 1700. Travel during these conflicts became dangerous for scholars. And with most universities co-opted by one warring sect or another, the Republic became a secular institution of learning, above the fray. Peiresc and others treated it almost like a cult, excited by the sense that they were producing knowledge in a kind of relay and passing it from one generation to the next. As René Descartes, the French philosopher and contemporary of Peiresc's, wrote, "With the later persons beginning where the earlier ones left off, and thereby linking the lives and the work of many people, we can all go forward together much further than each person individually would be able to do."

A glimpse into Peiresc's study in Aix would show just how much energy existed in the Republic and how eclectic its interests. The letters arrived at his town house in a constant flow, often multiple times a day, with the envelopes sometimes emanating the sickly sweet smell of vinegar, a disinfectant against the plague. Collect, observe, and compare. This was the ethic that guided the practice of the Republic's members, many of whom, like Peiresc, were antiquaries, possessors of cabinets of curiosities. There was the massive library of printed books, leather bound, on his shelves, loose-leaf manuscripts everywhere, next to ancient vessels and engraved gems. There were embryos preserved in jars and detailed drawings of both the real and the bizarre riches of nature—from bulbous mushrooms to hippopotamus skin. Sometimes a large object dominated his study, a mummy or an elephant's tusk. Drawers were filled with medals and coins going back through the centuries; there were seventeen thousand pieces in that collection upon his death. A quality of gift giving characterized the enterprise. At his feet and lazying about amid all this ephemera were the fluffy white-furred and blue-eyed Angora kittens that he loved to breed but was willing to part with if it meant he might add a precious piece to his cabinet ("If it were useful to promise one of the kittens in order to get the vase of Vivot, do not hesitate to commit yourself"). His interests extended outside, as well. He had vast orchards where he grew more than twenty species of citron and sixty varieties of apple. He grafted olive trees and made wine from the *malvoisie* grapes that were plentiful on his family's country estate.

Living at this moment, before scholarship developed into a specialized pursuit reserved for professionals, an amateur polymath like Peiresc went anywhere his curiosity took him—botany, zoology, numerology, and, of course, astronomy. The mechanics of everything—how a heart beat, how a flower reproduced, how a comet streaked across the sky—had to be examined. Even the fantastical: Peiresc took seriously reports of a man with a bush growing out of his stomach, a town in which every citizen claimed to be possessed by the devil, and a Frenchwoman supposedly pregnant for twenty-three months. Nor did he scoff at sightings of monstrous hydra-headed animals or giants. Why should he when news of strange and beautiful creatures like the long-necked horse known as a giraffe and the elegant, slender-limbed pink flamingo had turned out to be true? Peiresc wrote that because he had seen such marvels that he would have never previously believed, he tried "to neglect nothing until experience opens the way for us to pure truth."

This single-minded devotion to questioning the nature of everything was such that Peiresc chose consciously to have an ascetic life. When his father found him a good match for marriage, the daughter of the president of the Chambre des Comptes of Provence, Peiresc explained that he "could not care for a wife and children and be free to follow my studies and patronize learned men." He remained a bachelor his whole life.

But he was not alone in his intellectual pursuits. He wrote letters all day long (mostly in French and Italian and sometimes in Latin), and he could rely on an increasingly predictable and secure system to get them to their destinations. A letter from Aix to Paris took about a week, to Rome about two weeks, and to North Africa six weeks. And the routes were becoming more dependable, regular enough that he referred to letters to Paris as sent "par le Parisien"; the Avignon–Rome courier was simply "l'ordinaire."

These letters functioned as more than simply one-to-one communications. They were like messages carried along a stream with many tributaries—often copied and passed to readers beyond the originally intended addressee or read aloud at scholarly gatherings. This annotated excerpt from one of Peiresc's letters in 1635 shows just how far they could travel: "I opened a letter that Mr. Diodati [Paris] sent you, which included one that Mr. Schickard [Tübingen] wrote to Bernegger [printer in Strasbourg], asking him to send you his observations of the eclipse. I showed it to Gaultier [Aix] and asked Garrat [Agarrat, Peiresc's secretary] to have him [Gaultier] compare it with your observation. I used the same channel to send a second letter from Galileo, the original of which I had sent to Diodati and the copy of another letter from Galileo that Rossi [Galileo's relative in Lyons] sent."

It was to all these friends and collaborators in the Republic that Peiresc turned for help when he decided to rededicate himself to the longitude project. In early 1628 he organized a smaller recording of an eclipse—with just himself on his roof and friends in a village near Aix and in Paris—and this time the method worked. The measurements were "precise" despite, he quipped, "the barbarism and uncouthness in our poor country." Using the gathered data, he could correct the difference in longitude between Paris and Aix, which was then off by more than two degrees.

But he wanted more. His sights were still set on measuring just how far and wide the Mediterranean Sea stretched. The search was on for another lunar eclipse, and when he discovered that one would occur on the night of August 28, 1635, Peiresc got to work. To gather the observations he needed, he would reach beyond the cerebral confines of the Republic of Letters, to individuals stationed at the extreme edge of the map. Their value was their geographic location. But before he could recruit them, he would have to convince them. They would, in some cases, be taking an enormous risk.

REDRAWING A MAP might sound like a mundane cause upon which to concentrate such intense attention, but the letters tell a different story. Peiresc had to gently pull these potential observers toward a new relationship with nature, one not at all familiar or safe. Letters turned out to be quite useful in this conversion process. The medium was a conduit for slow thinking. Letters acted like oil in the gears of idea production: the throat-clearing pleasantries, the lines upon lines where a mind could wander, an informality that didn't demand definitiveness yet gave space for argument to build lightly. These were the qualities that made letters so critical to the community of protoscientists. But they also worked well for introducing a new worldview. The ruminative aspect of letters, the embedded patience of them, avoided what might otherwise feel like the locked-horn confrontation of one system of truth trying to overtake another.

Peiresc began by probing for possible participants. When two Portuguese traders in precious stones passed through Aix on their way to sail to India, he checked to see if perhaps they knew of some learned Westerner, Jew or Christian, in those foreign parts who could take measurements during an eclipse, whether lunar or solar, and send them back to him. Potential contacts were then vetted by Peiresc. Were they serious and dependable enough? Did they have the fundamental math skills to calculate distance? His letters are full of these urgent questions. When he learns, two months before the eclipse, of a new bishop named Isaac living in the foothills of Mount Lebanon, Peiresc writes to a third party to get any information he can about this interestingly situated man. He wanted to have "all the instructions you could provide concerning the age, country, good manners, and teaching of the bishop Isaac, in what place you have come to know him, and especially, of the knowledge that he might have of Arabic, Latin, and other languages. And if he has interests more curious than common, and where he obtained his title of bishop . . ."

In early 1635, Peiresc began a correspondence with Father Celestin de St. Lidwine, who was living in a Carmelite monastery in Aleppo. Peiresc's first letters are typical, giving Celestin a sense of his own interests. "If you would encounter, by chance, whether among the Greek monks or the dervishes, some book on music, a little old, not only in Greek, but in Arabic or other oriental languages, principally of those where might be preserved some notes of ancient music, I would willingly employ my money." Very soon, he is also trying to persuade Celestin to join the longitude project, promising that even one good set of observations could help yield the real distances between places and "an infinity of other great things praiseworthy in our century and to posterity." He also suggests that Celestin might involve local astronomers in the project, offering to make his own data available to them, "to give them pleasure in the comparison with ours."

But the biggest challenge before him was that educated men in these distant places were often devoutly religious. They were missionaries or solitary monks. And they were, by their very nature, resistant to such an enterprise. To interrogate the natural world on one's own—or worse, as a group—was a threat to the Catholic Church. This was especially true when it came to phenomena like comets or eclipses. The church's pared-down vision of Earth sitting immovable at the center of the universe was frequently complicated by these streaking events above one's head. Even curiosity seemed, at some level, suspect.

Though Europe had experienced the Renaissance and Reformation, both of which elevated subjectivity and individual will, this was a church that demanded deference to doctrine, with Saint Augustine's fifth-century dictum still standing: "It is not necessary to probe into the nature of things as was done by the Greeks. . . . It is enough for the Christian to believe that the only cause of all created things, whether heavenly or earthly, whether visible or invisible, is the goodness of the Creator, the one true God."

If this unease about the meddling of natural philosophy was not enough, there was also the cautionary tale of Galileo. One of the most famous men in Europe, at sixty-nine he had recently been forced to his knees before the Inquisition and made to denounce in front of ten cardinals his "errors and heresies," which he now promised to "abjure, curse, and detest" then and forevermore. His crime had been the writing of a book that argued forcefully (and in a way that seemed to mock the pope as a simpleminded idiot) that the church's static and geo-centric view of the universe was wrong. Galileo's book *Dialogue Concerning the Two Chief World Systems* was denounced and banned as blasphemous, and he was sentenced to house arrest for the remainder of his days. But the church's ire made the entire Republic of Letters shudder. Descartes, receiving the news in Protestant Holland, wrote to a friend in Paris that he might now need to "suppress" the publication of his own book *The World*, which would further elaborate on Earth's revolutions around the sun.

Peiresc had always looked to Galileo with awe and no small measure of envy, and he learned of his persecution with sadness. "Poor Galileo had to declare solemnly that he did not support the opinion that the earth moved, yet in his dialogue he used strong reasons to support it," he wrote in one letter following the verdict. But the main lesson he took away from this episode, coming after a lifetime in which both men had pursued very different paths toward the same ends, was that it was better to work incrementally and quietly. Peiresc managed to stay within the good graces of the church while also engaging with the intellectuals who questioned its most treasured precepts. If ever forced to defend himself, he could respond that he and his correspondents were simply exploring divine creation in all its manifestations. He trusted that even the church would eventually change its dogmatic approach. There were members of the Vatican hierarchy who discreetly corresponded from time to time with the natural philosophers of the Republic of Letters, covertly welcoming new discoveries even if tradition kept them from saying so openly. By pushing toward the outer limits of acceptable speculation, Galileo had exploded the old ways of thinking, and it's his name we remember today, not Peiresc's. But the patient antiquary had another approach—the hushed, discursive conversation of a letter versus the loud declaration of a book—one he thought preferable not only because it avoided certain risk but because of the collective insights it yielded, albeit "carefully and over time."

This cautious nature was on full display when Peiresc appealed to the powerful cardinal Francesco Barberini, a nephew of the pope's, to lessen Galileo's sentence. Peiresc knew that Barberini, though a pious upholder of his uncle's rule (he had personally sat in judgment of Galileo), was drawn to natural philosophy. To strengthen their bond, Peiresc would even send the cardinal the occasional rare specimen—he had once even passed along a gazelle, small and brown with sharp ribbed horns, which he himself had received from a North African correspondent who compared it to a unicorn. "Fragility is sometimes worthy of excuse and forgiveness," Peiresc pleaded in Galileo's defense. He tried to downplay the *Dialogue* as a lighthearted, almost comic, juggling of abstractions and not the clever indictment of the church that it most certainly was. When Barberini ignored his plea, Peiresc wrote again, intensifying his argument. The punishment of Galileo would one day seem as wrongheaded as what was inflicted on Socrates by Athens, "so much reproached by other nations and by the very descendants of those who caused him so much trouble." Peiresc was never anything but obsequious in his approach ("I stoop before you with the greatest submission of which I am capable," he began), but he couldn't and didn't hide that Galileo, in his eyes, was a mistreated genius. The arguments and gifts like the gazelle seemed to have an effect. The astronomer was granted his request to transfer his house arrest to Florence, and he thanked Peiresc profusely, describing his intervention as an "undertaking where so many others who recognize my innocence have remained silent."

When the men of the cloth resisted Peiresc's entreaties to join his experiment, he approached them in a similar spirit. He didn't shy away from engaging them in an exchange about Christianity and what it allowed. For him, there was little internal conflict. Natural philosophy was simply the process of uncovering more of God's glory. The church shouldn't resist these discoveries but rather expand in order to include them. It should delight in these new wonders and see in them a reason for increased faith. "The book of nature is the book of books, and there is nothing so conclusive as the observation of things," Peiresc wrote to Father Celestin in April 1635, four months before the eclipse.

He also appealed to practicality, as he did with another Capuchin missionary based in Aleppo, Michelange de Nantes. When the priest voiced theological concern, Peiresc responded that looking through a telescope would "not be injurious to your pious and charitable conquest of souls. On the contrary, this could one day serve as a lure to attract others to follow your example." He also stressed that his astronomical work could help in establishing a more accurate church calendar. For those still wary, he could point to the support of powerful cardinals who had ordered observations in Italy and the Levant and specifically directed priests and astronomers in Rome, Padua, and Naples to prepare their telescopes and abide by Peiresc's requests.

Encouraging their participation was only the first step. Peiresc still had to teach them how exactly to carry out a methodical observation. If he was going to trust their findings, he had to put some standards in place; this thinking, too, was an innovation of the age. He needed to guide them on how to hold their bodies when looking through a telescope, how to verify evidence. The lessons came in different forms. For those who passed through Aix, Peiresc was slowly setting up what would eventually be known as the École Provençale, a veritable training program for aspiring amateur astronomers. He had already built a simple observatory on his roof. Those who couldn't make it there or were already stationed abroad were sent detailed instruction manuals.

In one May 1635 letter to Father Agathange de Vendôme, who

would be viewing the eclipse from Cairo, Peiresc was quite explicit about where and how to observe: "You must try to view from above the pyramids or some other elevated site, in order to see the sun rise on the horizon, and to note the progression of the eclipse. But you should not simply trust the naked eye. You must use the telescope . . . because with the naked eye, the illuminated moon appears larger than it is in fact, and as a result, the eclipsed part smaller." Father Agathange would have to use a quadrant to take measurements of fixed stars and of the height of the sun at noon (for latitude), and it was best to do this, Peiresc wrote, the day before. The priest would need to be exacting about how he marked time, either with a well-calibrated clock or, better yet, by checking the position of the stars.

As it turned out, Agathange was not a quick study, and upon reading his disorganized report on the eclipse, Peiresc decided that he would have to better prepare him for the next one. In a letter, in which he managed to keep his annoyance just barely at bay, Peiresc wrote that he would be sending a new set of instructions.

One of Peiresc's more unusual eclipse observers was Thomas d'Arcos, a former secretary to a cardinal who had been taken captive by pirates and brought to Tunis, where he had been living as a slave for five years when Peiresc first contacted him in 1630. D'Arcos immediately attracted Peiresc's attention by describing how he had seen the bones of a giant, touched them with his own hands. Always on the lookout for curiosities, Peiresc was intrigued and wrote back offering to help gain d'Arcos's release and even involve high officials, up to the French king, if it proved necessary. By the time Peiresc's offer arrived, d'Arcos had managed to secure his own freedom, though he remained in Tunis and even converted to Islam a few years later, changing his name from Thomas to Osman.

D'Arcos would often send Peiresc mysterious material objects that were the subject of local folklore, and the natural philosopher took it as his job to demystify them. One exchange involved a strangely shaped stone that the Moors claimed contained the soul of a past emperor trapped inside. Peiresc examined it closely and wrote back that it was simply a fossilized sea urchin. D'Arcos wrote again, insisting that if the stone was washed in blood, the voice of the condemned emperor would sound. The letters usually had this dynamic: d'Arcos providing the local myths or "musings" and Peiresc searching for the verifiable. The giant, whose teeth (each weighing three and a half pounds) d'Arcos sent to Aix, turned out to be, upon Peiresc's close inspection, the remains of a long-extinct North African elephant.

Many items made their way across the Mediterranean. From d'Arcos came bejeweled dagger handles, live chameleons, and coins from ancient Carthage, and from Peiresc, barrels of wine, requests for specific Arabic books, and, eventually, thirty-five hundred words on the longitude project and how d'Arcos could participate.

Peiresc's obsession with observing the eclipse then dominated the correspondence, with a constant flow of lessons coming from Aix. Like the folklore and myth that Peiresc debunked, this was also a chance to nudge d'Arcos, a kindred if lost spirit, toward thinking like a natural philosopher. Peiresc wanted to station him in Carthage, believing the historic site would be an auspicious location. When d'Arcos failed to collect any data for an eclipse of March 3, 1635—a trial run for the August eclipse—complaining that his gout prevented him from taking part, Peiresc responded with irritation, asking that he do everything to observe the next one, which would begin "around 2:30 after midnight." Two weeks later, Peiresc wrote again, and his detailed explanation offers a hint of the type of instruction he was pressing on the other missionaries: "Since the last letter written in haste on the subject of the eclipse . . . I took it upon myself to send you in any case a small quadrant of cardboard that you can stick on a piece of wood or on stronger cardboard and raise the two sights that lay flat in order to bring them at a right angle to the plane of the instrument." And on and on he went. "Take the height of the top or bottom of the edge of the moon when you observe the beginning or progression of the eclipse."

It's exhausting to imagine the volume of words Peiresc committed to moving his collaborators along. All through the spring and summer of 1635, the letters nudged and cajoled and flattered the men. Peiresc was tutoring them not only in how to carry out a scientific experiment but in how to think differently, how to become scientists. And if, in his many modes, his ink bottle running dry, he sometimes veered toward the desperate, it was because he needed them—he simply couldn't uncover the mystery of longitude by himself.

ALL AROUND THE MEDITERRANEAN on the night of August 28, as Peiresc anxiously paced his roof, the amateur observers did their best to obey his detailed instructions. Some lacked confidence or the right equipment—Cassien de Nantes, in Cairo, had to admit that although he had tried to be meticulous, "absent the instruments, I could not notate the measurements you asked for." Some were bumbling; some lost interest.

In Aleppo there were a couple of participants. Father Celestin, the Carmelite monk, had tried to follow Peiresc's suggestion that he view the eclipse from atop Mount Casius, a small mountain on Syria's northern shore, high above any ground fog. He started gathering an expedition of a few dozen men in the weeks before the eclipse, but Peiresc grew wary of the plan, thinking it would be too expensive, "a bit too grand for me," and that Celestin and his crew might not be well received by the locals whose "jealousy and bad faith" would be dangerous to the project. "One must abstain from even the most innocent actions when they are a little outside the mainstream," the cautious Peiresc wrote about what would surely be the strange sight of monks on a mountain staring intently at the night sky. Peiresc sent a merchant friend headed to Aleppo to call off the trip. As it turned out, Celestin hadn't even received the telescope Peiresc had sent for him to use and had to view the eclipse with the naked eye. Looking at Celestin's observation notes, Peiresc despaired. Fortunately, there were two others that night in the Syrian city taking part: the Capuchin monk Michelange de Nantes and a merchant and chancellor of the French consulate, Balthasar Claret. Peiresc put a lot of faith in Claret, who had been an apothecary earlier in his life and so knew how to handle instruments and understood the value of accuracy. Claret stood on the roof of the consulate and took careful measurements that Peiresc would later find to be impressive and useful.

There was much anticipation in the months after the eclipse. Despite his misgivings, and the messages of mishaps and lost telescopes, Peiresc was still hopeful that taken together, the various observations would amount to some new discovery. But his letters are filled with anxiety, conveyed in endless questions back to his collaborators. Did they use their right or left eye? What kind of telescope? Who else was present? By November 1635 he had received most of the data from Italy and France. Early in December he wrote again to the Capuchin priests in Syria and Egypt urging them to send their observations and was frustrated when some of their notations arrived and seemed to be copied out of existing astronomical tables. Peiresc wondered to one of his collaborators how anyone could "prefer to believe what mathematicians say about longitude, latitude, and the dimensions of the stars rather than examine the truth."

By early 1636, he had begun using third parties to badger those who had still not sent all their notes to him. Some of the missionaries hesitated for fear that their work had not been exact enough. Peiresc assured them he wanted to see everything and begged them to send what they had. He dispatched a friendly merchant to Michelange de Nantes with the hope of "knocking some sense" into him, conveying that he shouldn't be inhibited by any worries about incompleteness. Peiresc hoped to see "the whole 'tissue' of his observation" because "even the faults and equivocations very often also serve." He wanted these missionaries, steeped as they were in infallible doctrines, to understand that arriving at knowledge often meant collecting broken shards.

When all the usable measurements were returned—from Rome, Egypt, Padua, Naples, Lebanon, Florence, Tunis, Paris, Holland, and Germany, among other places—Peiresc plotted these points on the existing maps of the Mediterranean and found something that he immediately declared in a letter to be "astonishing and worthy of being noted." Not only did he see how wrong was the accepted terrestrial longitude of numerous cities, but the entire eastern Mediterranean was revealed to be two hundred leagues (about seven hundred miles) shorter than had been assumed. And this made sense given the experience of sailors, who often had to deviate from their primitive maps, making adjustments to their routes based on their own knowledge of the sea and its coastline, maneuvers "for which they could never understand the cause and reason," Peiresc wrote. The new corrections had the effect of "reducing the space" of the sea, so that "there was nothing so easy to understand." It was a clearer transcription of nature.

Peiresc thrilled at how collaborative it had all been in the end, the work of serious, curious people joined together through him, the hub. And coursing through the many correspondences, in each exchange of letters, was his attempt to instill a sensibility. This mattered more to him than any specific skill. The reward of patience was the slow spreading outward of a net of common understanding. Through the letters, he was recruiting disciples to this new, and still perilous, way of testing perceptions against reality. In a way, it was this aspect of the experiment, that it was carried out by a diffuse group of missionaries and merchants, that had also most surprised sailors and cartographers. Gleefully, Peiresc wrote to d'Arcos, he was now able to explain to the "very most expert mariners of Marseille . . . and those themselves who made marine charts" why for centuries the maps used to sail the eastern Mediterranean were useless. And these men, so knowledgeable about the sea, upon hearing the way he had discovered its true shape, were "ravished and almost beside themselves."

THERE EXIST HALF A DOZEN portraits of Peiresc, drawn at different points in his life, capturing his fading vitality. But in all of them, his eyes are what overwhelm: they appear an almost solid black, pupil and iris nearly one. His lips form a straight line, his broad white collar and black skullcap, unchanging, simple, giving him the appearance of a weary monk. In the last portrait, done in charcoal by the French artist Claude Mellan on his way back from Rome in 1636, Peiresc's eyelids are even heavier, his aquiline nose points sharply down, his lips are still pursed: a tired, learned man, eager to get back to his letters. By then the many sicknesses that he had battled over the years—including terrible urinary tract problems—had taken their toll, and his bladder had almost completely disintegrated, leaving him feverish and in pain much of the time.

When he died on June 24, 1637, at the age of fifty-six, less than two years after the eclipse, it was in medias res. Almost all of his many projects were left incomplete. To others in the Republic, his death was a sudden void where there had been a flurry of activity. Tributes came from all over the Continent, from the learned community of men who had been his intellectual partners all those years, from merchants and sailors on the docks of Marseille, and from the intrepid explorers who had found a patron in Peiresc. Cardinal Barberini organized a memory book that lamented his death in all the known tongues of the world, elegiac poems in forty languages, including Quechua, Coptic, and Japanese—a "complaint of the human race."

More than anything else, those 100,000 pieces of paper that form his vast archive were his greatest contribution. They were remnants of communication, of the hours and hours he had committed every day to writing to his correspondents, collecting fragments of information, new objects, new theories, passing them along, swapping them with others, for decades. When his friend Gassendi wrote his biography, it was partly to capture the character of a man who was so influential and yet left no clear monument to himself. The book, one of the first major accounts of the life of a scholar, honored in Peiresc what he himself most valued: conversation as a conduit to knowledge.

Among the many unfinished projects left lying in his study after his death were his plans for mapping the surface of the moon. He had been trying to get an accurate rendering of the lunar landscape for more than two decades, ever since he first saw the moon through a telescope and was shocked to discover that it was as rough and misshapen as a giant boulder, not the smooth slab of marble he had always imagined. In the summer of 1636, Peiresc found the man for the job: Claude Mellan, the same French artist who would draw his portrait that year. When Mellan passed through Aix that August, Peiresc commissioned him to make copperplate engravings of the different phases of the moon, sitting with him on his roof as he looked into the telescope and sketched.

Mellan completed only three engravings based on his drawings from Aix—the moon when full, and in its first and last quarters. The images are incredibly exact for their time, capturing the pocked, glowing skin of a mysterious, unexplored world. But like so many other of Peiresc's endeavors, this project died when its patron did. The engravings were important to Peiresc, not as a prize to be captured and pinned to a wall, but as a lunar atlas of sorts, the first of its kind, a reference. With all the glorious imperfections of the moon's surface presented in detail—its craters and mountains—a group of observers could carry out their investigations with even more precision. Together with telescopes, they could use the map to track the progress of a future eclipse. And then do what they'd been taught: share with each other what they had seen.

Chapter 2

COHERENCE

———

MANCHESTER, 1839

UNSCROLLED, THE PETITION—pages upon pages pasted together and crowded with signatures—extended nearly three miles. The signers were men and women who sweated for their bread: a textile worker from Bradford, a south Wales coal miner, a group of weavers from Ashton-under-Lyne, a London cabinetmaker, an alehouse keeper. Altogether the names of 1,280,959 people were collected there. Rolled up and placed in a cylinder, the petition was enormous, almost immovable, the physical representation of a new constituency. And on June 14, 1839, when it was finally maneuvered carefully onto the floor of the House of Commons and up to the clerk's desk, it was met with laughter so resounding that the volume of the members' guffaws was set down in the House record. "That ridiculous piece of machinery," one member yelled out, pointing at the scroll and interrupting the speech by the Parliament member with the thankless job of presenting the grievances.

The laughter continued as a prayer composed by the petitioners was read out, beginning with their most radical hope: "That it might please their honorable House to take the petition into their most serious consideration, and to use their utmost endeavor to pass a law, granting to every man of lawful age, sound mind, and uncontaminated by crime, the right of voting for Members to serve in Parliament."

They were asking for universal suffrage. There was nothing new about this cry, even if the means of expressing it, essentially depositing a keg of gunpowder on the floor of the House, was shocking and unprecedented. For centuries—from the Magna Carta to Thomas Paine's impassioned defense of natural rights—British national identity was rooted in the fantasy of their island as a perfect democracy. But this was a lie; only a small upper crust had ever had access to the franchise.

That a petition capturing working-class desperation could barrel into Parliament at all was largely the result of one man's energy and ego, a man who both understood just how utterly quixotic this effort was and, nevertheless, pushed it forward with all his might. Feargus O'Connor, all Irish brogue and ginger muttonchops, was the bombastic, magnetic, loudmouthed leader of what could now be rightly called a movement. He had taken what was essentially a technicality of British law—enshrined by Edward I in the thirteenth century, allowing any subject to petition the Crown and Parliament for redress—and he had used it at a scale and toward a revolutionary purpose that was unprecedented. For a people excluded from political representation, who didn't matter to anyone in power because they had no power, this was a solitary but largely unused lever, "the only peaceable and constitutional mode," as Edmund Burke put it in 1775. Until then it had been employed mostly for small, local, and personal matters, and yet here they were, hoping this loophole would appear as menacing as a noose.

Instead, there was ridicule. The petition had given this newly self-aware working class an aim, had bound them together, turning the particles of anger that hung in the air above factory floors and in the small, dank living spaces of coal miners into something more. The act of signing their names to this document had unified them, taking their inchoate frustration, their resentment at a life of never-ending labor exacerbated by disenfranchisement, and sharpened it into a common purpose. This O'Connor could already claim as a victory. But what if this spear simply bounced off its target? He never imagined Parliament would just agree to their demands. But if they treated their efforts as nothing more than a joke, what would happen then? For all the petition had done to empower and embolden and cohere, O'Connor had also seen blood thirst in the eyes of these men and women, and he worried that if this effort—their last, best hope—failed, there would be chaos.

O'CONNOR HAD MANICALLY traveled the country making the case for signing. In the year before the petition was presented to Parliament, he gave 147 major speeches and spent 123 days on the road. Britain in the 1830s, even with its lengthening rail lines and proliferating national newspapers, was still a vast collection of atomized regions—culturally, economically, even linguistically isolated from one another. The man himself became an attraction—"brawny muscular figure, the big round shoulders, the red curly tresses overhanging the collar of his coat, the cajoling smirk, the insinuating manner, and the fluent tongue," as one of his fellow agitators described him. He was a born orator with natural charisma, scion of a family of wealthy Protestant landowners from County Cork, gentlemen radicals like his father and uncle who had suffered prison and forced exile for their embrace of Irish independence. O'Connor had trained as a lawyer and won a surprise election to the House of Commons in 1832, running on a platform of representing the unrepresented. But his tenure didn't last long. He had to leave his seat three years later when those in Parliament opposed to his radicalism successfully ousted him, claiming he didn't own the minimum amount of property to qualify as a member. Once out of Parliament, he took to the road promoting universal suffrage and other radical causes.

The push to organize a national petition was first proposed by a group of artisans and craftsmen in London, led by William Lovett, a cabinetmaker who was as coolheaded and cerebral as O'Connor was fiery and impulsive. At a mass meeting in February 1837 at the Crown and Anchor pub, Lovett presented a list of demands that, if met, would wrench away the entitled classes' monopoly on political power. In addition to universal male suffrage, they wanted to abolish the requirement that members of Parliament own property, to offer salaries for those who were elected, and to allow citizens to vote privately for their representatives. But the artisans of London were an elite among the working classes, and London too scattered a community—with four hundred different trades—to lead the cause. For this petition to live up to its ambition, it had to draw on the anger that pulsed most incessantly in the industrial north.

This is what Feargus O'Connor intuited. And he threw himself into promoting what became known as the People's Charter. He owned it, so much so that Lovett right away resented him, writing to O'Connor, "You carry your fame about with you on all occasions to sink all other topics in the shade—you are the great 'I AM' of politics, the great personification of Radicalism."

If O'Connor saw himself as "a sort of uncrowned king of the working classes," as one early historian of the movement put it, it was also because he was able to channel their frustrations. He knew their recent embittered history. Seven years before the petition, in 1832, Parliament had indeed passed a law to widen the franchise, but the promise of change raised hopes, only to quash them ("so generally popular a measure, so soon creating disgust," wrote O'Connor). The Reform Bill that passed still put heavy limitations on who was entitled to vote, keeping privilege in the hands of property owners and the landed class. In a nation of 13 million, the bill increased the electorate from around 400,000 to 653,000—still only one in six men. In Ireland the gulf was even more dramatic. Out of 7.8 million, only 90,000 could vote.

And this newly reformed Parliament, controlled by the ostensibly liberal Whig Party, continued to be blind to the realities of working people. In 1834, a new Poor Law created workhouses for the unemployed—humiliating institutions that shaved the heads of those who entered them, forcibly separated families, and then paid the lowest possible wages for manual labor. Some preferred starving to death. Trade unions came under attack, and some were branded illegal. In an infamous case, six farmworkers from Dorset were sent off to an Australian penal colony simply for swearing an oath to their local agricultural society. Any effort to lighten the lives of workers never made it past Parliament's doors. A campaign to limit the workday to ten hours equally went nowhere.

Industrialization, meanwhile, continued apace. More and more weavers found themselves displaced by mechanized looms. The bonds of family and community unraveled as women and children, in demand as cheap labor, went to work in the textile mills. In his study of Manchester from this period, Friedrich Engels, who would eventually become Karl Marx's collaborator, said he felt he was witnessing a slow form of "murder." Living conditions were abysmal. People were crammed together, "as many as a dozen workers into a single room, so that at night the air becomes so foul that they are nearly suffocated." They spent their days in damp, poorly ventilated dwellings that were themselves surrounded by piles of decaying animal carcasses and rotting vegetables. "They are goaded like wild beasts and never have a chance of enjoying a quiet life," Engels wrote. Even slaves and serfs seemed better off, he concluded. And in 1837 things got even worse when a transatlantic depression raised the price of grain and other basic goods. Increasingly, this working class had less and less to lose.

The cause grew through the late summer and into the fall of 1838, punctuated by massive gatherings. One in August in Birmingham drew 200,000 people. O'Connor was always the featured speaker and was dressed like a gentleman—dark waistcoat, cravat, and wide-brimmed top hat—but his words were aimed, as he once said, at those with "fustian jackets, blistered hands and unshorn chins." They came in droves. One meeting, in September, took over Kersal Moor, a green expanse just outside Manchester long ago trodden to a dusty brown by the weekly horse races. "By twelve o'clock," one newspaper reported, "one half of the ground was occupied, and the immense multitude even at that time presented a truly awful appearance." Vendors sold jellied eel and pea soup, baked potatoes and sheep's trotters. There were coffee carts and men clinking mugs of ginger beer and hot wine while the city was a silhouette in the distance—cylindrical smokestacks, puffing exhaust and poking up into the sky like organ pipes, feeding a thick black hovering cloud.

Sometimes the violence seemed only barely restrained in those last months of 1838. There were nighttime torchlit marches for men and women whose only free time was after the workday. An observer from Northampton captured a scene from one of these processions as it made its way through the city's streets, banners held aloft, "making the heavens echo with the loud thunder of their cheers." What he saw left an extraordinary impression: "The uncouth appearance of thousands of artisans who had not time from leaving the factory to go home and . . . whose faces were therefore begrimed with sweat and dirt, added to the strange aspect of the scene. The processions were frequently of immense length, sometimes containing as many as fifty thousand people; and along the whole line there blazed a stream of light, illuminating the lofty sky, like the reflection from a large city in a general conflagration." Soon, the sound of pistol shots could be heard as well.

As much as it excited him, O'Connor feared these bursts of emotion, worried that they could easily transform into recklessness and self-destruction. This all had to build to something. If not, where would this energy go? In December, Parliament outlawed what the local broadsheets had taken to calling "monster" demonstrations. O'Connor pleaded that now was the time to focus their anger and not let it dissipate into shouting. The goal was to add as many names as possible to the petition. The mass gatherings swept people up with such a feeling of strength that many failed to see the point of a plodding petition campaign. But O'Connor argued that this collective act was radically new and that it was their final gamble. "It is the last, the very last," he told one audience after another. "To silence them, give it to them: let every man, woman and child sign the Petition; disarm all your enemies at once. If it can be done by a dash of the pen, it is worth the experiment."

THE ANGER THAT was feeding the movement had been intensifying for a while. But it was disgruntlement without any organizing principle. In 1838 there were more than six hundred associations that had developed in response to the disappointing Reform Bill or had more recently been set up in support of the Charter. O'Connor himself had been seeding many of these groups in his years out of Parliament, like the Great Northern Union that he had helped establish—a collection of radical groups clustered around the manufacturing centers of Birmingham and Manchester. It was only now, though, that their cause became united enough to merit a name: Chartism.

In his memoirs, John Bates, who had been a Chartist in his youth, remembered the jolt that the petition provided: "There were associations all over the country, but there was a great lack of cohesion.... The radicals were without unity of aim and method, and there was but little hope of accomplishing anything. When, however, the People's Charter was drawn up ... clearly defining the urgent demands of the working classes, we felt we had a real bond of union; and so transformed our Radical Associations into local Chartist centres."

For O'Connor, the petition was more than just a performance of grievance, a rock to throw against the windows of an aloof and disconnected Parliament. Rather, he saw its real value in the actual, physical work of gathering the signatures—the need to go door-to-door, to convince others, to mark in ink one's allegiance to a cause. This would bind the disparate parts of the working class together, would allow them to see themselves *as* a distinct class. He tried to explain this at a Dewsbury meeting in April 1838, saying that what was important— what the People's Charter would help achieve—was "a union based on such principles as would not only enable Radicals to think alike, but also to know that they did think alike. Nothing was so necessary as that they should know how each other thought and with that knowledge they might almost attain any object upon which they set their wishes." The petition would allow them to recognize each other as bearers of the same burden, a community of the excluded.

But it did not have an easy start. In the spring of 1839, Chartist delegates from every corner of the United Kingdom converged on London to create a representative body, a national convention tasked with collecting and delivering the finished petition. And they right away encountered an unexpected problem. The numbers of signatures weren't quite adding up, nothing close to the hundreds of thousands they had hoped for. It certainly didn't reflect the enormous crowds who joined the demonstrations. The problem was in part logistical. There were only so many hours in a day to reach workers who toiled in factories from dawn to past dusk. In some cases, it was the National Rent, a small donation meant to support the convention, that proved prohibitive. But there was a mental barrier as well. This kind of proactive, aggressive push for full political rights was new and nothing like the local petitions people were familiar with. "Such is the enslaved state of the county of Gloucester that the people dare not sign a Petition," one Chartist wrote after trying to gather names from the Forest of Dean. Even in a county like Warwickshire, a center of radical activism, fewer than six thousand names had been collected from a population of seventy-seven thousand. "I am quite unequal to the task," the dejected local organizer wrote. "We can no longer call it a 'National Petition.' The assumption on which we proceeded has proved false."

O'Connor was deployed by the convention to persuade the reluctant, and it was while on these trips in the spring of 1839 that he saw with his own eyes the purpose the petition served, what it could do for working people despite its current difficulties. It was a medium with almost zero cost. "Wherever there is a halfpenny sheet of paper, a pen and a few drops of ink, there are the materials for a petition," wrote one Chartist. But the act of picking up these materials inspired solidarity—among those who worked with rulers to draw up the sheets by hand, went door-to-door to canvass, snuck onto factory floors, or set up tables in busy marketplaces. When a Chartist activist had to argue his case, he was reinforcing his *own* beliefs, talking himself into deeper commitment while convincing others. And for the deliberating worker who finally signed, this was a pledge taken, a contract entered into, an act more official and solemn than almost any other in these impoverished people's lives. The petition arrived at a moment when a largely oral culture was becoming more literate. The petition lay at this intersection. Half the job was to convince neighbors and friends and fellow citizens with words; the other half was to get them to sign their names. It was through signing that they felt consecrated in the cause.

According to Malcolm Chase, the scholar of Chartism, gathering signatures was an "educational process central to building political awareness." In much the same way that Peiresc's letters opened up new channels of conversation and thinking for his correspondents, the petition was a knock on the door, but it also did something else: as quickly as it brought new ideas and feelings to the surface, it also provided a unitary outlet, a way for all this talk to have a point. In his autobiography, William Lovett, the London cabinetmaker who had first dreamed up the petition, described it as "the most efficient means of creating, guiding, and ascertaining public opinion." The more they engaged in it, the more signatures they gathered, the more they identified themselves as a class with imagined rights. To put your name on a petition was, in a sense, to vote—the only kind of voting the working class was allowed. "Petitions parade Chartism in open day," observed O'Connor, "and bring us under the eye of the heretofore blind."

Communities constituted themselves around this activity. It gave them form and purpose. In a town like Kidderminster, not far from Birmingham, when local workers heard of the petition, they established what they called a "provisional committee" to organize a "preliminary meeting of the Working Classes." There they read the petition aloud and then held another meeting to formally adopt it, the group of these 150 initial petition signers now calling themselves the Kidderminster Working Men's Association. Each member pledged to collect even more signatures. Over the next eight weeks they managed to gather twenty-five hundred.

A whole culture spun out from this central, intimate act carried out one person at a time. When the Charter was in trouble for lack of names, yet more associations and canvassing groups formed. Because the Chartists conceived of this petition as expressing the will of "the people" writ large, it also made room for children and women, who were previously excluded from political activity of this sort. Earlier, smaller-scale petitions had explicitly barred women. What was happening now was an unprecedented shift. "Wherever I have been, I have got women to sign it," one activist told a Midlands crowd. "They are more interested than the men." And they did more than sign. They started their own committees and pulled in their friends and neighbors, even though any new electoral reforms were bound to apply to men alone. Of the 1.2 million names that would eventually be collected, 200,000 were estimated to be from working women.

Newly formed Chartist newspapers reported on this massive effort, with no publication more important than O'Connor's own *Northern Star*. Started in 1837 and run out of an office in Leeds, it had within a year become the most read newspaper in Britain, surpassing *The Times*, with a weekly circulation that hit fifty thousand. Besides elevating O'Connor, who wrote a regular column filled with Irish jokes and poetry and whose profile appeared in the fifth issue in a steel engraving meant for cutting out and hanging in Chartist homes, the paper reported in detail the goings-on in every Chartist enclave, listing tallies of collected signatures, setting targets, and creating a sense of momentum.

By the spring of 1839, the convention in London started sounding more positive reports. In Glasgow, twenty thousand signatures were collected in four days. And in the town of Hayle in Cornwall, Chartist representatives found people waiting in line until ten at night to sign. "There is now more of a political feeling in this country than ever existed, perhaps, in any nation in the world," declared one editorial in a radical newspaper. "It would seem that every man has become a politician."

THE LAUGHTER IN PARLIAMENT was followed, unsurprisingly, by rejection. On July 12, a month after the petition was presented in all its bulk, a vote was called over whether the petition should be considered. The debate over this question lasted only a few hours and, with the exception of speeches from a handful of passionate radical members, was largely dismissive. Dejected Chartists stood in the gallery watching as an overwhelming majority voted against even discussing the petition, 235 to 46.

And then came the crackdown. "As the object of the Chartists was to knock us on the head and rob us of our property," an influential Whig cabinet member, Lord Broughton, recalled telling the prime minister around this time, "we might as well arrive at that catastrophe after a struggle as without it; we could only fail and we might succeed." Arms and soldiers began flowing across the country. A shipment from the Royal Armouries arrived, for example, in the small Lancashire town of Leigh, with 150 swords, 300 long sea pistols, 300 flintlock pistols, and 6,000 rounds of ammunition.

Even in those summer weeks after the petition was wheeled into Parliament but before it had been voted on, there were signs of where things were headed. On July 4, a few hundred Chartists milled around the Bull Ring, a square at the center of Birmingham, dominated by a bronze statue of Vice Admiral Horatio Nelson, one hand resting on a giant anchor and the other tucked into his vest. There were banners and flags, including a skull and crossbones. And then, suddenly, there was chaos. Sixty officers with the London Metropolitan Police, wielding truncheons and led by the mayor on horseback, had been dispatched by the Home Office and empowered to arrest any Chartist caught addressing a crowd. For half an hour, until a local military unit, the Fourth Dragoon, arrived and took control, the Chartists threw rocks and were beaten bloody. Three police officers were stabbed. And by the end of the night, eighty Chartists had been arrested, forced to empty their pockets of stones, and marched to jail.

The leaders were arrested next, including William Lovett. His alleged crime was sedition for writing, in the wake of the Bull Ring incident, that "there is no security for life, liberty or property, till the people have some control over the laws they are called upon to obey." He would spend the next year in jail.

What would happen now? O'Connor himself was in York facing charges of libel for a column he'd written. In his absence, there was no one to speak up for the use of "moral force," and the voices of more militant Chartists took over. There had always been, among the working-class leaders, men who were impatient to tap into the movement's wilder instincts. A committee that met in Birmingham after the failure of the petition decided to call for a monthlong general strike in which every man and woman, in every factory and workshop, would abstain from work. It was to start on August 12, in a few weeks.

O'Connor was appalled. A strike was not a bad tactic, but unless the hundreds of Chartist communities acted in concert, with the same will and method they had mustered for the Charter, he knew it would be a disaster. There was no mystery how the authorities would perceive it. As *The Scotsman* put it: the Chartists, "if not downright insane, are certainly under the influence of the most diabolical malignity, and are pursuing a course that is beyond all possible doubt *intended* to lead to *insurrection* and *anarchy*." And if the strike failed, it would take away their last remaining leverage. "Once let them be defeated in this, and they were lost forever," O'Connor explained.

A sign of his power over the nascent movement, he managed to significantly reduce the length of the strike—proposing instead that it last three days, a far less threatening prospect. When it finally did take place, in mid-August, it was done in such a scattershot way that it left little impact, just as O'Connor had feared.

As the summer of 1839 turned into fall, the movement collapsed into uncertainty and dissolution. Chartism had once been spoken of "as a thing in the clouds," O'Connor wrote. And now he feared it would return to this airy state. The movement would be "left to local discussions and sectional power, which above all things must be avoided because nothing is more necessary than that all the currents of public opinion should so harmonize and blend together as to bring them in now overwhelming tide against the enemies of the people." Only the petition had so far achieved anything close to this.

THE AUTHORITIES WOULD later try to pin the violence that followed on O'Connor, incredulous that the great "I AM" was not the guiding force behind every plot. But anyone could see that it was the result of a vacuum, of hands now fidgety and without aim.

In the early hours of November 4, rain pelted the Chartists who had gathered in the hills overlooking Newport, the industrial center of south Wales. There were a few thousand, mostly coal miners and iron-workers from the valley's surrounding towns like Nantyglo, Pontypool, Blackwood, Newbridge, and Risca. In their pockets, they carried homemade cards recording their number and division in the ragtag army. For weeks they had been dreaming up an attack on Newport that might cut it off from London and ignite other revolts throughout the country. The weather made communication difficult, and the largest group of about five thousand men stood freezing and wet most of the night outside the Welsh Oak, a small village pub, passing around drinks and occasionally firing off nervous shots. It was already light by the time their leader, a fifty-five-year-old linen draper named John Frost, onetime mayor of Newport turned militant Chartist, had them begin moving out in military formation, bearing down on the town from the west. Those who saw them marching through the hills were frightened by the rage finally released. "On they came, many of them half drunk, yelling, swearing, and waving great cudgels, a terrifying mass of men," wrote one witness remembering what he saw as a boy hiding behind his father, who was protecting his family with a wooden-handled blunderbuss.

The current mayor of Newport, learning at dawn about the approaching armed men, preemptively arrested a few local Chartists. He held them at the Westgate Hotel, which he had declared his headquarters, fortified by the presence of thirty-one infantrymen from the Forty-fifth Regiment stationed nearby. They locked themselves up and waited, listening to the terrible sound of Chartists smashing windows with the butts of their guns and loudly chanting as they made their way through the town. When they got to the hotel, they demanded the release of the prisoners and the surrender of the mayor. More men were coming down toward the square facing the hotel and pushing their way into the entrance hall. As the bodies pressed closer and closer, a mass of pikes moving up and down, a shot was suddenly fired in the air.

The soldiers in the hotel had a good view of the street and the armed crowd below and they began firing their muskets, stepping to the large window, two at a time, shooting into the crowd, then reloading as two other soldiers took their place. People fell, screaming, and the Chartist troops began stampeding in retreat, colliding with their own comrades in the rear, and leaving in their wake streets littered with pikes and guns. The Chartists still imprisoned in the hotel meanwhile began tearing apart every piece of furniture, raging against the soldiers who had just fired on their friends. The infantrymen then opened the locked door and discharged their weapons on their captives, the air choking with gray smoke.

It all lasted about twenty minutes. "There was a dreadful scene," wrote a special constable who remained inside, "dreadful beyond expression—the groans of the dying, the shrieks of the wounded, the pallid, ghostly countenances and the bloodshot eyes of the dead, in addition to the shattered windows and passageways ankle-deep in gore." Some of the injured and the dying were crawling away in search of hiding places.

The Chartists who had attacked the town, their weapons now abandoned, didn't stop running until they reached the countryside. Of those who could be counted, there were twenty-two dead and fifty seriously injured. The pocket of a young man who had fallen contained two cards. One, for his position in the uprising, reading "No. 5 of H Division"; the other, tattered proof of his membership in a local Chartist group, the Aberdare Working Men's Association.

In the winter of 1839, with the nation still recoiling from the Newport Rising, Thomas Carlyle, the Scottish essayist and historian, published a pamphlet titled *Chartism* in which he tried to determine, with some sympathy, the cause of all this working-class agitation. The rebellion had devolved into chaos, and yet he desired, he wrote, "a clear interpretation of the thought which at heart torments these wild inarticulate souls, struggling there, with inarticulate uproar, like dumb creatures in pain, unable to speak what is in them!"

The great virtue of the petition had been to make the working class legible to itself and to the upper and middle classes. The violence had now scrambled this legibility. It made Chartism look, indeed, "inarticulate." It allowed its many critics among the political and business elite to dismiss it as unfocused and impotently raging. "They call themselves the masses but they are no more the masses than the dust in a whirlwind," editorialized the London *Examiner*.

O'Connor was devastated by what had happened in Newport. On

the same day that the Welsh Chartists began gathering in the hills with their guns, he had just returned from a monthlong stay in Ireland. It's unclear how much if anything he knew about what was to occur—no more "than the man in the moon," he insisted—but it's highly unlikely he would have supported violently taking over a single town. O'Connor had always thought, after the petition failed, that Chartism had to build on the national campaign, expand its ambition and its reach, not contract into factions that whispered and stockpiled arms. During his travels in Ireland that fall, he had been trying to establish a system of interconnected Chartist clubs that would help elect radical candidates in the next general election to Parliament. Constitutional means backed up by tough words still seemed to him the clearest path.

What the Chartists needed was a new national goal, to pull back into concert all the various activists and communities that had seemed to spin out of control over the past several months. And O'Connor realized that the crisis presented him with an opportunity: their objective could be to save the life of John Frost.

THE LEADER OF the Newport Rising had fled the scene of the massacre with tears in his eyes. He hid for a day in a coal truck, but when he emerged wet and tired at night to visit the home of a Chartist printer and change his clothes and eat something, he was arrested. His two collaborators were soon caught as well: William Jones, a traveling actor, hiding in the woods clutching a pistol, and Zephaniah Williams, a freethinking innkeeper, a few weeks later in Cardiff with a bag of gold coins aboard a ship bound for Portugal. The government called for an expedited trial. And so Jones, Williams, and Frost found themselves on the last day of 1839 in a courtroom in Monmouth, being judged for the rare charge of high treason—no one had been tried and punished for such a crime since 1820.

In the weeks leading up to the trial, O'Connor threw himself into raising money for a legal defense. This, after all, was what he did best, in front of different audiences every night, moving from town to town. He even had the profits of the December 21 issue of the *Northern Star* donated to Frost's legal team. It was a tense time, with many Chartists assuming that a conviction would finally signal total and national armed revolt. A rumor spread that the *Northern Star* would be printed in blood-red ink as a sign for the revolution to commence. But O'Connor had no such plan. In the January 4 issue, while he himself sat in the courtroom observing the trial, the *Star* editorialized that any talk of violence would be "ill-advised in the extreme, and must be everywhere carefully suppressed. The time for big words and loud talking is gone by."

After a week of hearings in which Frost's face in particular was scrutinized for the slightest twitch, the jury deliberated for less than half an hour. The three men were found guilty. "It was then, for the first time, that his countenance changed," reported *The Observer* about Frost's demeanor. "His excessive agitation was betrayed by the convulsive movement of his lips, and as the fatal words resounded through the Court, he sank back into the dock overwhelmed with grief." Then came the punishment. Death alone was clearly too light a sentence. The judge read out the details a week later: "You, John Frost, and you, Zephaniah Williams, and you, William Jones, be taken hence to the place from whence you came, and be thence drawn on a hurdle to the place of execution, and that each of you be there hanged by the neck until you be dead, and that afterwards the head of each of you shall be severed from his body, and the body of each, divided into four quarters, shall be disposed of as Her Majesty shall think fit, and may Almighty God have mercy upon your souls."

The Chartists were confirmed in their feelings of sheer helplessness. There was no recourse for them, no political power they could yield, no vote they could cast. Even the money they had contributed to Frost's legal defense would be for naught. Many wanted vengeance. But O'Connor returned to a means he had come to trust: the best, maybe only, way, to remind the Chartists that they were Chartists, part of an aggrieved collective who must be heard. He called for another petition.

———

EVEN THOUGH THE CHARTER had failed, it had undoubtedly given shape to the movement—growing it and setting its direction. The emotional response to Frost's fate, properly channeled, could
inspire a similar effort, though one with the more particular goal of
commuting a death sentence that the Whig government was eager to
carry out quickly. The court decreed the three men's punishment on
January 16, and even with an appeal pending, it looked unlikely they
could be saved. Behind closed doors, the government was intent on
using this sensational form of execution to send a message to the
working class. The cabinet member Lord Broughton recorded in his
diary that there was unanimity as to this point and that even the prime
minister, Lord Melbourne, felt that such measures "were indispensable
to prevent anarchy."

This time, the collection of signatures happened swiftly and at a
tremendous scale. Whereas it had taken weeks and months for the
national petition to reach a critical mass, now Chartists were accumulating similar numbers of supporters within days. In Sunderland,
17,000 names were gathered in three days, in Oldham 18,000 in just
two, and in Birmingham 30,000 in six. Scotland proved particularly
fruitful: Chartists in Aberdeen, using their door-to-door tactics, collected 15,000 signatures, and in Edinburgh 5,000 more people signed
for Frost than put their names on the 1839 petition. Dundee also
brought in more than 20,000 signatures, and in Paisley, where the
town council took the lead on canvassing, 14,784 signatures were
amassed in the span of fourteen hours.

This was a sign that the petitioning was creating something dura-
ble, a movement capable of snapping to attention when needed. Over
the past year and a half, the culture that had first fused around work on
the Charter—all those small local associations—now seemed self-
sustaining. There were temperance societies, groups that raised money
for funerals, collective newspaper-reading clubs, lectures, and garden
parties. That one gesture of putting your name to paper created a new
sort of allegiance to a set of values and those who shared them. There
were Chartist songs, weekend gatherings, and massive picnics. Many
pubs self-identified as proudly Chartist, and one could find the *North-*

ern Star there on every table wet with beer suds. Chartists decorated their homes with those prints of Chartist leaders that came with special editions of the *Northern Star*. They could order Chartist products from Chartist stores—Chartist shoe polish, ink, textiles, or a powdered corn concoction for breakfast. They signed their letters "Yours in Chartism" or "Your brother in the Cause of Right against Might." The fanatically committed even named their children Feargus, though not without some repercussions. One little boy, Feargus O'Connor Holmes, the son of wool combers from Keighley, spent his school years referred to only as "F" by a headmaster who wouldn't utter the radical's name. When little Feargus O'Connor Mabbot was baptized, the vicar of Selby deadpanned, "I suppose they want the child hanged."

The press reported with awe on the enormous number of signatures so speedily gathered by these communities. And in the end, it made a difference. The gallows were already set up outside the Monmouth jail when the government suddenly relented. There was the matter of Queen Victoria's wedding to Prince Albert, taking place on February 10, and the worry that all that pomp would be spoiled by the gruesome reports of the men's beheading and quartering. But the main reason lay elsewhere. The petition campaign made it impossible to ignore the large constituency opposed to such a punishment. The memory of the Newport Rising still sizzled. It seemed good sense to listen. In a letter to Parliament in early February, a government minister, Lord Normanby, explained his logic to the queen and how "the proceedings which have taken place since their trials" had made it "advisable to recommend to her Majesty to extend the Royal mercy to the said prisoners, on condition of transportation for life." They would be exiled.

Within a day of her decision, Frost, Jones, and Williams were woken up in the middle of the night and taken in chains to Portsmouth without a chance to say goodbye to their wives or children. A few weeks later they were placed on the *Mandarin*, a convict ship headed for Van Diemen's Land, today known as Tasmania. They were condemned to spend the rest of their lives there in hard labor. The ship was delayed for a few days for repairs after one of the masts was damaged at port during a storm. A sympathizer snuck on board in the guise of a missionary, and he caught a glimpse of Frost chained in the hold, his face "wan and haggard and indented with deep furrows." There was no escaping this voyage, but it was a far better fate than the punishment the state had intended to mete out.

For O'Connor, the result was an invigorating boost. Though the victory might have felt small to some—replacing execution with a life of hard labor in a foreign land—for him it was clear validation of the petition as a tactic, of the power it could exercise. It was no small thing to shift the government from its resolve, and O'Connor considered this the Chartists' first real success. They had focused their collective attention, avoided disintegrating as a movement, and emerged with new strength. Dorothy Thompson, a scholar of Chartism, saw the commutation as a turning point, an act that, being "the result of peaceful constitutional pressure," undermined the greatest threat and biggest advantage the authorities had, their "fundamental violence." O'Connor quickly pivoted to another petitioning effort, to win a complete royal pardon for the three men. By May of the following year, 1841, the Chartists had collected nearly 1.5 million signatures to deliver to Parliament, surpassing the People's Charter and nearly gaining approval (the Speaker's deciding vote broke a tie, and clemency was ultimately rejected).

But O'Connor would not be presenting that petition. Not long after Frost's ship set sail for Van Diemen's Land, five hundred Chartists were thrown into prison, including most of the leaders. O'Connor was put on trial again in March for seditious libel. One of his speeches and another printed in the *Star* were said to promote violent rebellion. O'Connor, true to his character, turned the courtroom into a stage. "I shall console myself with the reflection that I have perfumed the whole atmosphere with a scent—the essence of Chartism," he wrote after his trial. His opening remarks, delivered as if he were standing before a crowd of hundreds of thousands at Kersal Moor, lasted nearly five hours.

There was little question he would be found guilty and sentenced. In many ways, he had been waiting for this moment, the final station in his ascendance as the one and only Chartist leader. He was, he told his followers, innocent of the charges, of course. His persecution was an unjust reaction to the Newport Rising, but he was willing to claim his martyrdom. "This is my last letter for some time," he wrote in the *Star* after he'd been sentenced in May. "In a few hours after you shall have read this, I shall be consigned to a gloomy dungeon, not for any particular merit of my own, but in consequence of your disunion. Under these circumstances, you will suppose that I am about to scold and chide you; but no, my friends and companions, the last glimmer of my lamp shall be devoted to lighting you on the road to freedom."

He was to spend eighteen months in York Castle, behind the imposing stone wall and moat that guarded the complex originally built by William the Conqueror. His cell, though roomier than all the others, was damp and dark, and at first, despite his status as one of the country's most well-known political figures, he was treated like any other prisoner, his only special privilege the ability to wear his own clothes. But O'Connor being O'Connor—ever the influential and persuasive gentleman—he was soon allowed to bring in some of his furniture and even a few exotic caged birds to keep him company. He had wine and his own food ("His meals are, we understand, served up from one of the inns in the city," reported the *York Gazette*). Even the one prohibition explicitly spelled out by the government was flouted: he was back to writing his column for the *Star*. He could read its pages too, smuggled in weekly. And what he read was gratifying. Chartism, though still far from its goal, was maturing in all the ways he had hoped.

The future looked clearer, too. In July he received news that a Manchester meeting of activists had established the National Charter Association. They had created what was, in effect, the first working-class political party in history. Building up from the canvassing groups, small cells of activists would make up local chapters, with individuals paying a quarterly subscription of one penny, which would earn them the right to elect the national leadership. The collected dues would then be split between these local Chartist councils and the national organization. This was O'Connor's vision of a movement that was locally rooted but unified nationally in its mission. The founding president, a Manchester mill worker, was the first political leader in Britain of any party to be popularly elected, chosen through the votes of individual members and not in a smoky back room.

O'Connor himself would not live to see the ultimate realization of the Chartist mission. That would take a long time. But he did see many more petitions. In 1842, the movement tried again to assemble signatures for a national charter and outdid themselves, gathering 3.3 million, a third of Britain's adult population. Weighing six hundred pounds, that rolled-up petition did not actually fit into the House of Commons. The doorframe had to be taken apart, and when this failed, the sheets, six miles long, had to be unfurled and piled in front of the clerk's desk under the astonished eyes of the members. William Lovett, who watched from the gallery, said it looked as if it were raining paper. It was then rejected by a vote of 287 to 49. There was even a third petition, in the revolutionary year of 1848, that gathered six million signatures, though that number was disputed by the clerk. By then, O'Connor had made it back into Parliament as a member, only to succumb precipitously to drink and depression. He died in 1855.

It took until the Reform Bill of 1867 for the right to vote to be granted to some working men—and even then, not all—and only in 1918 was there a semblance of universal suffrage, including for women. But while this took long to achieve, the immediate impact of Chartism was to elevate petitioning as a political act, one that bound the signers together and amplified their voice. Petitioning reached its height during the Chartist years of struggle. From 1838 to 1848 there was an average of 16,000 petitions every session of Parliament, compared with only 4,498 in the entire five-year period ending in 1815. In 1843 alone there were 33,898 petitions. This new constituency petitioned against unsafe labor conditions. They petitioned to limit the number of hours in a workday. They petitioned against debilitating tariffs that raised the price of grain. They petitioned against the persistence of the Poor Law. They made themselves legible.

Chapter 3

IMAGINATION

MORE THAN SIX THOUSAND spectators crammed into the Teatro Verdi that evening, packed like "anchovies in a tin," reported the *Corriere della Sera*, "a restless and electrified public" equipped with eggs, dried pasta, and rotten fruit. They would hate what they heard and knew it before they entered the hall. The young men who took the stage were on a never-ending tour of incitement that had begun three years earlier, featuring evenings like this one, a *serata*, a theater of contempt. The target was their fellow Italians in the audience: for their way of life, their fecklessness and passivity, their old-fashioned habits, and their slavish worship of the past, embodied by their devotion to Florence itself, which the young men spat on, claiming the city was a graveyard suitable only for the living dead.

Squeezed among the theatergoers that night was Mina Loy, a thirty-year-old British artist, who had recently stumbled, by accident, into the passionate circle of these men, the Futurists. She wore flowing dresses and dangling earrings, her long black hair in a loose chignon and a perpetually eager look on her face. Mina had come to Florence five years earlier with a husband who had since abandoned her with two children. Her career as a painter, once promising—she had even exhibited in the Salon d'Automne in Paris—was now foundering. It was a time, she wrote to a friend, "of shilly-shallying shyness—of an utter inability—to adjust myself to anything actual." The artists onstage—a sculptor, a poet, a painter—were completely unafraid before their public, declaiming their radical visions by reading from manifestos that smashed to pieces all the old pieties. Looking up at them, she felt what she would come to call a "risorgimento": a resurgence.

She was desperate to extract herself from her creative rut. How else to explain why just a few months before, in the fall of 1913, after meeting all the most prominent Futurists at the Giubbe Rosse, a café on the Piazza della Repubblica, she had found herself emotionally entangled with two of them? They were rivals of a sort, and both present onstage that December night. One was the movement's ringmaster, Filippo Tommaso Marinetti, who dubbed himself the "caffeine of Europe," with his handlebar mustache and bowler hat, like a silent movie villain about to tie a woman to the railroad tracks. The other was Giovanni Papini, the brooding, serious leader of the Florentine faction and editor of the literary journal *Lacerba*, who self-consciously referred to himself, due to his toady scowl of a face, as the "ugliest man in Italy."

Mina watched, astounded, as they addressed the roiling theater. Ardengo Soffici, one of the Florentine Futurists, later described the scene from the stage. It looked, he wrote, like "an inferno. Even before any of us opened his mouth to speak, the hall was boiling over, becoming agitated, resonating with savage voices, almost like a piazza full of people awaiting an execution." This was the enraged catharsis the Futurists had hoped for. And as cauliflower and slices of cake rained down on their heads, they read out their manifestos and proclaimed their utopian (or dystopian, depending on the listener) visions. They hoped their ideas—radical, degrading, terrifying ideas—would wake the sleepy Italian people. It's hard to know if the audience gleaned anything other than the impression of insult through the deafening boos, the toy trumpets and cowbells and whistles and rattling door keys, but the Futurists persevered. They wanted a modern, youthful

Italy and a new sort of Italian, one who would mirror all that was thrilling about the twentieth century's new machines, which were gleaming, metallic, pulsating, fast. By the time Papini read his manifesto on Florence, a city, he said, "marked by the past as by a disease," the stage was slathered in food. "Throw an idea, not a potato, you idiot!" yelled Carlo Carrà, the painter in the group.

In spite of herself, Mina found the spectacle exhilarating. The evening ended with a lightbulb smashing against the side of Marinetti's face as he tried to read out a political statement and a man being dangled by his feet over the balcony. It took the police, jumping to the stage with clubs in their hands, to end the show. If these intellectuals were driving so many people crazy, their art must be of the sort that crushed illusions, she thought. Mina swooned in a letter to a friend that the evening was as restorative "as a fortnight at the seashore." The manifestos of Marinetti and his merry men were the clearest window into their minds and their aspirations for their movement. Public by nature, the texts also functioned as a sketch pad, an imaginative space where individuals or factions could dream out loud, elaborately.

But for all that was liberating about their ideas, the trashing of convention and tradition that resulted in their being showered with food, Mina found something disturbing there as well. Their ultimate ambition was a war that they hoped would be so cataclysmic it would purify the country and allow them to start from zero. The violence of that night was the point. Pain and blood were the quickest way to revitalize man—and it was men who were their sole concern. Mina found the superpowered machismo that ran through their writings ugly: it came at the expense of women's humanity (a typical Marinetti taunt at a *serata:* "I've had enough of the femininity of the crowd and the weakness of their collective virginity"). The only real role for women in their idealized future was procreation.

Mina couldn't deny that the Futurists were having an effect on her—"Personally I am getting very young," she wrote to a friend—even as she recognized that she might be "the only female" to be so beguiled by them. Was there a way for her to extract all that was invigorating while leaving behind what demeaned and dehumanized her? Marinetti had birthed the movement through his manifestos, and every one that followed added a new dimension to the collective picture, another breath in its existence as a movement. If it was possible to bend their violent impulses toward a vision that might include her, that might ensure her own salvation not just as an artist but as a woman of her time, it was through the sort of writing she heard read at the *serata*. To begin a conversation with them as an equal, Mina would have to learn to speak the language of the manifestos.

IN 1909, MARINETTI had taken a medium that had lain mostly dormant since 1848, when Karl Marx and Friedrich Engels wrote their *Communist Manifesto*, and revived it to spectacular effect. The manifesto, with its future imperative tense, gave a writer the freedom to exercise his radical imagination, almost demanded it. This is what we *will do*. This is who we *will be*. Marinetti's "Foundation and Manifesto of Futurism," as he called that original document, was more than just a matter of personal expression. He needed the first-person plural. "We had stayed up all night, my friends and I," Marinetti began. The form allowed him to speak immediately for a generation and make claims way beyond what was within his power to achieve—yet. "We intend to exalt aggressive action, a feverish insomnia, the racer's stride, the mortal leap, the punch and the slap," he wrote. The manifesto was a perfect medium for conjuring. If Chartists gained from petitions the ability to cohere as a movement, manifestos provided the Futurists with a place to articulate their fantasies, always the first step to making them come true. The manifestos were part of an iterative process, each one instigating another that would build on the boldness of the previous one, expanding and sometimes correcting the vision and the tone they were determining together.

Marinetti set off a chain reaction. His first manifesto would pull in some of the most brilliant and promising young artists and writers then at work in Italy, who would in turn churn out dozens more manifestos over the next couple years, each articulating another aspect of the group's core principles. After Marinetti's initial salvo came the

"Manifesto of the Futurist Painters" in February 1910, which was signed by five artists—including Umberto Boccioni, creator of some of the most lasting Futurist works. It demanded that artists take on more relevant subjects. In the same way that religious themes had inspired painters in the past, "we must breathe in the tangible miracles of contemporary life." The proper Futurist subject, in other words, was new technology—factories and trains and airplanes—painted with a reverence once reserved for the infant Jesus. This manifesto was then elaborated on a few months later with the "Futurist Painting: Technical Manifesto," which introduced the idea of "dynamism." Like the newly emerging cubist works, art should capture movement rather than stasis, the experience of shouldering your way through a bustling city. And, in Futurist fashion, the painters laid down some precepts. "We demand, for ten years, the total suppression of the nude in painting," they wrote—not because it was immoral, but because it was a tired subject best given a break.

And so it went. A manifesto about sculpture pointed back to an earlier one about music, and still another, about the state of architecture, alluded to the previous two. Marinetti was the catalyst, but each imaginative leap stimulated another, with dozens of manifestos landing week after week, each pushing things further. Their typography brought to mind this wild, internal conversation, using capital letters, words climbing and falling all over the page, as disorienting and exciting as the experience of standing amid a gaggle of feverish speakers. Marinetti's original manifesto set out the structure and pattern, complaint followed by radical prescription, but then the form just reverberated. Each manifesto's vision might read as far-fetched and nearly impossible to picture (music should do away with the "tyranny of rhythm," and they wanted sculpture in which "the sidewalk can climb up your table"), but there were steps—here they were—for how to seize modernity. And art was only the immediate target of their sledgehammers. The cracks would spread throughout society, into the very way Italians saw themselves and their destinies.

This will to destruction had roots that were both philosophical and nationalistic. Marinetti was born in Alexandria, Egypt, his father a lawyer who had hoped to make his fortune there. The deracinated young man grew up in Jesuit schools and from a young age wrote a constant stream of poetry. Later, as a student in Paris at the Sorbonne, he was drawn to the most popular and provocative fin de siècle ideas then in circulation—Friedrich Nietzsche's notion that the world needed supermen who would be "brave, unconcerned, mocking, violent," and uniquely constituted to lead, combined with Georges Sorel's anarchism, rooted in disdain for the compromises and incrementalism of liberal democracy. It was a heady and emotional mix, drunk by many young men at the time. Marinetti chased it all down with operatic notions of glory and sacrifice. Predictably, he loved Wagner, the grandiose, myth-obsessed composer, who "stirs up the delirious heat in my blood, right down to the most hidden heartstrings of my very being."

In 1905, Marinetti founded a journal, *Poesia*, run out of his apartment on Via Senato in Milan. When his father died two years later, leaving Marinetti an inheritance that suddenly made him a rich man, he started a publishing house and even created a literary prize with a thousand-lira reward. He became a cultural impresario, well known for attracting the most avant-garde and anarchist writers and for needling the stifling conformism of the bourgeoisie. When his play *La donna è mobile* was received with loud jeering on its opening night in Turin in early 1909, Marinetti jumped on the stage and thanked the audience for "this whistling, which does me great honor." Their anger enlivened him; it was an emotion he considered healthy for Italians. The next day the local paper, *Il Lavoro*, had a verdict on the strange man in a bowler hat who had confronted the crowd: "Not all of the nuts are in the nuthouse."

Marinetti felt that Italy itself had let his generation down. A fairly new nation-state, then only fifty years old, it had yet to achieve greatness in his eyes. To the Futurists, the country was led by cautious, impotent leaders, too reverent of the papacy and paralyzed by a parliamentary democracy that didn't provide national unity or a sense of purpose to its citizens. What Marinetti and his crowd wanted was something epic, and fast, a patriotic cause that might lift Italy out of its stupor. The cultural annihilation was only a prelude to actual, bloodletting violence, the quickest path to rejuvenation, as he saw it. Marinetti threw around words and images that now sound obscene. "We will glorify war—the world's only hygiene," he wrote in his first manifesto. "Militarism, patriotism, the destructive gesture of freedom-bringers, beautiful ideas worth dying for, and scorn for women"—the last point not an afterthought but a prerequisite for the creation of a new man, one not hobbled by what he saw as the crippling effects of femininity.

That initial manifesto, which appeared in newspapers in Bologna, Naples, and Verona, and then, explosively, on the front page of the French daily *Le Figaro* on February 20, 1909, was Marinetti's attempt to instigate demolition so that something new might rise. The details about what that would be were still fuzzy. Aside from the incessant call to raze everything to the ground—"We will destroy museums, libraries, academies of every kind," Marinetti exclaimed—the emphasis was on modernity and youth. "The oldest of us is thirty," Marinetti, then thirty-two, wrote, "so we have at least a decade for finishing our work. When we are forty, other younger and stronger men will probably throw us in the wastebasket like useless manuscripts—we want it to happen!" But other particulars were left to later manifestos. The medium, by design, trafficked in yearning. The Futurists were a bunch of struggling artists and, as such, were in no position to impose their prescriptions beyond their small circle. "Manifestos frequently overcompensate for the actual powerlessness of [the writers'] position with theatrical exaggerations, and their confidence is often feigned rather than grounded in real authority," wrote the literary critic Martin Puchner. But it is in the crafting of these texts, with their wild visions, that manifesto writers come to believe in their own ability to "create points of no return; to make history; to fashion the future."

Marinetti's "Manifesto Against Past-Loving Venice" was a perfect example of just how bombastic these documents could be. He introduced it in 1910 by climbing with his friends to the top of the clock tower over the Piazza San Marco and raining down thousands of copies on the tourists below as they returned from the Lido at dusk. The Futurists' hatred of the city was florid. "Let us hasten to fill in its little reeking canals with the shards of its leprous, crumbling palaces," the manifesto read, topping itself with every sentence. "Let us burn the gondolas, rocking chairs for cretins, and then raise to the heavens the imposing geometry of metal bridges and howitzers plumed with smoke, to abolish the falling curves of the old architecture." A few months later, Marinetti returned to Venice for a *serata* at the Teatro La Fenice, and this time he went even further, reading from another manifesto in which he called the Venetians themselves prostitutes, their lives good only for servicing tourists as guides and hotel waiters. If they could not contribute to the glory of Italy's future, he told the crowd, "you should throw yourselves down, one on top of the other, like sandbags, to make a dike at the outer limits of the Lagoon, while we prepare a great, strong, industrial, commercial and military Venice on the Adriatic, our great Italian lake."

These abhorrent flights of fancy and the belligerent tone fit within the bounds of this medium, but the manifestos also absolved the Futurists of responsibility. They were able to profess their brutal thoughts and claim it was just art—and in fact the manifestos themselves remain the most distinct aesthetic legacy of the entire movement. But they also put these ideas into circulation, the swaggering words fueling a swaggering feeling that the world could be dragged, kicking and bloody, into the future. Offering some advice about "the art of making manifestos," Marinetti said they required "violence and precision." They must be clear and accessible—an explicit series of steps for arriving at implausible futures—but also capable, at the same time, of prodding and irritating their audience, of driving them off a cliff.

MINA COULDN'T LOOK AWAY. The Futurists had ignited something within her. But the misogyny of "the bombastic superman," as she called Marinetti, continued to bother her. When she confronted him about his "scorn" for women, he claimed that he rejected the binary categories of femme fatale and Madonna that were thrust onto them, and men in relation to them. It was not individual women who bothered him but women "as the divine reservoir of Amore."

She didn't buy it. There was something about the way he casually juggled these dangerous beliefs that suggested immaturity: boys tinkering with toy soldiers while rolling their eyes at the girls. "I am in the throes of a conversion to Futurism," she wrote to her friend. "But I shall never convince myself. There is no hope in any system that 'combat le mal avec le mal,' that fights evil with evil. And that is really Marinetti's philosophy—though he is one of the most satisfying personalities I have ever come in contact with." Satisfying and apparently irresistible, since Mina soon began a playful affair with him in the fall of 1913 shortly after they met—"his tactile adroitness equalled his conversational celerity," she wrote in a roman à clef about her time on the edges of the movement, giving Marinetti the elaborate pseudonym Brontolivido and, most tellingly, changing "Futurists" to "Flabbergasts."

She had been in Florence for five years, a long stretch in a life that had been peripatetic ever since her escape from England at eighteen. Her father was a Jewish Hungarian immigrant who worked as a tailor, and her mother was a working-class Englishwoman who, ashamed of her husband's religion, tried to hide it for most of her life. Mina was born with the last name Lowy, unmistakably Jewish, which she changed to Loy when presenting her paintings for the first time in Paris. Her parents wanted her to marry respectably and lift the family into the middle class. This was the extent of their hopes for her. But Mina had other plans and used her painting as a way to gain distance from the stifling environment at home, attending art school, first in London, then in Munich, and finally in Paris, where she was drawn into a community of eccentric artists and thinkers, including Gertrude Stein. In 1903, she married Stephen Haweis, an English painter and photographer, but the relationship curdled after Mina's first child, a daughter, died of meningitis two days after her first birthday. They each took lovers, and she got pregnant again, but not by her husband. She was overwhelmed by grief and a tormenting self-pity that felt, she wrote, like "some terrible Golem of doom shattering my aspirations."

Mina would have divorced Haweis, but that path was closed to her. Her main source of income came from her father, who made her promise that in exchange for the money she would maintain a stable marriage. It was in 1907 that the couple moved to Florence in an attempt to revive their relationship, joining the expatriate community and art scene then flourishing in the Tuscan city. It would at least be warm there. They did reach a bitter détente for a few years and even had another child together. But Haweis decided at the end of 1912 that he was restless, and he soon sailed for Australia, leaving Mina and the two children in a large villa in the Costa San Giorgio neighborhood, just across the river Arno from the city center, struggling to find her artistic footing again.

But now, in the presence of Marinetti, who, following the rousing *serata* in the Teatro Verdi, visited Florence frequently to see her as 1913 turned into 1914, she began to feel her creative energy return. It was no longer painting that called to her but the manifestos. She too wanted a medium that would allow her to reinvent herself. And if these men could help shape their movement through the back-and-forth of these declarations, why shouldn't she take part as well?

Marinetti had left for part of that winter on a trip to Russia to meet artists intrigued by the manifestos and *serate,* eventually launching what would become a Russian arm of Futurism (made up of painters like Kazimir Malevich and poets like Vladimir Mayakovsky, some of whom would soon produce their own founding manifesto, "A Slap in the Face of Public Taste"). Mina found a way to continue her intellectual wrestling with Marinetti and with the parts of Futurism that repelled her. She too wrote a manifesto, entering the imaginative space that had been opened up by the men. It was an unusual choice for someone who had always seen herself as a visual artist. The risorgimento was also turning her into a writer and a poet, and the manifesto she produced in January 1914 would be her first published work, soon appearing in America in a small journal, *Camera Work,* run by the photographer and art promoter Alfred Stieglitz.

What immediately stands out about Mina's "Aphorisms on Futurism" is how much more personal and self-affirming it is than other manifestos; instead of devising a despised "they" (as in, "we are of the future, but they are stuck in the past"), Mina is addressing a "you," which could easily be imagined as her own conscience or, perhaps, women in general. There is much less "precision" in these sometimes cryptic lines and certainly less "violence," but she is attempting to use the tropes of the movement, the spirit of the other manifestos, toward a new end: self-liberation. Though it begins with a sentiment that aligns her with Marinetti—"DIE in the Past / Live in the Future"— she moves into a deeper register. She is fixated on the problem of living in good faith, trusting one's feelings, and not being hampered by social and cultural conventions. It's a Futurist theme—cracking the shell to get to the yolk of authentic experience—but she's applying it much more sharply to her own existence as a woman. "LIFE is only limited by our prejudices," she writes. "Destroy them, and you cease to be at the mercy of yourself." The manifesto demands changes not from some external force but from an internal one, the "you" she addresses. Clear out the "fallow-lands of mental spatiality" in order to make "place for whatever you are brave enough, beautiful enough to draw out of the realized self. / TO your blushing we shout the obscenities, we scream the blasphemies, that you, being weak, whisper alone in the dark."

Who is this weak, whispering being she is addressing? This is not the collective, assertive voice of the other manifestos. This is unmistakably a woman struggling with questions the men aren't asking themselves, about whether they are *mentally* prepared to be new people in a new world. She is suggesting a shift, from the annihilating spirit that wants to smash all the physical surfaces—all those doomed libraries and museums—and toward a psychological reckoning, dismantling past attitudes and certainties. She cannot march alongside the Futurists to level cities or prove herself in war. But if the struggle is an inward one, a question of conquering oneself, that is a battle she can join. Mina ends by returning to the mode in which she started, a demand to "ACCEPT the tremendous truth of Futurism," a truth she has just reinterpreted for herself through her own manifesto. "Leaving all those / Knick-knacks."

Mina was not the first woman to use a manifesto to try to edge her way into the movement. Valentine de Saint-Point was a French poet and artist at the center of Parisian salon society—a model and muse for Rodin and an experimental dancer—who often appeared in extravagant costumes that included high-necked beaded bodices and elaborate ostrich-feather headdresses. Not long after Marinetti's initial manifesto, she wrote her "Manifesto of the Futurist Woman," which opened by directly responding to his "scorn": "Humanity is mediocre. The majority of women are neither superior nor inferior to the majority of men. They are all equal. They all merit the same scorn." She rejected the notion that masculinity and femininity resided respectively in men and women. Everyone had both of these qualities, and everyone needed more masculinity. "What is most lacking in women as in men is virility. That is why Futurism, even with all its exaggerations, is right. To restore some virility to our races so benumbed in femininity, we have to train them in virility even to the point of brute animality. But we have to impose on everyone, men and women who are equally weak, a new dogma of energy in order to arrive at a period of superior humanity." The nudge her manifesto hoped to provide Futurism was, in the end, an affirmation of its basic assumptions and mode as set by Marinetti; she just wanted it applied equally to women—"let woman find once more her cruelty and her violence that make her attack the vanquished because they are vanquished, to the point of mutilating them."

Mina took a different tack. In her manifesto she removed from Futurism its most troubling illiberal, antihumanistic aspects. In a way she intuited what Marshall Berman, the cultural historian, would later see as the danger of an ideology that perceived modernity as a relentless and cleansing wave. "What happens to all the people who get swept away in those tides?" Berman asked. "Their experience is nowhere in the Futurist picture. It appears that some very important kinds of human feeling are dying, even as machines are coming to life." Mina's manifesto was her attempt to bring human feeling back into the movement, into its purpose, turning it away from a death cult and emphasizing all that was life-affirming in what the Futurists were saying—what it could mean for a woman if the old societal conventions were obliterated.

Did "Aphorisms on Futurism" make her a Futurist? In a way, yes. By writing her own manifesto, she had entered into a conversation with the others. But she still had to contend with domineering men who would not easily alter their thinking. For them, modernity would be achieved by making themselves harder, by taking apart the material world around them, and not, as she had suggested, by scrutinizing their preconceptions and value systems.

She was hopeful, though, about Papini, the subdued and self-conscious Florentine intellectual at the center of the movement, and she was also fascinated by his face, which he allowed her to paint in the winter of 1914. "His mass of curly light brown hair shot up from the deeply lined enormous forehead in a tall surprise," she wrote in her notes. His mouth seemed to belong to "an impertinent gamin." Their flirtation proceeded much more quietly (and Mina thought, deeply) than her ongoing affair with Marinetti. Papini's memoir, *The Failure,* revealed a prodigiously intelligent man who nevertheless struggled to come to terms with his own "concreteness," with the limitations of his class and his strange looks. In Papini, Mina recognized her own dilemma. She too felt pulled between a drive for greatness and a frustration with her lived existence as a woman. Papini also seemed, at heart, much less doctrinaire than his Futurist comrades. Like Mina, he was more interested in how manifestos could allow you to test propositions, squeeze and pinch reality, and less in how they could produce directives. It was possible, from a distance, to hear only shouting in the manifestos, but closer up and looked at as an ongoing exchange, they revealed a working out of ideas, a sense of process. And it was this unfinished quality that appealed most to Papini; as he wrote in the opening manifesto of *Lacerba,* the journal he started in 1913, he preferred "the sketch over the composition, the potsherd over the statue, the aphorism over the treatise."

She saw in him a possible ally. But Papini, cerebral and distant and envious of Marinetti's charm and hold on the movement, would disappoint her, personally and ideologically. For all his philosophizing, Papini was so obsessed with Marinetti and so competitive that he lunged toward extremes, behaving impetuously, often in self-defeating ways. Just at the moment when Mina began an impassioned relationship with him, Papini retreated to Paris. In a poem she would later write, "Songs to Joannes," Marinetti appears as "a boy"; Papini is "a haloed ascetic" but too preoccupied with the other man to recognize her love. At the very moment he left, in March 1914, Marinetti steamed in, inviting Mina on a trip to Rome for the opening of a Futurist art gallery that would feature one of her paintings—a portrait of him, Marinetti. "His proximity was in a manner thermal," she wrote about the mustachioed dynamo. "Raw" from her "aborted love" for Papini, "she felt the salutary jar of being lifted up and let down." She was willing to give in to that "liveness of his."

At the gallery, Mina presented herself as a Futurist for the first time, mingling with the others who all hung on Marinetti's every word. At one point the conversation turned to Papini and a recent essay he had written for *Lacerba,* one that Mina was trying hard to pretend did not exist. It was a vicious, almost homicidal, attack on women, one she could not reconcile with the man she had started to fall in love with. Titled "The Massacre of Women," the article was clearly Papini's effort to outdo Marinetti: "Women must disappear. It is useless, my Futurist friends, to preach scorn for women if we then continue to live together. Living together, one can hardly avoid loving them—and loving them, one can hardly avoid serving them—and serving them, we are cowards, the betrayers of our true destiny."

Standing before his acolytes in Rome, Marinetti took the opportunity to publicly attack Papini (who he guessed by now was vying for Mina's affections). The other man's ugliness, Marinetti announced, was such that "it is a physical commotion to sit in the same room with it." He then turned, perhaps for Mina's benefit, to the subject of the article. "A woman," Marinetti said, "is a wonderful animal, and when I put into print any part of her body I choose, it is in purest appreciation." He enjoyed women, he said. Why should he be able to describe everything that gives him pleasure, except "a vagina, which gives me infinitely more," he said, stunning the room. "This is a beautiful word."

Mina couldn't help but be impressed by how little Marinetti cared about conventions or propriety in that moment. In her own manifesto,

Mina was desperate for such "obscenities" to be shouted and not whispered, and that's what Marinetti was doing. "He had said one word—distinctly, unaffectedly; and it had crashed down the barriers of prudery," she later wrote, examining the evening. "Such primordial pokes of simplicity might redirect the universe"—and perhaps the goals of Futurism as well. But, then again, he had also crudely reduced women to their body parts, their ability to satisfy *his* desires. There was no real reason to think the supermen would make room for her.

AND THEN, ALL OF A SUDDEN, in the summer of 1914, the work of defining Futurism's true aim became moot. War, a real war, had arrived. Bloodshed had featured in Futurist manifestos from the very first. If war came, they would approach it "dancing and singing," Marinetti wrote. In war there would be an opportunity for renewal, for regeneration, for the kind of chaos where men could prove themselves and achieve glory: an "apocalyptic transition," as one manifesto described it. Blood was invoked so often that it barely seemed to refer to what actually flowed through human bodies. In 1913, Papini wrote, without any sense of irony, that "blood is the wine of strong peoples; blood is the oil for the wheels of this enormous machine that is flying from the past into the future—because the future quickly becomes the past. Without the sacrifice of many men, humanity will go backward; without a holocaust of lives, death will defeat us."

When a European-wide war broke out in August, drawing in every major country from Russia to France, the Futurists felt history had finally shown up. The abstract became real. And their persistent argument about the redemptive power of war turned them overnight into Italy's leading voice for intervention. More manifestos followed and now dropped the pretense of being just about art. "Only war knows how to rejuvenate, accelerate and sharpen human intelligence, to make more joyful and air the nerves, to liberate us from the weight of daily burdens, to give savor to life, and talent to imbeciles," Marinetti wrote in a manifesto directed at students a few months after the guns of August.

The Futurists wanted war for war's sake and so the question of which side to support wasn't as important as whether to jump in. The Italian government, acting exactly as the Futurists feared, declared itself neutral, neither joining Germany and Austria (its allies since 1882) nor opposing them. For the Futurists, and all fervent nationalists, the choice was made simpler because they had long sought to wrench the Italian-speaking cities of Trento and Trieste away from the Austro-Hungarian Empire. Burning Austrian flags was a regular feature of Futurist *serate*. Marinetti and his friends wanted to back the entente, led by France and England, and take by force land they believed belonged to them. The Italian government's tentativeness on this matter was another sign of a liberal order in decay.

There were other reasons that France appealed. The home of the avant-garde, it was where Marinetti's original manifesto was printed on a front page. The country seemed more primed for the upheavals of modernity. As Papini saw the debate, it was the choice of "invigorating wine against indigestible beer." In a new sort of manifesto, "Futurist Synthesis of War," which doubled as a wall poster, the argument for the entente was presented as a free association of adjectives divided by a giant "greater than" sign pitting the future against the past. On one side were the Central powers, Germany ("sheepishness," "crudeness," and "heaviness") and Austria ("idiocy" and "filthiness"). And on the other, France ("intelligence," "courage," "speed," "elegance," and "explosiveness"), alongside England ("practical spirit" and "sense of duty"). It was manifesto as reductive schematic and evidence that all the creativity the medium had opened up—so attractive to Mina—was closing. This manifesto literally resembled an arrow dumbly pointing in one direction.

The outbreak of war found Mina summering with the children in Vallombrosa, a village in the mountains to the east of Florence, home to a monastery turned resort surrounded by a forest of tall pine trees. She was annoyed at the absence of news from the front (the Italian press was censored) and the general complacency and lack of interest among the expatriates and rich Italians sunning themselves around her. War, the consensus went, would end fast, and there was no reason to think it would affect them. Among the poems she began writing at the time was one that captured the atmosphere: "While round the hotel / Wanton Italian matrons / Discuss the better business of bed-linen / To regular puncture of needles." Most days Mina spent walking through the woods, still dressed stylishly in dramatic woolen cloaks, long beaded necklaces, and oversized hats trimmed with flowers and feathers. She was anxiously waiting for mail—particularly for news from Marinetti or Papini.

Her affairs seem to have precipitated open conflict between the two Futurist leaders. Now fully aware they were rivals, they came to hate each other, with Papini taking to the pages of *Lacerba* to denounce Marinetti as a domineering force who had harmed the movement. After his trip to Rome with Mina in March, Marinetti had been on the road constantly. He had spent a few weeks in London, releasing his long poem *Zang Tumb Tuuum*, a war epic composed in a style he called "words-in-freedom," which, as he had explained in a recent manifesto, did away with syntax, grammar, and punctuation ("These weights thicknesses noises smells molecular whirlwinds chains webs corridors of analogies rivalries and synchronisms"). Papini was also far from Florence for most of the first half of 1914. When Mina did briefly see him, he acted distant and fixated on Marinetti, as if testing her allegiances.

The war, when it came, slowed down the growing rift. All these thinkers, whatever their slight political and artistic arguments, were firmly on the side of intervention and obsessed with the challenge of bringing it about. It diminished the small differences and even, momentarily, some of the personal clashes.

For Mina, too, the war in its first months seemed exciting and galvanizing, a prophecy fulfilled. It allowed her, if not to ignore Futurism's misogyny, then to get swept up in the intensity of the approaching conflict. She began fantasizing about going to the front to see battle up close. Marinetti, she soon learned, was busy secretly organizing a volunteer legion to fight alongside the French until Italy gave up its neutrality. He was so eager to experience combat that he was willing, he wrote to a friend, to offer himself up "as a volunteer or as an ordinary bullet to be placed into an enormous, long-range cannon." It was overwhelming to suddenly see before them the war they had always wanted, and Marinetti and his comrades went into a frenzy of activity to try to take advantage of the moment. In the middle of all this, though, he took time that August to drive up to the mountains and surprise Mina with a visit, their first reunion since their trip to Rome in the spring.

They walked underneath the canopy of pine trees, and Mina felt the usual push and pull in his presence. He was as obnoxious as ever. "You've got a wonderful brain," he told her. "But it's like a gimlet. I wonder it doesn't hurt you!" It would do you a lot of good, he told her, "if only you could stop thinking." He had arrived with an offer to her: himself, "as a poor thing but a genuine article," she wrote. He promised even that he'd been faithful since Rome—a claim she found laughable. All his gestures, his proclamations—he was impossible to trust. "I have quite a few sympathies with my sex," she said to him by way of explaining why aligning with him would force on her a sort of betrayal.

She immediately regretted it. All her expatriate friends were making plans to board ships heading for America before transatlantic sea travel became too dangerous. There was little solid ground beneath her feet. Her connection to the movement had at least thrust her into the middle of a drama, one she wished to sustain. An American in Vallombrosa even overheard her say that she was going to go to Milan and have a child with Marinetti before he headed off to war. This momentary delusion ended up as a piece of gossip that made its way to a columnist for *The Chicago Evening Post* who, a month later, published the story of Marinetti, "a manifesto writing painter," and Papini, a "pragmatist philosopher," and Mina, "the woman who split the Futurist movement." The column described Mina as having caused the two bohemians "to attack each other in their periodicals." This woman "who loves Marinetti voiced, albeit a little theatrically, the august desire, so marked in ancient Hebrew literature, to 'preserve the seed' of valued men."

She returned to Florence that fall, a year now since she had first met the Futurists and they had shaken up her creative life. The children would stay in Vallombrosa with their nurse. She was now almost entirely devoted to poetry, a highly abstract free verse, which she used to deconstruct her feelings about Marinetti (rendered "Raminetti") and Papini ("Miovanni," a man "outside time and space"). Some of her poems even appeared that year in *The Trend,* a small New York City journal, in which she was cited in the contributor notes as someone who "has interested herself in the Italian Futurists, led by F. T. Marinetti, and for them has renounced the brush and taken up the pen." She was amused by this description, which made it seem as if she were part of the movement when in reality, as she wrote to her agent, correcting the record, she was "in no way considered a Futurist by Futurists. . . . If you like you can say that Marinetti influenced me—merely by waking me up." But to what, she still wondered, had she awoken?

AS THE WAR ground on, the manifestos became manic, even more outlandish, panting at the chance to meet a world-changing moment when the Futurists, sanctified by battle, would emerge as the first men. How to make this renewal happen? How to imagine it? Above all, how to push their countrymen toward the necessary war, how to raise patriotic spirits and steel the nation? Their treatises now zoomed in on the logistics of reengineering society—the subtext of the earlier manifestos now became text—starting with the most trivial, superficial elements of everyday life.

There was Giacomo Balla's "Futurist Men's Clothing: A Manifesto," which railed against attire that was "tight-fitting, colourless, funereal, decadent, boring and unhygienic." He got more specific in his second manifesto, written the month after war broke out: "The Antineutral Suit: A Manifesto," which demanded clothes patterned with bright, geometric shapes. Marinetti walked around in one of these garish "anti-neutral suits" in Italian red, green, and white. There was the jointly signed "The Futurist Synthetic Theater," from early 1915, which prescribed how to use theater "to influence the Italian spirit in favor of war." One manifesto, issued in March 1915, was simply called "The Futurist Reconstruction of the Universe" and covered a range of reforms, large and small, including the form and purpose of children's toys. The Futurist toy must lead the child to "completely spontaneous laughter," must have "maximum elasticity (without resorting to thrown projectiles, whip cracking, pin pricks, etc.)," must be centered on his "imaginative impulses" and the "continual exercise and sharpening of his sensitivity," but must also prime him for "physical courage." A proclivity for fighting and war was best encouraged with "gigantic, dangerous and aggressive toys that will work outdoors." The manifestos could still be a fertile sketch pad.

Marinetti was no longer onstage dodging vegetables. The *serate* had been, in retrospect, dress rehearsals for the combat now taking place in the streets. The first demonstrations against neutrality happened in Milan at his urging, and in September he was locked up for six days. Mina followed his exploits and after he got out of jail wrote about "the Brute," who is "probably ... dreaming of becoming Emperor of Italy." Many more protests followed. The fight between neutralists and interventionists was taking place not on a grand scale but between groups of elites and intellectuals, students and political cadres. Marinetti's skill at goading and rousing an audience made him particularly influential.

On April 11, 1915, after months of protest, Marinetti was arrested again at the Piazza Barberini in Rome at the head of a demonstration of thousands. Alongside him was Benito Mussolini, the dynamic Socialist activist who had recently been expelled from his party after he embraced the interventionist cause. The two men, both charismatic, both pushing for war, had praised each other in the lead-up to the rally. A few weeks before their arrests, Marinetti even claimed Mussolini as a follower, saying that "his recent actions, his attitudes and his rebellion are clear demonstrations of a Futurist consciousness." The next day, Mussolini in his paper, *Il Popolo d'Italia*, said, "We are sympathetic to Futurism and understand what it stands for and its strength." And in Mussolini's speeches, one could hear what sounded very much like the tenor of a Futurist manifesto: "We want to act, produce, dominate matter, enjoy the kind of triumph that exasperates illusions, that multiplies life's energies, and reaches toward other ends, toward other horizons, toward other ideals."

As war approached, Mina still struggled to understand what she had gained from the movement. She was alone, watching Marinetti frantically egg on the fighting ("he's getting fat & his eyes are brutalized," she wrote to a friend) and feeling distant from Papini. She was starting to realize that Futurism's greatest impact on her was in opening her eyes to her own exclusion. Even in these intellectual spaces of unfettered thinking, in the cafés where all was permitted—where you could even say "vagina"—the most exciting vision of the future these men could conjure demanded the relegation of women to the home. There was Papini and his sick fantasies of destruction or Marinetti telling her that even if women did one day get the vote, the average woman would still continue to exist only within the limited boundaries of femininity "as a mother, as a wife, and as a lover."

The manifesto still appealed to her in this moment of crisis. One could say she had so internalized the syntax and semantics of the movement that, even in opposition to it, she could only stake her claim by using its language. But it was more than that. She saw the manifesto as a medium that gave her some freedom, a way to think through what she really wanted and then assert it, to let loose the urgent and fantastical. Even if she couldn't move the men toward what she sought from Futurism, her attempt to do so, to remain part of this dialectic, was exhilarating to her. After all, it had given the men a tool for pushing each other and eventually the entire nation toward a previously unimaginable war. Maybe it could help her, too, to achieve things yet unseen and unknown. So one day in November 1914, she pulled out a sheet of white paper and in an emphatic cursive wrote "Feminist Manifesto" at the top.

The conflict that mattered to her now was the "sex wars." The manifesto begins with a declaration: "The Feminist movement as at present instituted is Inadequate. Women if you want to realize yourselves you are on the eve of a devastating psychological upheaval, all your pet illusions must be unmasked—the lies of centuries have got to go. . . . There is no half-measure—NO scratching on the surface of the rubbish heap of tradition will bring about Reform, the only method is Absolute Demolition." This was insistent and direct and much less opaque than her earlier manifesto, and her audience was, explicitly, women.

The categories of "mistress and mother" needed to be discarded, Mina wrote. But this was just the beginning. A feminism centered simply on achieving equality was misguided. There would never be any. The two sexes were in a state of permanent war, and this was the most important fact to see. "Men & women are enemies, with the enmity of the exploited for the parasite, the parasite for the exploited," she wrote. "The only point at which the interests of the sexes merge—is the sexual embrace." Women needed to stop "looking to men to find out what you are *not*," and instead "seek within yourselves what you *are*."

She insisted that women grab liberation with their own hands and stop waiting to be seen by men. In her eagerness for independence, she let the manifesto and the freedom it permitted take her to some radical conclusions. Women were being deprived of the chance to cultivate themselves, partly because they leaned on their "physical purity" as a source of value. Her solution? "The unconditional surgical destruction of virginity throughout the female population at puberty." (Mina later discovered she wasn't even the first woman to propose this—testament to just how desperate feminists of the period were to free themselves from the confinement of their circumscribed roles.) This was undoubtedly a Futurism-inflected approach—brutal, revolutionary means, sapped of human feeling—but it was also her own take, a way for women to recapture power over their bodies and self-worth. She also asserted the right to enjoy sex and motherhood regardless of whether it was outside or inside the institution of marriage. For a woman, children should be "the result of a definite period of psychic development in her life—and not necessarily of a possible irksome & outworn continuance of an alliance."

If Marinetti had used the manifesto to heap "scorn" on women, she had taken the form, bent it, and then used it to hurl her own scorn back on his limited, sexist vision of their potential. The manifestos were in conversation with one another. They could be used to modify old ideas, or even negate them—this was the process. And it's what Mina had done with hers, signaling her indebtedness to Futurism while definitively breaking with the movement and all it represented to her.

BY THE TIME Italy had entered the war in May 1915, Mina no longer had anything to do with the Futurists. Papini had finally split from Marinetti the year before, writing in *Lacerba* a series of articles denigrating him and his ideology as "juvenile, crowd-pleasing, propaganda . . . amateurism." Mina, too, had come to realize how little her two lovers had ever recognized her as a full person; she was simply a conduit for their jealousies and hatred of each other. "Don't ever live to see the day when the man you want sobs out the other one's name in the ultimate embrace." In the depths of her initial sadness, she expressed a sentiment that could not be more anti-Futurist: "The future has ceased to be as a future. One can only know that for the present one's heart continues to beat."

Mina volunteered as a nurse at a local surgical hospital in order to prepare herself to serve in the Italian Red Cross. She spent her days assisting doctors and feeling, strangely, animated by the dramatic scenes, an inkling of what she expected the men would see on the battlefield. "You have no idea what fallow fields of psychological inspiration there are in human shrieks & screams," she confided to a friend in New York. "I'm so wildly happy among the blood & mess for a change & I stink of iodoform—& all my nails are cut off for operations—& my hands have been washed in iodine—& isn't this all a change."

Italy finally joined the European battle in response to a crescendo of interventionist agitation, including the return to the country of the alluring poet and nationalist Gabriele D'Annunzio, who toured cities and towns rallying the people, as well as secret negotiations with the entente powers to grant Italy the land it wanted from Austria. The Futurists felt as if they had achieved a great victory. In that hinge, after war was declared but before the troops began heading off to the reality of battle (to experience genuine bloodletting), there was the sense that an aspiration, imagined and hoped for, was being realized. The manifestos seem to have manifested it all. In the next issue of *Lacerba*, which Papini declared would be the last, a banner headline cried, "We Won!"

Marinetti, then thirty-eight, two years away from his self-imposed expiration date, hurried to enlist in early May, as soon as war seemed imminent, but he was deemed unfit because of a hernia. He had a rushed surgery, and then another for an attack of phlebitis, all so he could get into uniform—the thing he'd most lusted after. When Italy entered the war, he was convalescing in bed, and his followers had to carry him over to his balcony, where a crowd below yelled out the news.

The manifestos had created an opening for the Futurists, allowing them to envision a world that would be violently propelled toward the new, creating rubble and ash without a thought for what would come next or what might be lost on the way there. It was an alluring opening for Mina as well, but she couldn't and wouldn't walk through it. And, in any case, her mind was fixed elsewhere. While the man who had "invigorated" her was heading off to war, and she was forced to stay in Florence, she told her agent in a letter, "What I feel now are feminine politics, but in a cosmic way that may not fit in anywhere."

With her "Feminist Manifesto" unpublished and tucked away in her suitcase, Mina set off for New York the following year, leaving Marinetti, Papini, and now Mussolini to encounter their future without her.

Chapter 4

DEBATE

—————

ACCRA, 1935

THE BRITISH IMAGINED themselves benign imperialists, and when it came to freedom of speech, they wanted to believe that the same liberal ideals that guided their own society prevailed even for their subjects. The officials who ran colonial policy were mostly smart enough to understand that controlling a population through censorship could easily backfire. "On general principle, legislation interfering with the liberty of the Press is highly undesirable and provides an effective target for public criticism of the Administration," is how one 1934 memo put it. Better for the colonized to have at least some opportunity to vent. As a result, in Accra, the capital city of the British colony known as the Gold Coast, local newspapers had existed from the mid-nineteenth century and into the twentieth as places where respectful yet scant disagreement with the colonial authorities could be found. This was tolerated.

The smudged newspapers of West Africa, produced in tiny batches on ancient printing presses and issued irregularly, functioned as another sort of loophole—much like petitions in nineteenth-century England, an exception allowing a bit of voice to the voiceless. In the newspapers, there was a chance at least for those literate West Africans to set their own agenda despite their subordinate roles. This was how J. B. Danquah saw it when, in 1931, he brought his ambition to bear on the creation of the Gold Coast's first African-owned daily, *The Times of West Africa*. Danquah was a star of Accra "society," the minuscule African elite, children of rich coastal families, who in the years after World War I had begun studying in Britain, becoming doctors and lawyers, and then returning to the colony highly educated and restless. Indirect rule, divided between the capital's white colonial administrators and a few trusted and unthreatening traditional chiefs in the agricultural hinterland, left little room for agency on the part of this elite, and also benefited the colonial power by preventing the formation of any true national identity that might transcend tribe.

It was this logjam that Danquah hoped to break with his newspaper. Accra itself had experienced a profitable cocoa boom in the 1920s, and the city was now home to a new class of locally educated Africans, the first in their families to go to public schools or those run by missionaries, becoming literate Anglophones—teachers and accountants, police officers and mining clerks, telephone exchange operators and midwives. Together with Danquah's own small community of professionals, this was a growing population that wanted to do more than just subsist. They congregated at the new Palladium on Saturday night to watch films like Busby Berkeley's *Gold Diggers of 1933* or browsed at the Methodist Book Depot (which sold English novels, transistor radios, maps, and pens) or gawked at the Accra Race Course, where elites gathered on the weekend in their hats to watch the horses. Self-improvement clubs guided these newly literate Accrans through the works of Shakespeare. And Danquah's newspaper provided the forum for shaping a common sensibility about the future. Those who had experienced life in England wanted a fast track to modernity, to discover their own analogues to European nationality and society. The locally educated meanwhile were still attached to the old ways. An issue like polygamy, for example, could become highly contentious, and *The Times of West Africa* was where the debate could take place. At bottom these were arguments about what independent African identity might look like, released from British domination.

London, grasping that the newspapers had become a space of true ferment, quickly realized the limits of its liberalism. At the end of 1932, a new governor arrived in Accra, Sir Shenton Thomas, intent on cracking down on what he saw as too much discussion and agitation in the local papers. "A greater measure of control is now necessary," he insisted to his superiors, "in view of the irresponsible and misleading matter which is continuously appearing in the local papers and which is readily believed by the half-educated classes." The governor's inspector general of police agreed, adding, "There is not a single editor of repute or sense of responsibility on any one of the local newspapers." As long as the elite remained a small and select group, their airs were tolerated. But the "half-educated classes" were now joining in the conversation. Thomas was explicit on this point: "It is the illiterates who are affected most, and young semi-educated men. They have the paper read to them and lap up all they hear."

A set of restrictive bills was announced in early 1934 to quiet the cacophony. The owners and editors of these newspapers, Governor Thomas told senior officials at the Colonial Office, "could hardly be described as civilized." The proposed rules were met with an unprecedented public protest at the Palladium. The newspapers were offering these colonial subjects an outlet they had never had before. Banning the press ("a harmless organ and the only means through which our cries are sometimes heard") would constitute a grave injustice "meted out to a very helpless people." The papers themselves were filled with letters and commentary. Many writers, as if they were in their last days of freedom, mocked Governor Thomas mercilessly, using the newspapers in precisely the way the Colonial Office feared.

Danquah joined a small delegation to go to England and confront the colonial secretary in person. The meeting was a disaster. Thomas, who had quit his post as governor in the middle of the protest, was waiting for the group and had attempted to prejudice the secretary in advance of their arrival. Danquah, he wrote, was "a dangerous man in conversation" who was also "pronouncedly Anti-White and Anti-Government," and *The Times of West Africa* was "renowned for its venomous and scurrilous attitudes towards the Government and the

European race generally." The delegation was treated like a rabble of troublesome children. They barely got a word in, and when the lunch hour began to approach, "the Colonial Secretary kept on looking at the clock as if to say, 'Oh, get on with it and be done,'" Danquah wrote in his published report. The meeting was all the proof Danquah needed to conclude that the supposedly gentle reign of the British, which seemed to offer the possibility of eventual self-rule, was a sham and the idea of gradual autonomy one they should consider "dead." It was the newspapers, Danquah could now see, that had made the British aware that "the Colonies are dangerously, perilously becoming self-conscious."

Just as they were boarding their ship back to Accra, dejected, one of the proposed ordinances was shoved through the Gold Coast's legislative council. Sedition was now illegal in the colony, a criminal offense, a blade that could drop at any moment. A publication deemed seditious could be shut down. Editors were liable and could be locked up in prison and fined. Danquah had had enough. He soon closed *The Times of West Africa* and decided to remain in London, where he set to work researching the history of the empire called Ghana, which lasted until the thirteenth century after hundreds of years of rule. When he returned to Accra two years later, it would be with the name he hoped to give his country, if it ever managed to free itself.

But in his tenure as editor, Danquah had shown what a small newspaper, bursting with many loud voices, could do for a disempowered community, how it could be a place to work out their differences and debate their identity. And just as the respectable Danquah, always in a tailored suit and striped tie, left the scene, a new editor—a radical-minded transplant from Nigeria who had spent the past few years in America—was sailing into Accra harbor, looking to go further, to create a newspaper that would be the crucible for producing the New African.

WHEN NNAMDI AZIKIWE arrived in Accra on October 31, 1934, he gave little thought to the new law or what it might mean for his plans. He wanted to change how the continent saw itself. Next to that, what was the pronouncement of some British official? He had swerved away from the comfortable life and academic career on offer to him in America to fulfill a promise he had made to himself, typed out and sworn "before God and man" on the last day of 1933, when he was still teaching political science at Lincoln University in Pennsylvania. "I shall dedicate my life to the emancipation of the continent of Africa from the shackles of imperialism, and to the redemption of my country from the manacles of foreign rule," he wrote. He wanted to coax out a "new Africa," bursting with self-respect. And the only tool available for fulfilling this mission was the new daily newspaper he was about to helm: *The African Morning Post*.

For Azikiwe (or Zik, as his reading public would soon come to know him), this was a return. The last time he had seen the Gold Coast was as a tired and hungry nineteen-year-old stowaway ten years earlier. He and two friends, all dreaming of America, had paid a sailor to hide them under a lifeboat on a ship headed from Lagos to Liverpool, where they planned to work for passage across the Atlantic. But one terrible bout of seasickness sent them ashore farther up the West African coast, not far from Accra, and soon Zik's mother, having traveled all the way from Nigeria in pursuit, was kneeling before him, tears in her eyes, begging him to return home.

It was an ignominious beginning to his life's adventures. But Zik did soon make it to America, and his years there had shaped him. He had arrived clutching a well-worn biography of James A. Garfield he'd been given as a teenager in the Nigerian province of Onitsha. It told the story of a poor boy, born in a log cabin, who had pulled himself up through education and hard work to become the twentieth president of the United States. The actual country, however, when he finally encountered it in all its messiness, knocked this sweetly naïve preconception out of him. At moments, he felt the promised freedom and possibility. He was present for FDR's first election win and the New Deal. He'd visited Harlem and seen the Sugar Hill neighborhood, where the strivers lived in large brick town houses. But from his first moments in the country—arriving at a preparatory school in

Harpers Ferry, West Virginia, site of the abolitionist John Brown's ill-fated raid—he'd been equally affected by the near-constant news of lynchings. He was lonely and poor, doubly alienated as a Black man and a foreigner. One summer in Pittsburgh he lived on lemonade and bread, working on a ditch-digging gang. He felt so depressed that he tried to kill himself, lying across train tracks late one night. A stranger pulled him off just as the conductor hit the emergency brakes. He captured his state of mind in a blues-tinged poem: "Friendless, dejected, / Sorrow fills my mind, / All hope is gone, and now: / I want to die."

From there, his situation improved. He began studying at Howard University, where he took classes with some of the greatest African American minds of that generation—political science from Ralph Bunche and philosophy from Alain Locke. In his anthropology courses, Africa, his home, was presented as the cradle of the human race. He tapped into the ferment of the late 1920s and the 1930s—the Pan-Africanism of Marcus Garvey, the writings of W.E.B. Du Bois and George Padmore, the Trinidadian-born anticolonialist. Always in need of scholarship money, he transferred to Lincoln University in 1929 (where his classmates included Thurgood Marshall and Langston Hughes) and received a master's degree there in religion and then a second in anthropology from the University of Pennsylvania, and was preparing to start a PhD at Columbia University, in political science.

It was just as he was about to make this move to New York City that he decided to stop and take stock. He had learned how to play football and was even initiated into the Phi Beta Sigma fraternity, but he was, emphatically, not of this place and never would be. His fate was always to return to his people eventually. There was one problem, though: he was now overeducated and too Americanized for British authorities, who would surely bristle at his independent mind and his ambitions. What meaningful work could he possibly find in colonial West Africa? His ideal was to return to Nigeria. Zik's mother was Igbo royalty, and his father was a functionary in the British administration, a job that had taken Zik all over Nigeria in his youth, so that he was fluent in Yoruba, Hausa, and Igbo—all three of the country's major tribal languages. But his queries for jobs back home were ignored. The civil service did not want him. Neither did the mission schools.

Newspapers were a last resort; he had dabbled as a journalist in America, writing, among other things, about sports for *The Philadelphia Tribune.* In one of his letters to various editors, Zik presented his political philosophy as more "pragmatist" than "radical" (or, rather, a "sane radical," as he put it). "I am returning semi-Gandhic, semi-Garveyistic, non-chauvinistic, semi-ethnocentric," he wrote. This was met with silence. There were few job opportunities for a self-described "budding leader."

Then he tried Alfred J. Ocansey, a Gold Coast businessman who in a short time, through trading cars, trucks, and other goods, had become one of Accra's most successful African merchants. Ocansey had branched out as well to entertainment, opening his hugely popular Palladium movie house and music hall (inspired by his visit to the London Palladium). He saw opportunity in the new, educated middle class of civil servants and clerks: here was a market in need of amusement. The Palladium became their center, a place where musicians pioneered highlife, the unique blend of fox-trot and calypso that made for a twangy guitar-heavy African version of big band. Accra's high society lined up in evening dress, top hats, and tails to hear bands like the Jazz Kings and the Cape Coast Sugar Babies, while schoolteachers and nurses sat in the balcony and Ocansey, the impresario, made money.

Zik had a proposition for the entrepreneur: fund a new newspaper and let him, Professor Azikiwe, be the editor. He even promised he could make the venture profitable. To Zik's surprise, Ocansey said he liked the idea, and on the day of Zik's return he was waiting for him onshore. As Accra harbor came into view, from the white fortress of Christiansborg castle to the clock tower of the new Achimota School, opened only a few years earlier, Zik's head was filled with his hopes for what he could do with his newspaper. "I whispered to myself that, one day, I would be in position to guide the public opinion of the country whose capital was then before me," he later wrote of that heady moment.

Accra had no landing facility, so passengers climbed onto surfboats manned by Ga boatmen, who sang as they rowed, stopping to take bites of *kenkey,* corn dumplings. Zik got in one of the bouncing boats. He was the only African, projecting seriousness with his owlish glasses and a stylish part shaved into the side of his head, all just barely compensating for his soft boyish face. As the surfboat neared the shore, the boatmen lifted each passenger on a chair over the waves the last few feet to the customs wharf. One by one they picked up the white passengers, and it soon dawned on Zik that he would be last. When he protested, a bare-chested young man looked him in the eyes with surprise and indignation. You have to wait, he told him. We first have to serve the "masters."

THERE WAS A LOT of work to do. And, in early 1935, as soon as Ocansey set up the presses and Zik, now installed at the Trocadero Hotel, hired a small staff of half a dozen secondary school graduates, *The African Morning Post* began rolling. Its print was often smeared, and readers complained about the typesetting, which left individual letters and sometimes whole words off the page, but the *Post* quickly gained a circulation of two thousand in just a few months, matching the four or five other city papers. Zik's purpose scrolled across the top of every day's front page: "Independent in all things and neutral in nothing affecting the destiny of Africa." It was easily the most stridently political of the Accra papers, shaped by Zik's anticolonialism, his nationalism, his exposure to socialism, his deep African pride, and his cerebral sensibility.

An African newspaper at this time was nothing like the professionalized and well-staffed publications that existed in the United States or Europe. The author Richard Wright, who visited Accra more than a decade later, reported that the offices of newspapers were "tiny and cluttered; many of the presses are hand-powered; the staff, in terms of quality, is extremely poor; and the salaries of the reporters are unbelievably low." These were not newspapers, he wrote, "in the sense that the West uses the term."

But there was something else that truly defined the paper as different from the Western press. A newspaper like *The African Morning Post* was made up almost entirely of contributions from its readers. It contained some hard news—a combination of wire copy from Reuters and local reports about weddings and dances. But mostly it was filled with letters and opinion pieces and freelance articles by its small community of educated English-speaking readers. This was partly out of necessity: Zik simply didn't have a budget to fill the pages with original reporting from his own journalists. "We shall be happy to place as much space in this journal as we possibly can at the disposal of the contributors," one editorial declared. The staff also solicited these contributions to encourage personal investment on the part of their readership. If they saw their own words on the page, they might be more inclined to remain loyal buyers of the paper. Often this meant coaxing reluctant writers, shaky in English, to enter the fray, advising them, as *The Gold Coast Leader,* one of the other local African-owned papers did, to "be yourself, imitate no one, say what you wish to say in your own way and leave it there: you need not ransack tomes of dictionaries for words to suffocate your readers with."

But if the newspaper's form—more a message board than a one-way conveyor of information—was largely a function of economics, it also served Zik's purpose. Much like Danquah's earlier effort, Zik imagined *The African Morning Post* primarily as a place for conversation, where Accra's literate population, its aspiring intelligentsia, could come together. Its centerpiece section was dubbed "Grumblers' Row" and was intended for debate and complaint. The quality of the writing here was surprisingly loose and unguarded. It's not that contributors had forgotten their British overlords but that almost all submissions were anonymous or pseudonymous (attributed to portentous names like A. Native or ridiculous ones like Lobster). This gave people a chance to speak their mind, unhindered, to test out higher degrees of daring. Danquah had opened the door to this possibility, but Zik was now barging through, every day bringing another argument or counterargument about the nature of their existence as colonial subjects and the need to see beyond their fractured state as a collection of tribes.

In one of the paper's first columns Zik wrote that the New Africa he envisioned "must consist of Africans and human beings, not just Fanti or Ga, Temne or Mende, Yoruba or Ibo, Bantu or Tuareg, Bubi or Hausa, Jollof or Kru." Danquah, with his vision of a modern West African, would have agreed. But whereas he had worked toward self-improvement and British recognition, Zik wanted Africans to see themselves differently—a point he and his reader-contributors reinforced in every issue—as proud and worthy, at this moment, of running their own affairs.

Zik set the table every day with his column, "Inside Stuff," and editorials. But any number of writers could then take over, usually disguised, to advocate for or condone or contradict on any topic, from the scourge of unemployment, to the pros and cons of egalitarian marriage, to the increased, possibly nefarious trend of cinemagoing among young people. *The African Morning Post* became the closest thing to a public sphere that had yet existed on the Gold Coast, at least as it would later be defined by the German philosopher Jürgen Habermas. For Habermas, the public sphere was where citizens could show up as individuals, independently, outside government control and any allegiance to clan, and deliberate together about the news of the day, forming collective opinions that could then act as a countervailing political force. In his account of the public sphere's birth, this unique environment first came together in the coffee shops of England and France in the seventeenth century, facilitated by newspapers, which provided a focal point for discussion. Habermas's vision has come to be seen as blinkered and utopian—for one thing, despite writing his formative work in the 1960s, he failed to acknowledge all the people left out of those coffeehouse conversations. The public of his "public sphere" signified a very specific slice of society, which was true as well for Zik's readers, a minority amid the illiterate masses. But the concept helps us see just what was being created on the pages of "Grumblers' Row."

In 1937, for example, British companies formed a cartel, or "Pool," to set a lower price for the cocoa they were buying from African farmers. Their alliance seriously compromised the livelihoods of powerless Gold Coasters, who depended on the cash crop. Soon enough, *The African Morning Post* erupted with dozens of pseudonymous columns from readers, including one that lamented how the cartel would "let down the African into a state of distress" and another that argued the next day that the farmers themselves were guilty for not pushing back enough: "I must say that whatever may be the case against the Pool, the European is not solely to blame. When he sees that we are up for our own rights, he steps back a little. It is our own kith and kin." Five thousand cocoa farmers eventually joined a boycott and managed to hold a united front, bringing the sales of cocoa down by 90 percent and refusing to buy European goods—except for essentials like sugar, kerosene, matches, and tobacco—until the buyers accepted a deal on their terms.

It was more than just solidarity that the quarreling voices on the page built. Being able to see differences of opinion also established common ground. Each writer was equally invested in the same project of creating a new relationship to the land and to their oppression at the hands of the British. It was the arguing that allowed them to peek over the dividers of tribe or social status and establish new allegiances, to create "indefinitely stretchable nets of kinship," as Benedict Anderson, the political scientist and historian, put it. Like Habermas, Anderson saw newspapers as the nucleus for these newly politically awake publics and would have understood exactly what was happening in the pages of *The African Morning Post*. "These fellow-readers," Anderson wrote, "to whom they were connected through print, formed, in their secular, particular, visible invisibility, the embryo of the nationally imagined community."

A TYPICAL ISSUE: Tuesday, June 4, 1935, a day of "fair sky" over Accra. The front page touts some news, both extremely local ("Christiansborg Youth Earns His B.A. Degree") and international ("Socialist

Party Forms New Cabinet in France"), but the inside pages are where things get interesting. A reader named "Angelina" fills one column with her thoughts on life insurance, a novel concept for her, which she learned about from a purloined copy of *Time* magazine. "Angelina" urges African women to "induce their husbands to take an insurance policy" so they can protect themselves in case of any tragedies. Another piece, headlined "A Disclaimer," is by a reader responding in "this popular and highly respected daily" after he was accused in a different newspaper of assaulting a woman ("Victoria Mahney is not my wife and was never brought by me from Sierra Leone and starved"). Alongside ads for the new 1935 Chrysler Plymouth Six and Satab blades ("The blade that will laugh at any beard"), most of page 6 is taken up with a political screed from someone using the byline Gump. Under the headline "What Is Civilization?" he attacks white superiority and calls Christianity itself a hypocritical religion for preaching equality but keeping the African subjugated. "They speak bitterly of the Negro; they say the Negro is mentally unfit to rank with the white man. Missionaries and non-missionaries have a bitter hatred against the Negro, yet the former is persistently promulgating the principle of 'love thy neighbor as thyself.'" Gump ends by exhorting his fellow Gold Coasters "to extinguish tribal differences and silly whims if our nation must progress on our own lines."

The concerns and opinions of readers of all sorts made it into the pages—the first priority being to fill them—but Zik clearly chose submissions to bolster his own project of raising up a New African. That June 4 issue has an unsigned lead editorial titled "African Mentality" that echoes Gump: "That the brain of the African is capable of accomplishing and, at times, surpassing, the achievements of other races, is being vindicated day by day." In Zik's own column, which he penned under the name Zik, he writes at length about the "Gold Coast scholar" touted on the front page that day for graduating from Lincoln University, Zik's own alma mater. "The African is essentially a fighter. He believes that what is willed can be," he writes.

The other regular column besides Zik's was "Men, Women, and Things," by the pseudonymous Dama Dumas. In that day's column,

Dama Dumas, who had a playful, scolding tone, pushed the need for education, reprimanding young urban women who "despite their Parisian chic and flair for intrigues are totally illiterate." Dama Dumas was Mabel Dove, the daughter of a prominent lawyer who had attended finishing school in England. She was at the very center of Accra's tiny high society and had been briefly married to Danquah. It was in his *Times of West Africa,* in a column called "Ladies' Corner," that she first perfected the judgmental but droll and clever voice that became a perfect foil for the paper's readers. Her opinions, on everything from the chicness of certain frocks to the need for young women to resist premarital sex, were never predictable and always elicited either angry or approving responses. She was a feminist who also urged cultivation, with suggestions on which Dickens novel to read. Her elitist sensibilities, aimed at lifting up the newly educated class, were largely gleaned from her time in England but were balanced by deep African pride. Most columns would land on a question: "If an Indian lady of rank could appear at Buckingham Palace in her own national costume and look perfectly appropriate and in good taste, what is to hinder us women adopting a similar attitude?" And the pages of the newspaper often turned into a forum on positions she had taken, such as when the Young People's Literary Club held a debate on the question, "Is the European form of marriage beneficial to the African?" The initial vote was no, but she disagreed and thought "native marriage," by which she meant polygamy, to be "old" and "primitive" and "a trifle distasteful to us modern women." For weeks, the opinions of readers and her rebuttals filled the pages.

This printed back-and-forth was good for keeping readers hooked, but it also allowed for a reconciling of different visions of independence. What would that New African be like? How much of traditional culture and practice would have to be thrown off to seize upon a modern national identity? These questions snaked through every column and reader response. A figure like Zik had already crossed the Rubicon. A Nigerian, educated in America and living in Accra, he saw himself as embodying something much larger than tribe or even colonial territory. He wanted a future of independent African countries, on equal footing with a France or a Germany, each state held together by a set of common values as much as a rootedness to soil.

Mabel Dove was much closer to being a New African, which is why one of the biggest debates she ignited, when she was still writing as Marjorie Mensah in Danquah's paper, was about whether she actually existed or, more precisely, whether a woman could really be behind her column. Many readers saw her as an aspirational fiction, created by the elites. They were dubious that a woman with such sharpened wit and intelligence could be real and, if so, whether this would even be desirable. The argument began with a contributor claiming that "the diction and firm grip" that she possessed as a writer were impossible to imagine in a Gold Coast woman. Another man speculated that she might just have had a lot of training in Europe. Underneath the surface controversy about who really wrote the columns was a debate about future gender roles: If Africans embraced independence and modernity, would they have to contend with equality of the sexes as well? These attacks were parried in the column, of course, with Mabel defending all women. "What do you think of us, after all? You, and a good many others like you, have the most peculiar notions of women— especially Gold Coast women—that I have ever heard of. Do you really think that none of us is capable of writing up a column in a Newspaper?" The controversy was so intriguing—"Print her picture!" was the demand in many letters—that there was even a local cabaret show featuring a man in drag as "Miss Marjorie Mensah" in the skit "Of Course I Am a Lady."

Though it might not have felt like it to the many readers who were writing in and choosing grandiose pen names to voice their opinions, they were creating a public sphere and one that Zik understood to be doing significant work. These debates in the pages of the *Post* were sometimes serious—one forum straightforwardly asked the readers, "Is the Gold Coast a Nation?"—and sometimes trivial, but they were the only way to move an anti-imperialist movement forward. As long as the British set the terms of identity, exploiting tribal divisions to keep the nation fractured and precluding any kind of national consciousness or civil society from taking shape, they could argue that there was no leading, educated class prepared to grab the reins. It was the act of wrangling with each other on the pages of the newspaper that not only built that class but provided the proof that it existed.

WITHIN A YEAR, Zik had kept his promise to Ocansey and had increased circulation far past the point the businessman thought possible. By 1936, the *Morning Post* had ten thousand daily readers, some subscribing from Nigeria, Sierra Leone, and the Cameroons. With a small, inexperienced staff, the work was never ending for Zik. He would wake before dawn and rush from his room on the top floor of the Trocadero Hotel to the office, where he'd take a magnifying glass to the proofs of each day's paper. He would then make his way to the dusty printing workshop, where he would yell orders at the workers manning old presses that often broke mid-printing. Zik could be aloof and dictatorial with his staff, who never seemed to live up to his standards. He felt himself a professional, a man of the world, working in an environment that continuously sabotaged him.

Because of his education and his bearing, Zik had been accepted by Accra's high society, playing tennis every other day at the Rodger Club with members of the elite and even a few white colonial administrators. But he was never truly comfortable there and remained a largely solitary, driven figure behind his glasses. As his assistant editor at the paper put it, Zik was "ill at ease in this society in which he was still both a 'stranger' and also something rather special. He was admired and cheered by thousands, but most people stood in understandable awe of him when in close, personal contact. They flocked around him smiling broadly and shaking hands after his lectures, but that is different than intimate small talk on equal terms." His was the loneliness of the New African, as he saw it. In his mind and in the pages of his newspaper, he lived in the future, but day to day the old allegiances and power structures, reinforced by tradition and the gun, still seemed to dwarf him.

There was, however, some proof of his success, that he was moving people in his direction, if only in the irritation of a growing number of detractors. Despite the chummy tennis matches, Zik had a harsh opinion of what he thought of as the old African establishment, both the elite he felt were too passive and the tribal leaders who were complicit in British rule—they had become too comfortable with the way things were. Or perhaps they benefited too much? In his lexicon, all of them represented the "Old Africa" that he repeatedly insisted in his columns "must be destroyed because it is at death grips with the New Africa." He opened up his pages to the frustration of a younger generation who saw no prospects for themselves and resented the status quo and anyone, Black or white, who seemed to profit from it. Zik even successfully used the *Morning Post* to promote a new populist political party, the Mambii Party (from the Ga word for "people"), against the establishment party, vying for seats on the colony's legislative council, a largely ceremonial body meant to offer the illusion of political participation (its constitution guaranteed a British majority and gave final word to the governor).

To the chiefs, who had gained most from indirect rule and wielded even greater power than they had before colonialism, Zik was nothing but an outside agitator. At a session of the legislative council, one of the most respected chiefs in the Gold Coast, Nana Sir Ofori Atta (also, coincidentally, Danquah's half brother), spoke of Zik without mentioning his name. "We have heard so much of a 'New Africa' coming to birth," he said. "The protagonists of the New Africa are spreading doctrines which can only tend to cause trouble in this country." He saw real danger in the way the young were being "educated to disrespect and show open contempt to the Chiefs and Elders."

Zik liked what was happening in his pages, the way it seemed to be building up the self-esteem of Accrans and challenging the elite to think more expansively. If it meant that sometimes his readers expressed themselves bombastically or with too much violence—criticizing administrators, condemning colonialism, embracing Pan-Africanism (and sometimes even Communism)—it was all part of the healthy friction he was hoping to create.

So free and lively were the *Morning Post*'s pages that Zik could be said to have forgotten the threat that hung over him from the very first issue: the ordinance passed through the legislative council (even though it was opposed by all the African members), which gave the governor the right to determine whether a publication had "seditious intention" and then impose fines and jail time on writers and editors. It left wide open to interpretation exactly what was meant by "seditious." This could be anything from inciting rebellion against colonial rule to simply provoking "hatred or contempt" and "disaffection against the administration of justice in the Gold Coast."

The reviled governor Shenton Thomas had been replaced by Sir Arnold Hodson, who had a very different approach to his role. Hodson had gained the nickname Sunshine Governor at his previous post in Sierra Leone, and his governing philosophy soon became clear. He would give the press some room to do its thing. Aside from blasting pro-British propaganda over the state radio, he would practice benign neglect. He was confident that a venue like "Grumblers' Row," with all its jostling argumentation and passionate opinion, was simply too clamorous to present a real threat. "It is well known," he wrote shortly after taking over as governor, "that overstatement and exaggeration eventually defeat their own ends and exert little influence on the great mass of public opinion."

With Hodson installed, there were very few reasons to worry that the bubbling disquiet in the *Morning Post* would create any problems for Zik. Into the second year of the paper's life it seemed he was able to do just what Danquah had done and much more, with no real pushback. Zik had even struck up an acquaintance with the new governor, and in April 1936, when Zik got married to Flora Ogoegbunam, a young woman from his city of Onitsha, Sir Arnold was in attendance. Underneath the redbrick clock tower of Accra's Methodist church, with Zik dressed in black tails and striped pants, the governor handed him a gift: the gathered speeches of Britain's Conservative prime minister, Stanley Baldwin, in a book titled *This Torch of Freedom*.

THE ARTICLE THAT nearly brought Zik's experiment to an end was published in the May 15, 1936, issue of the *Morning Post*. It was part of the regular volley of columns and counter-columns. In this case, the writer, identified only with the pseudonym Effective, was responding to an earlier editorial that posed the purposefully provocative question, "Do the Europeans believe in God?" Effective said yes, they did, but it was a god "whose name is spelt Deceit" and whom Africans had no business worshipping. The white man "believes in the god whose law is 'Ye strong, you must weaken the weak.' Ye 'civilized' Europeans, you must 'civilize' the 'barbarous' Africans with machine guns. Ye 'Christian' Europeans, you must 'Christianize' the 'pagan' Africans with bombs, poison gases, etc." Nothing was held back. The racism of the colonizers was rancid: Europeans "put a monkey on a chair with a chain around its neck and let an African child hold fast to the chain and take their photographic picture and write an inscription underneath—'two monkeys'—so that the African realizes that to the Europeans he (the African) is classified as a monkey. Yes, this is the god that the European knows and believes in."

By the article's end Effective asserted that he prayed only to "the god of Ethiopia, whom my forefathers worshipped at a period when the Europeans were living in caves," and that he felt himself to be on equal footing with any white man who might claim superiority. "The European respects me and I respect him in turn. In the event he oversteps his bounds and becomes insulting, I often put him in his place in a jiffy. He does not controvert with me because he knows what the result would be."

Zik had had reservations about running this piece. It wasn't that some red line had been crossed—the anonymous opinions in his pages regularly stretched to these extremes—but the identity of the man writing as Effective made him wary. It was Isaac Theophilus Akunna Wallace-Johnson, a self-described "international African" who was born in Sierra Leone and spent most of his life traveling in trade union and Communist circles, even studying at a Comintern-sponsored university in Moscow in the late 1920s (where Jomo Kenyatta, the future Kenyan leader, was his roommate). When Wallace-Johnson landed in the Gold Coast around the same time as Zik, the colony's attorney general wrote that the writer had been trained in Moscow "in the art of subversive propaganda" and that he had "returned to West Africa as a professional agitator." Copies of *The Negro Worker* proliferated in his wake.

Zik didn't mind Wallace-Johnson's radicalism—after all, they shared the same anticolonial goals—but they differed greatly on tactics, on how to get to where they wanted to go. Wallace-Johnson desired immediate revolution. He looked to Lenin, Stalin, and Trotsky and valorized the idea of a vanguard leading the way. Zik disagreed and thought an "intellectual revolution" was needed first—and that his newspaper was doing the work of bringing it about. "I referred him to the history of modern Italy," Zik wrote, describing his first encounter with Wallace-Johnson. "How it took a Mazzini to revolutionize the thinking of the Italians, and a Cavour to plan the future of Italian nationalism, before a Garibaldi came on to the scene as a man of action." Wallace-Johnson responded that Zik's method would take centuries; his could accomplish independence in decades.

What Zik couldn't abide was Wallace-Johnson using his radical approach to sabotage Zik's, planting a bomb in the middle of his public sphere. And so when Alfred Ocansey, the paper's publisher, passed along the article and asked Zik to run it, Zik pushed back. He did not trust Wallace-Johnson, and he also knew that without a name attributed to the piece, he himself would be responsible for its possible "seditious intent." But Ocansey insisted and Zik, frustrated, passed the piece along to one of his assistant editors to handle.

What Zik didn't know was that Governor Hodson, despite his genial presence at Zik's wedding, was looking for just such an opportunity. In February 1936, several months before Zik published Wallace-Johnson's piece, Hodson had made a request to the Colonial Office that had shocked his superiors. He wanted "absolute power to suppress a paper at once, if, in my opinion, such action is warranted." The radio propaganda campaign had failed, and the newspapers seemed beyond reform, "controlled by the Red element" and seeking, through the publication of many angry, disgruntled voices, "to stir up trouble and break up the Empire." He had a specific disdain for Wallace-Johnson, who, though he didn't run a newspaper, seemed to always be involved in every provocation. Increasingly irritated, Hodson wrote home that he was certain that, unlike the British rulers, "the French would not tolerate it for one second."

THE KNOCK ON Zik's door came eight days after Wallace-Johnson's "Has the African a God?" appeared in the *Morning Post*. It was early on a Saturday morning at his suite at the Trocadero. Standing there, flanked by a number of armed officers, was the superintendent of police, D. G. Carruthers, who also happened to be one of Zik's regular tennis partners at the Gold Coast Lawn Tennis Club at Adabraka. Carruthers looked as if he didn't know the man before him. "Are you Mr. Nnamdi Azikiwe?" he asked. Zik responded that he was. "Are you the editor of *The African Morning Post*?" "Yes," Zik answered again. "I have a criminal writ for you." And with that Carruthers handed over a document charging Zik with four counts of violating the sedition ordinance, all related to Wallace-Johnson's article. Zik scanned the page and quickly saw that each count carried a maximum penalty of two years' imprisonment or a hundred-pound fine. He broke out in a cold sweat, his thin shoulders hunching forward, and Carruthers suddenly abandoned his impersonal pose. "Zik, I hope you realize that I am doing my duty," he told him. "Of course, D.G., I do." Carruthers then smiled and asked if they were still on for tennis that evening.

Wallace-Johnson was soon also arrested after detectives uncovered proof that he was Effective. His trial came first, in the fall, and ended with a guilty verdict, though the radical was able to avoid prison (he was given two weeks to raise a fifty-pound fine instead of a three-month sentence). The light punishment so angered Governor Hodson that he began drafting new legislation allowing him to deport from the colony anyone charged with sedition.

Zik's ordeal dragged out much longer; the trial was delayed nineteen times over the course of 1936. These were long months of waiting and uncertainty. He tried to run the newspaper as before, populating it with as many voices as possible. But he felt the chill of Hodson's crackdown. When Zik did finally come before a judge, in January 1937, it didn't take long for him to be declared guilty. Wallace-Johnson's trial had already established that the *Morning Post* had published seditious content, and as the editor Zik was complicit in the crime. "It is a very serious offense for an editor of a newspaper to commit in a largely illiterate country like the Gold Coast," the judge told Zik. He received a six-month sentence and was fined fifty pounds, but a technical mistake on the judge's part spared Zik from prison, and he emerged on the steps of the courthouse looking rattled but resilient. He was prepared "for the inevitable," he told the crowd, if it helped to speed Africa "on its way toward redemption and self-determination."

He embraced his martyrdom. The day after his judgment he wrote a column describing himself as the "living spirit of an idea—the idea of a New Africa," now faced with "the travails and tribulations of Gethsemane, and Golgotha and Calvary." He had arrived in the Gold Coast, "this Galilee of my life," at the age of thirty and he was now thirty-three, "on the brink of my 'crucifixion.'" His readers, also the paper's main contributors, who owned it as much as he did, now felt embattled along with him. They were his strength, he wrote. "Why then should I be daunted when I know that Renascent Africa feel with me, and sigh with me, and dream with me, and vision with me, at this thirty third age of my fleeting existence on this planet?" If the *Morning Post* had managed to create a new public, Zik was speaking to it and for it.

Zik appealed the ruling a few months later, in March, and it was then that the special character of the newspaper revealed itself. "Grumblers' Row," and much of the rest of the paper, had a trickster quality in its anonymity. Writers darted out from behind trees, threw rocks, and then retreated. And this, in the end, is what saved Zik and his entire endeavor.

He was represented by Frans Dove, the most highly respected West African lawyer (and the father of Mabel Dove, a.k.a. Dama Dumas). Dove decided to question a fundamental assumption of the Crown's case: that Zik was in fact the editor of *The African Morning Post*. Before the appeals procedure could begin, Dove asked the three judges of the West African Court of Appeal (made up of the chief justices of Nigeria, the Gold Coast, and Sierra Leone, three knighted white Englishmen in wool wigs) if he could first raise a preliminary but basic objection. He wanted an explanation for why Nnamdi Azikiwe had any connection with this case.

The attorney general huffed that this was an absurd question. He said that, of course, Nnamdi Azikiwe was "Zik" and that every school-boy in the country knew who Zik was: the editor of *The African Morning Post*, which published a seditious article in its pages. Dove answered that though he understood "the popular identification of Zik with Azikiwe and Azikiwe with the *African Morning Post*" and that this might mean something to the average person, it "meant nothing to the law." In the paper, the pseudonyms separated the pen from the body. The name Nnamdi Azikiwe appeared nowhere, even if "Zik" did. Unless the Crown could properly identify the man before them as the editor, he was not answerable to the charges that had been brought against him.

Dove had come up with a checkmate, using the logic of the British court system—which determined guilt through identification and confession—against itself. The attorney general jumped to his feet and said he was surprised that Dove was trying to deceive the court in this way. He would gladly provide legal proof of identity. He then called into the record Zik's original arrest by his tennis buddy D. G. Carruthers. In the transcript read aloud, Zik was clearly asked both whether he was Nnamdi Azikiwe and whether he was the editor of *The African Morning Post*. "That was the record, my Lords," said the attorney general with triumph in his voice.

Dove was prepared for this. The courtroom grew quiet, and all three judges peered down from their benches with real curiosity about the lawyer's next move. He stood up and said in a quiet voice that it was true that on the occasion of his arrest, May 23, 1936, Nnamdi Azikiwe had admitted he was the editor of the paper. But that was irrelevant. Had the prosecution established anywhere that he was the editor on the material date of Friday, May 15, 1936—that is, when Wallace-Johnson's article appeared in print? "Even breathing seemed to have stopped in the court," one of Zik's friends reported. The judges posed the question to the deflated attorney general, who had to answer that no, he could not offer any proof that Zik had been legally identified as editor on May 15. That, one of the chief justices then said, was "fatal" to the Crown's case.

The trial was over in a matter of minutes. The president of the West African Court of Appeal threw out Zik's conviction and ordered that the fifty-pound fine be immediately refunded. Zik hardly had a moment to take it all in when what he later described as a "hilarious uproar" broke out. He was lifted on the shoulders of his friends as the police shouted, "Order in the court!" They carried him out and then down Pagan Road to the offices of *The African Morning Post,* where, he later wrote, "the staff joined with the mob as we milled through the streets of Accra, singing, dancing and merrymaking at my acquittal." The grumblers had come in person to celebrate their win.

THE TRIAL AND ZIK'S VICTORY over the colonial masters had made an impression on the growing community of newspaper readers in Accra. They had affirmed their right to their public space, the small freedom to debate among themselves. Kwame Nkrumah, a young teacher trained at the Achimota School who had visited Zik the previous year looking for advice, later wrote in his memoirs that his own feelings of nationalism were "revived at about that time through articles written in *The African Morning Post.*" Nkrumah had thought of becoming a Catholic priest but decided to study in the United States instead. Zik wrote a letter to Lincoln University, and Nkrumah set off, starting his studies there in the fall of 1935. But he followed the events back home very closely—as did Langston Hughes, who wrote a poem about his old college friend. Nkrumah, the man who would eventually become the first prime minister and president of Ghana (and one of the first leaders of any sub-Saharan African country to gain independence), wrote that Zik's sedition case was "the first warning puff of smoke that a fire had been lit, a fire that would prove impossible to extinguish."

What was this fire? Those first flickers of a national identity, born of opinions rubbing against each other in ways they never had before, as citizens of a shared nation argued about their present and their future. Zik was pleased, of course, but he also took the moment to stop and ask himself what he was doing in the Gold Coast. It had been an exhausting year. His wife, Flora, missed her family, missed Nigeria. And his own relationship with Ocansey had become strained. He didn't know whether he would have the same sort of editorial control over the paper that he had enjoyed before his arrest. With these doubts already growing, he learned of a small newspaper going out of business and selling its press. He quickly found investors and took the opportunity to buy the steam-powered machine, a Wharfedale Stop Cylinder, invented in the mid-nineteenth century and already out of use in Europe and America. This one was well worn but functioning. Zik had all the parts delivered on a truck to Accra, and as soon as he set it up, he registered a new company: Zik's Press.

Soon, just three months after his acquittal, he was on a boat in Accra harbor, looking again at the coastline. This time, though, he had his wife with him and a printing press on board, as well as a reputation for being more than just a sharp young man with an American education. He had proven himself capable of bringing together a readership, a self-aware community that didn't mind irritating the British authorities as it groped toward its own independence. Now he was headed to Lagos, where he would start a new newspaper, the *West African Pilot*, hoping to continue what he'd begun. It would take another quarter century before Nigeria would declare its independence from Britain, and when it did, Nnamdi Azikiwe was sworn in as the republic's first president.

Chapter 5

FOCUS

Moscow, 1968

IN THE YEARS following Stalin's death in 1953, the Soviet Union exhaled. It was a period known as the Thaw, and like many in her generation Natalya Gorbanevskaya was shaped by the sliver of openness it brought after the long years of pervasive fear and murder. Nikita Khrushchev, the new leader, delivered his "secret speech" in 1956 denouncing Stalin's cult of personality and repressive rule. New thinking, new shapes and colors, made their way in. Picasso's paintings were exhibited in Moscow and Leningrad, and Natasha, as she was known to all, rushed to see them with her friends from university.

But for the urban intelligentsia this dizzying moment also presented a new set of complications. Just a few months before cubism made its way to the Hermitage, Soviet tanks had brutally crushed the Hungarian revolution. It was no longer obvious anymore exactly what would set the regime on edge. Under Stalin, testing the limits of freedom meant possibly being sent to a Siberian Gulag or marched downstairs to a prison basement and shot. But how far could you go now? The landscape, though cleared of land mines, still had plenty of holes to fall into and sharp rocks to trip over. What would set off the regime? How critical could you be, and what exactly could you criticize?

What art was permitted? And what kinds of difficult truths could be uttered above a whisper?

The testing ground for these questions was samizdat. The word was a contraction of "self" and "publishing," usually by typewritten manuscript, and it was in every way a unique product of the Thaw. By the early 1960s it was the underground method for reading the novels, short stories, poems, political essays, and memoirs that would never make it through the Soviet state censors. Samizdat writing quickly became the most interesting writing, passed from hand to hand illicitly, a sort of forbidden fruit. (A famous joke from the time recounts a mother saying that when her daughter refused to read *War and Peace*, she gave it to her to retype as samizdat, and she grabbed it and read every word.)

For a burgeoning poet like Natasha, who had been writing verses since she was a young girl, the Thaw made her feel she could express herself more openly, but the options for having her work read were still few. When she was a linguistics student at Moscow University in the late 1950s, her first poems appeared on the university's wall newspaper—pages of printed broadsheet pasted up around campus, to be read while standing. Other students attacked her as "decadent and a pessimist" for her dark, lovelorn sentiments. She also learned just how dangerous poetry could be in the Soviet Union. After the quashing of the Hungarian revolution, some of Natasha's friends were arrested for their poems, and she even found herself at the notorious Lubyanka prison (the place where, in fact, inmates *had* been shot in the basement not long before). Under KGB pressure, she revealed everything about the creation of the pamphlet that had contained the offending poems. In her mind then, at twenty-one, she still imagined herself a good Soviet citizen, a member of the Komsomol, the young pioneers. But afterward she was filled with remorse and never forgave herself for betraying her friends.

By the early 1960s, her writing life benefited from the spread of samizdat, giving her a chance to add her verses to the stream of underground poetry. At first, she would copy out her poems by hand and share them with friends. But after she purchased an old Olympia for forty-five rubles to write her thesis, she began typing them out. She used carbon paper that could create four copies at once. Natasha would reproduce the same collection as many as eight times, to "publish" an initial samizdat run of thirty-two. Her poems of alienation and loneliness would then spread as her readers made their own copies. "I enter my being like a plane going into a spin," she wrote in one poem, part of her first samizdat publication from 1964, the year when she began putting together annual compendiums. In another she is "not a flame, not a candle, but a light, I am a fire-fly in the damp, tangled grass."

Increasingly, the samizdat drew Natasha into a community of dissidents. Just by virtue of engaging in an artistic act, even if its subject was more personal than political, she found herself in defiance of a regime and an ideology that wanted control over all cultural production. In the early 1960s she helped organize two samizdat poetry magazines, *Syntax* and *Phoenix*, both of which so riled the authorities that they arrested their editors, charged them as criminals, and sent them away to prison camps. Natasha continued to write. In 1962 she was even taken by a friend to meet Anna Akhmatova, a godmother to the country's dissident poets. Akhmatova's circle of young acolytes then included Joseph Brodsky, who would soon be denounced and put on trial for what were deemed "pornographic and anti-Soviet" poems. Then in her seventies, Akhmatova's regal, uncompromising presence made a strong impression on Natasha, and she became set on her identity as a poet, with all the difficulties this life would entail.

If samizdat started this way for her, as a form of self-expression, Natasha was also beginning to see how it could unify the community of dissident artists and writers then increasingly under attack. It fused them together, providing a form of currency when all the usual avenues of culture were closed. But just how instrumental it could be in helping their burgeoning opposition to home in on a clear purpose, hammering away day after day at the same immovable force of the state—that only became evident once the aperture that had allowed some light into their creative lives began to close.

THE THAW ENDED for Natasha and her friends on the day Andrei Sinyavsky and Yuli Daniel were arrested in September 1965. Both were respected and established writers. Whenever purveyors of samizdat had been prosecuted before, it was almost always for invented or planted crimes, but Sinyavsky and Daniel were put on trial specifically for their words. They were charged under a new Article 70, which made "anti-Soviet propaganda and agitation" illegal and punishable by prison sentence.

On December 5, 1965, an official holiday celebrating the Soviet constitution, the dissidents gathered at Pushkin Square in central Moscow in protest, a terrifying prospect coming just a decade after Stalin's death. The banners they unfurled gave an indication of their strategy: not to call for revolution or overthrow, but simply to ask the Soviet state to abide by its own laws—the civil and human rights principles codified in the country's guiding charter. "Respect the Constitution, the Basic Law of the USSR," they insisted, and "We Demand That the Sinyavsky-Daniel Trial Be Public." A couple months later, Sinyavsky was sentenced to seven years and Daniel to five in the notorious labor camps in Mordovia.

Natasha knew both of them well. She had often visited Sinyavsky, whose seminar in Soviet poetry she had taken as a student, and she had once met Yuli Daniel at his home. This was her community, with all of its squabbles and love affairs, and the sentencing fell on her hard. What followed over the next two or three years was best captured in the title of one of the samizdat books about the various repressions: "The Process of the Chain Reaction." There would be an arrest and a trial and then exile or imprisonment, and samizdat began to serve as a way to document it all, the facts of it, including secretly gathered testimony from trials, and the accounts of those few open displays of protest that were often dispersed in seconds. The appearance of the samizdat in turn led to more arrests, leading to even more samizdat. In this way, throughout 1966 and 1967, Natasha saw many of her friends either sent to prison camps themselves or taking care of those who were—not to mention the families they had left behind. The days of poetry deemed subversive simply because its themes were not cheery enough, those days were over. They were now fighting a war with the regime and their only real weapon was onionskin paper.

Natasha made her part in this battle public in February 1968, when she signed a letter addressed to the troika of leaders then running the country and guiding the crackdown—Nikolai Podgorny, Alexei Kosygin, and Leonid Brezhnev—to demand that her friends, arrested for producing samizdat, be given an open trial, as mandated by law. "As long as arbitrary action of this kind continues uncondemned, no one can feel safe." Natasha knew she was taking an enormous risk and that she was in a particularly vulnerable situation. She was living with her mother and her son, Yasik, in one unit of a noisy, dimly lit communal apartment with shared bathrooms and kitchens. Natasha's father was killed at the front in 1943, and she had grown up with a single parent. Her own decision now to raise a child by herself—with the help of her mother, of course—was voluntary but unusual. There was a pervasive eccentricity about Natasha. In a photo from 1968, when she was thirty-two, she is dressed in baggy pants, a formless dark, knitted sweater, and tennis shoes. Her hair is messy and comes down only to her chin; cat-eye glasses dominate her face. And now she was pregnant again, once more without the child's father's involvement.

Two days after sending off her protest letter, she felt the hand of the state slap her down, and in the strangest, most unsettling way. Early in the last trimester of her pregnancy, she woke up ill one day and, fearing there was a problem with the baby, checked herself into a maternity hospital and was diagnosed with anemia. As in a horror story, once admitted, she wasn't allowed to leave. In a series of notes that she managed to smuggle out, she described the ordeal in real time. "Why are they keeping me here?" she wrote. "After each 'Wait until tomorrow' I collapse like an empty sack." After a few days, a psychiatrist examined her and deemed her insistence on being discharged a symptom of schizophrenia. She was then forcibly strip-searched and placed in an ambulance, where she was taken to Moscow's main psychiatric institution, known as Kashchenko.

The nightmare continued with the clothing: "Another way of crushing and humiliating one. Knickers (knitted ones) down to the knees, stockings without elastic which keep falling down . . . So we all go around looking uniformly awful, scarcely human in appearance, let alone feminine." Most of the women were indeed mentally ill: "There's a recreation room here, with a television and a radiogram. I glanced in, thinking I might pass the time watching television. The television was not yet switched on, and two couples were moving round to the radiogram, to the sound of some post-war tango: poor, miserable women, in frightful gowns, twined together, languorously swaying their hips."

This was the KGB's way of punishing her. Only the pregnancy had dictated she land here and not in a prison camp. She tried to be strong. "If they did want to frighten me, to throw me off the rails, to traumatise me, they did not succeed," she wrote in her last note. "I am waiting for the birth of my child quite calmly, and neither my pregnancy nor his birth will prevent me from doing what I wish—which includes participating in every protest against any act of tyranny." After nearly two weeks, she was suddenly and without explanation sent home.

It was in the days following her release, regrouping with friends, and still very pregnant, that she began imagining some further use of samizdat, extending its role of documentation, creating one central place to compile a detailed list of wrongs committed by the Soviet Union.

NATASHA LIKED THE TONE captured in the protest letters written collectively by dissident friends—cold as ice, precise, almost legalistic, placing state actions alongside citations of law. She had a love of objectivity, as she later put it. She wanted to use this approach in the creation of a samizdat "journal," one that would capture the way her community was, by 1968, being regularly battered. Even though some news of the arrests and trials was making it out to the West, and sometimes even being broadcast back into the Soviet Union on the BBC or Voice of America's shortwave frequencies, these were only the most well-known cases. Natasha wanted to gather everything that was happening, the full experience of living through what they were beginning to think of as a neo-Stalinist moment. It was easy to lose track of the many injustices in the day-to-day reality of their persecution, to feel many darts landing but not know how to move beyond an emotional response, or do more than gird themselves. This journal would help them focus—allow them to pick up the scattered pieces and put them together, fixing their attention on the construction of an ongoing argument. It would also allow them to bring together the various strands of dissidence throughout the empire—those persecuted for their religion, those treated with suspicion for their allegiance to their national or ethnic group, and, of course, the political outcasts, some beaten down simply for insisting on truthfulness, others just for being slightly out of step with the unitary vision of the Communist Party. Each saw their plight as unique. Now they would literally be on the same page.

In this journal, Natasha and her friends resolved, they would excise all personal opinion and let the facts speak. Western journalists would take them more seriously as a result, but this decision about style was also a form of resistance. For a regime that, going back to Lenin, valued the press primarily for its propaganda potential, a neutral news source like the one she was envisioning, committed to a clinical, dry recitation of information, was subversive.

Natasha had time on her hands; her due date fast approaching, she was on leave from her job as a translator at Moscow's State Institute of Experimental Design and Technical Research. She also had editorial skills from years of producing samizdat, and she was a quick typist. There were other intellectuals who had more standing among the dissidents, but they saw the job of compiling and retyping as menial. Natasha was not afraid of work, and she was eager to do something. And so that spring of 1968, at the end of March, feeling her child move inside her, Natasha slipped one of the pages of carbon paper into her Olympia and started to type.

At the top of Issue No. 1, Natasha had given the journal a title, half-ironic and half in earnest: *Human Rights Year in the Soviet Union*. The Universal Declaration of Human Rights (not exactly commemorated in the Soviet Union) had been signed twenty years earlier. For good measure she added Article 19 as an epigraph: "Everyone has the right of freedom of opinion and expression; this right includes freedom to hold opinions without interference and to seek, receive and impart information and ideas through any media regardless of frontiers." The name that stuck was the one she used as a subtitle, *Chronicle of Current Events,* after a BBC Russian-language news roundup. It would become known simply as the *Chronicle.*

Natasha composed the first issue in her apartment on her typewriter, though she had paid someone on the black market to alter the keys on her Olympia to keep the authorities from connecting her political samizdat to her poetry samizdat. It was twenty tightly spaced pages, with seven carbon copies. She finished by the end of April and gave it an issue date of April 30, 1968 (from then on, issues would appear every other month on the last day of the month). Six of the copies were spread among friends to be retyped in turn, and one was given to a Western correspondent. The scribbled notes containing all the information that went into the issue were immediately burned.

From that first edition, Natasha and her friends used the *Chronicle* to unload the burden of all the harm that had been done to them. In that sense it was fairly parochial. All the events described at first concerned the small circle of intellectuals in Moscow and Leningrad, starting with an account of the trial of four among them who had been prosecuted for creating samizdat. Even Natasha's recent ordeal made it in: "Without any warning and without her relations' knowledge, Gorbanevskaya was transferred on 15 February from maternity clinic No. 27, where she was being kept with a threatened miscarriage, to ward 27 of the Kashchenko Hospital."

The journal felt new. It presented itself as a value-free receptacle. The sparse writing was refreshing, almost elegant. Later, Ludmila Alexeyeva, one of the dissidents who most helped with the typing of the *Chronicle,* described what she called the "wooden, impersonal style" this way: "It would offer no commentary, no belles lettres, no verbal somersaults; just basic information." The absence of embellishment felt to Natasha like a creative act. Not the experience she had writing poetry, which, she often said, felt to her as natural and necessary as breathing, but a willed sort of chiseling away at emotion that was satisfying in a different way—that sharpened the focus.

Two weeks after disseminating the first issue, she decided to do another press run, which meant sitting down and typing it all out again. Her friend Pavel Litvinov, grandson of Stalin's foreign minister, Maxim Litvinov, had become a prominent dissident who had contributed a lot of the information for the first issue. He let Natasha use his family's apartment during the day as a place to type, mostly to keep the project away from Natasha's mother. While working there on the afternoon of May 13, she felt the first contractions of her labor. She kept at it a bit longer, but when the pain became too much, she simply left the page in the typewriter and a note for Litvinov to finish the work. She took herself to the hospital, where she gave birth to her second son at 1:30 in the morning. Weeks later when she recovered and went to visit Litvinov, she found the page in the typewriter exactly where she had left it. It was her project, her initiative, appreciated perhaps by the other dissidents, but not yet deemed essential. She would have to prove its importance to them. She finished retyping Issue No. 1 and started on Issue No. 2, which would be dated June 30, 1968.

By the second issue, Natasha began to innovate, adding more features to the journal. The most important was "News in Brief," a kind of catchall for violations of every sort and updates on the various cases and prisoners. The first item in Issue No. 2, for example, read, "A lathe tore fingers from the hand of Vadim Gaenko in Camp No. 11 in Mordovia. Gaenko from Leningrad is serving four years under Articles 70 and 72 of the RSFSR Criminal Code for taking part in an illegal Marxist circle and issuing The Bell periodical." She also included a long list of "extra-judicial political repression," with the names of ninety-one individuals who had been expelled from their workplaces or kicked out of the party for various perceived offenses like signing protest letters or teaching outlawed books.

Most of the material came from friends who wrote what they knew on slips of paper or committed it to memory and then told it to Natasha, whose identity as the editor was an open secret. With this second issue, Natasha also moved outside the urban centers, with a letter from a group of Crimean Tatars who described the lingering psychic pain from the forced and brutal Stalin-era expulsion from their land. For the *Chronicle* to convincingly act as a legal brief for the aggrieved Soviet citizen, for it to focus dissent, it had to extend beyond the concerns of Moscow and Leningrad's intelligentsia.

Natasha was now devoting most of her time to the journal, running around the city collecting material, meeting with relatives of prisoners to debrief them after visits to the camps in the east, and then scrambling to type it all out in the *Chronicle*'s accumulating pages. It was arduous, secretive work. Her one consolation was that at the time she did not believe the KGB cared much about the *Chronicle*.

Just as she became comfortable in her identity as the hidden editor, furtively typing alone in borrowed apartments, Natasha felt called to take part in a more physical form of protest. On August 21, Soviet tanks rolled into Czechoslovakia to crush the Prague Spring. She still felt guilty about the way she had turned on her friends in the wake of the Hungarian revolution. This was her chance to redeem herself. She had to show solidarity with the people of Czechoslovakia and the liberalizing moves of the country's new leader, Alexander Dubček.

Natasha and a group of her friends, including Litvinov and Larisa Bogoraz, the wife of the imprisoned writer Yuli Daniel, decided they would stage a sit-down protest in Red Square. An act of such flagrantly public dissent had never been attempted on what was essentially sacred ground, mere feet from Lenin's mummified body. They prepared by making Czech flags and banners with slogans like "For Your Freedom and Ours," which she then folded up and placed beneath the mattress in her three-month-old son's pram. Just before the appointed time at noon on August 25, she rolled sleeping baby Osya toward Red Square, an extra pair of cloth diapers and pants at his feet.

They met at Lobnoye Mesto, the stagelike raised circular stone platform in front of St. Basil's Cathedral, where Ivan the Terrible was said to have carried out beheadings. And when the bell struck noon, the seven friends took out their banners and flags and sat in silence in the middle of the bustling square. Within minutes they were shut down. Natasha recorded her memories right away for inclusion in the next issue of the *Chronicle:* "People had hardly begun to gather round us when those who were intent on undoing our demonstration came racing towards us, beating the nearest onlookers to it. They leapt on us and tore down our banners without even sparing a glance for what was written on them. I shall never forget the sound of ripping cloth."

A crowd organized by the KGB to rile up the mostly confused pedestrians began shouting at the protesters, "They're all Jews!" and "Beat up the anti-Soviets!" Meanwhile, black Volgas, the cars of the KGB, sped through the square and police hopped out, roughly pulling the seated protesters off the ground and into the vehicles. Only Natasha was left, standing by her baby's pram as strangers yelled at her. The screaming woke him up, and she quickly changed his diaper in the middle of the frenzied crowd. Then another Volga pulled up, and Natasha was lifted up and thrust into the car, her baby just barely pushed into her arms before the door slammed shut and two not-so-random bystanders joined them as witnesses. "I threw myself at the window, lowered it and shouted: 'Long live free Czechoslovakia.' Halfway through the sentence the witness took a swipe at my mouth. The man got in beside the driver and said: 'To the 50th police station.' I lowered the window again and tried to call out: 'They're taking me to the 50th police station.'" The witness seated next to her in the car then hit Natasha again, "which was both humiliating and painful."

Natasha, because she was still nursing an infant, was almost immediately released. A few days later she wrote a letter that appeared in *The New York Times,* among other publications. As the only participant "still at liberty," Natasha described what happened in Red Square and expressed pride that, as she put it, "we were able even if briefly to break through the sludge of unbridled lies and cowardly silence and thereby demonstrate that not all citizens of our country are in agreement with the violence carried out in the name of the Soviet people."

With her closest collaborators, Litvinov and Bogoraz, now jailed and soon sentenced to Siberian exile, Natasha felt increasingly alone. She was ordered to present herself at the Serbsky Institute for Psychiatric Medicine, where a committee of psychiatrists and KGB officers deemed her "non-responsible for her actions—the possibility of low-profile schizophrenia is not excluded." The committee recommended that "she be declared insane and lodged in a penal category psychiatric hospital for compulsory treatment." But the state prosecutor simply ordered the case closed and appointed her mother as her official guardian. Natasha threw herself back into the *Chronicle* work, not knowing how long she had.

BY THE END OF 1968, the *Chronicle* was a fixture in the Soviet Union, a regularly appearing samizdat publication that told a continuing and highly detailed story of repression. In the way a small local newspaper can endow meaning to a group, much as *The African Morning Post* did, the *Chronicle* helped the dissidents see themselves fully as a community at war with their own state. The harassment and nighttime searches and exiles and long prison terms gained new significance in those typewritten pages. By recounting it all there, as evidence, the dissidents came to feel part of a single narrative in which they alone were demanding accountability. And, by the fifth issue, the circle of readers had greatly expanded, so much so that most did not know of the existence of the small, harried single mother of two who was pulling it all together.

It was in Issue No. 5 that Natasha addressed her readers as a distinct audience for the first time. The "Year of Human Rights," 1968, was coming to an end, and she wanted to explain that the journal would persist: "From the five issues of the *Chronicle* to date, one may form at least a partial impression of how the suppression of human rights and the movement for them has been taking place in the Soviet Union. Not one participant in this movement can feel his task is ended with the end of human rights year. The general aim of democratization, and the more particular aim pursued by the *Chronicle*, are still to be achieved. The *Chronicle* will continue to come out in 1969."

Natasha began receiving the most unexpected kind of positive feedback. The publication she had created was as neutral and open as a bulletin board, and soon strangers were pinning up their own items.

The crumpled pieces of paper started arriving almost as soon as the first issue was released, containing details large and small of offenses individuals had witnessed or experienced themselves. If they seemed credible, Natasha included them in the "News in Brief" section. Soon, the pieces of paper were feeding the *Chronicle* with much of its content. The notes were passed down a chain, hand to hand, much the way the *Chronicle* itself was disseminated. And based on what was getting to her, the chain was lengthening, with news arriving from cities like Kiev, Kharkov, and far-off Perm, long train rides away from the capital.

Every link in the chain knew only the two other links to which it was attached. Natasha wanted to keep it that way. In that same Issue No. 5, she made explicit what had already become practice. Anyone who is interested "in seeing that the Soviet public is informed about what goes on in the country may easily pass on information to the editors of the *Chronicle*," she wrote. "Simply tell it to the person from whom you received the *Chronicle*, and he will tell the person from whom he received the *Chronicle*, and so on. But do not try to trace back the whole chain of communication yourself, or else you will be taken for a police informer."

This system's only downside was that it had the taint of being secretive and conspiratorial, and that was not a message Natasha wanted to convey. She didn't see the *Chronicle* as an illegal enterprise. Its entire modus operandi was transparency—"glasnost" in Russian—uncovering the inner workings of the Soviet Union for the benefit of vigilant citizens. The concept of an underground newspaper had a major archetype in Lenin's own prerevolutionary propaganda organ, *Iskra*, printed abroad and smuggled into tsarist Russia, where it had to be hidden and spoken about in hushed tones. The *Chronicle* was fueled by a different impulse, not building up a shadow revolutionary army, but rather exposing to light, one abuse at a time, the repressive quality of the Soviet state. If a revolution of sorts was envisioned as a result of this process, it was to come from this slow peeling away of obfuscation and illusion that the state used so adeptly to hide its repression.

Natasha wanted the reporting to strive for total accuracy. In Lenin's view, articulated in 1901, the press was "not only a collective pro-

pagandist and collective agitator, but also a collective organizer." The
dissidents weren't looking to propagandize or agitate or organize. They
were interested in shattering the distinctly Soviet feeling of having
two selves—one that whispered truths in private and another that was
regularly called on to deny reality out loud. Lyudmila Alexeyeva, who
by 1969 was retyping issues and also providing information from her
contacts in Ukraine, described working on the *Chronicle* as pledging
oneself "to be faithful to the truth." It was almost a religious feeling:
"The effect of the *Chronicle* is irreversible. Each one of us went through
this alone, but each of us knows others who went through this moral
rebirth. This creates among people who scarcely know one another, but
who were connected with the *Chronicle,* very strong spiritual ties, the
kind that probably existed among early Christians."

For Natasha this faith took the form of being fastidious about
corrections. As early as Issue No. 2, there was a section for pointing
out misspellings of names or wrong dates in previous issues. Natasha
kept this up. And she also wanted her reader-contributors to understand that accuracy was a critical aspect of their work. Natasha was
frequently shocked to see fifth- or sixth-generation recopied editions of the *Chronicle* with mangled names and figures. This was inevitable with samizdat, which could be like a written version of the
game telephone. "In those instances when it is not absolutely certain
that some event has taken place," Natasha told her readers in Issue
No. 7, "the *Chronicle* indicates that the piece of information is based
on rumor. But at the same time, the *Chronicle* requests its readers to
be careful and accurate in the information they provide for publication."

These were essentially journalistic ethics that were most adhered
to and respected in the West and not at all part of how Soviet media
functioned. In its insistence on transparency, the *Chronicle* was shaping sensibilities. When readers reported some mistreatment they had
witnessed—a colleague being unfairly fired or a KGB search of a
neighbor's apartment—they joined this shadow fellowship of truth,
what in other countries might simply be called civil society. The act of
jotting down this news on a piece of paper in the pared-down, legal-

istic language of the *Chronicle* and then moving it along the chain of like-minded *Chronicle* readers connected each of these individuals to a network that was trying to live by different values.

Into 1969, the size and breadth of the issues grew. Now at least thirty pages of tightly packed news, the journal was covering occurrences that spanned the Soviet Empire. The initial items of Issue No. 7 (dated April 30, 1969) were the accounts of trials, the first in the southern Crimean city of Simferopol of a Tatar, Gomer Bayev, who was accused of distributing "deliberate fabrications defaming the Soviet State and social order," and the second in Jurmala, on the Latvian coast, of Ivan Yakhimovich, who was arrested after he wrote a letter protesting a political trial. There was also a piece on the persecution of Greek Orthodox priests. The "News in Brief" section included eighteen short items, reports from readers drawing on the local experiences of various marginalized communities—Tatars, Soviet Jews, Russian Orthodox priests, and Ukrainian nationalists.

Natasha was still at the center, quilting every issue together, a careful assembler of a pastiche of reports, large and small, making their way to her in Moscow. She depended on her mother to watch Yasik and Osya. The *Chronicle* took up nearly all of her time. She was often lugging her twenty-pound typewriter in its case through the Moscow metro and down the wide snow-covered boulevards and up stairways to the empty apartments she borrowed for her work. Hitting the keys hard enough to make an impression that would show up through six pages made considerable noise. She already stood out as suspicious and didn't need the sound of banging keys through thin walls to further implicate her. So she had to keep moving. The number of pieces of paper she dealt with had also grown by 1969. Holding on to them for too long put her and the writer in danger.

The *Chronicle* was demanding more and more of a sacrifice from her, but this was also because it was becoming more important. She felt this acutely when the mother of a political prisoner just off the train from having visited her son rushed to meet her in secret so she could unload all she had learned. Natasha would take notes about who was having their food ration cut in that camp, who had been injured recently while carrying wood, who was sick and not receiving medical care. It all went into the next issue's section on news "from the camps."

Or there were the trials, another major target of the *Chronicle*'s attention. The inside of a courtroom, especially in a political trial, was a cordoned-off space in the Soviet Union. Like the prison camps, it was where the crushing machinery of the state was on full display. Natasha would debrief individuals who had managed to sneak in and take notes, sometimes making audio recordings, but more often than not, committing entire bits of testimony to memory. She copied down all these details—of arbitrary rulings, invented laws, and defense counsels never allowed to present evidence—and then put them in the *Chronicle*. Sometimes the journal even reconstructed the entire proceedings of a political trial.

Readers were able to see how the courts functioned. Issue No. 6 revealed, for example, the way in which the authorities constructed a fake "public" for ostensibly open trials, busing in pliant individuals to attend them and keeping out the friends and families of dissidents: "All those chosen to represent 'the public' at the trial turned up at the Proletarsky District's party committee building at 8 a.m. on October 9th; there they were informed that they would be present at a trial of 'anti-Sovietists.' Then they were taken to the court in a bus which drove straight into the yard and they entered the building by the back door." The *Chronicle* further reported that the source of this information, one of those planted audience members, "felt embarrassed when in the course of the trial he recognized the falsehood of the information he had been given, and ashamed when, with the rest of the audience, he walked through the saddened crowd—which sympathized with the defendants—after the verdict."

Natasha now relentlessly searched out new information. It made her less than completely careful at times. In an episode from the summer of 1969 that would soon reverberate off the red marble walls of a Moscow courtroom, an ex-convict named Vilko Forsel met Natasha at an apartment of friends while she was vacationing with her older son in the Estonian city of Tartu.

As soon as she heard that the man had spent ten years in Vladimir prison, she perked up and began peppering him with questions about the conditions, particularly about the well-being of the political prisoners: How many were there? Were they housed together? What kind of food were they eating? Were the guards more aggressive with them? Then she turned to the case of a Tartu schoolboy who had recently been beaten for passing out leaflets connected to the anniversary of the Soviet invasion of Czechoslovakia. Did he know anyone with more information about this? Forsel, a little tipsy from his afternoon of vodka and pickled mushrooms, didn't know what to make of this tiny and slightly disheveled Muscovite lady. Then she pulled out a few issues of the *Chronicle* and handed him the most recent. He leafed through them and stopped when he saw an article about the Crimean Tatars and their struggle to "return to their native land." Forsel wasn't too drunk to understand the danger, and he angrily shoved the issues back at Natasha. "I didn't like the way a man who had just come out of prison was being drawn into some risky enterprise, being hindered from living in peace," he later told the court. He was asked whether he reported the exchange to anyone. Yes, he said, I went and told the KGB.

NATASHA HAD ALWAYS FIGURED it was a matter of time. With every added *Chronicle* reader, her chance of arrest increased. After ten issues, the KGB and its head, Yuri Andropov, had upgraded the threat level of the journal. And then there was the matter of the BBC and Voice of America, which would broadcast readings of entire issues. The stations saw the journal's reporting as a reliable news source, a contrast to the Potemkin paradise presented in the pages of *Pravda* and *Izvestia*. Their frequencies were jammed from transmitting into Soviet territory, but they still managed to reach wily Soviet citizens with shortwave radios.

When her apartment was searched in late October 1969, Natasha knew she had to pass off her editorial duties to someone else, and quickly. It was difficult to give it up, but she had also come to see herself as a conduit for a collective voice. Someone less compromised could now perform that role. The essential thing was to keep the journal going.

Her first successor had an eventful start to her editorship. Galina Gabai, the wife of a political prisoner, had taken over the work of Issue No. 10 and had already collected much of the material for the following issue when the KGB arrived early one morning. Before opening the door, she had the good sense to stuff a handful of the most sensitive notes inside her bathrobe. And then, as ten KGB agents, some undercover in sweat suits and others in dark ties, filled her small apartment, she edged into the kitchen and toward a large steaming pot of borscht cooking on the stove, dropping the pages into the bubbling red soup before they could see. After that close call she decided to relinquish her responsibilities.

So on the freezing morning of December 24, Natasha herself had in her apartment the scraps of paper and longer reports that would make up Issue No. 11, including a long piece about Vladimir prison, incorporating the bits of intelligence she'd gleaned from the stranger she'd met in Estonia, Vilko Forsel. That's when the knock came. She had an envelope crammed with handwritten notes that was in the center drawer of her desk, and a few other crumpled pages stuffed in the pocket of her coat hanging by the door; the KGB would pounce on any handwriting to try to track down contributors. She watched the agents shake out books, hammer their fists against the floors and walls to find possible hollow hiding spaces, cut through cushions, and pour her kitchen utensils out of their drawers.

At one point, as Natasha sat at her desk trying to calmly sharpen a pencil with a safety razor, one of the agents started flipping through what was perhaps her most treasured possession: a manuscript copy of Anna Akhmatova's *Requiem* with a personal inscription by the poet herself. She leaped up to grab it from the agent's hands, forgetting she was holding a razor, and cut a deep gash across his fingers. Blood began dripping down to the floor. Natasha immediately apologized, but it seemed a particularly bad omen.

By the time the search was done, the agents had gathered a pile of paper a foot thick and dozens of books. Only then did they let

Natasha know that she was under arrest. Three friends had stopped by during the search, and still concerned about leaving any incriminating papers and not sure if the KGB had found them, she whispered, "Go through the desk," before she was taken away. She also grabbed a light coat and left the one she hoped still had the scraps in its pocket, though she felt the painful chill of December slap her in the face as soon as she walked outside and was shoved into the waiting black Volga.

What she'd feared most was that the authorities would once again simply declare her insane. Having already been confined to a mental hospital and then diagnosed again following the Red Square demonstration, she knew there was an obvious solution for dealing with her. Other dissidents had suffered a similar fate, like her friend Pyotr Grigorenko, the major general turned activist who was at that moment locked in a psychiatric ward. The KGB officers brought her to Butyrka prison, where she was charged with slander of the Soviet system under Article 190-1, as well as resisting arrest for the incident with the razor blade.

In April, after three months in prison, she was taken to the Serbsky Institute as she had suspected and examined by a commission of psychiatrists including Professor Daniil Lunts, who had become infamous for liberally diagnosing dissidents with "sluggish schizophrenia," a mental illness newly invented by Soviet doctors. Lunts joined in the conclusion that Natasha had a "slow progressive" case of this schizophrenia. Though she was described as being completely normal—"converses willingly, calm bearing, a smile on her face"—her unwillingness to perceive her behavior as wrong was proof of pathology: "Does not renounce her actions, but thinks she has done nothing illegal. Unshakably convinced of the rightness of her actions, she moralizes a great deal, in particular saying that she acted thus 'so as not to be ashamed in the future before her children.'"

The trial took place on July 7, without Natasha. As a rule, mental patients were not allowed to be present in court proceedings. The prosecution used Forsel, the man Natasha had met in Estonia, to prove that she was at least spreading the *Chronicle*. Copies of the journal had also been confiscated from her exiled friends Litvinov and Bogoraz (Natasha had visited them in Siberia that fall). This particular issue, the prosecution argued, could be traced back to Natasha's typewriter— it had been grabbed during the search, and they could now match the keystrokes. And finally there was her own account of being forcibly confined in the beginning of 1968, called "Free Health Service," which had been smuggled to the West and broadcast over shortwave radio. This evidence, together with the testimony of the KGB agent who had been accidentally cut during the search, was enough for the prosecution to declare that she had "systematically prepared and circulated slanderous concoctions defaming the Soviet political system."

Natasha's mother was allowed to speak from the stand. Weepy and exhausted, she made a plea: "If my daughter has committed a crime, sentence her to any punishment, even the most severe, but do not place an absolutely healthy person in a psychiatric hospital." The defense lawyer's only argument—echoing the one heard in the case against Nnamdi Azikiwe—was that the *Chronicle* was entirely anonymous. No proof had been given that Natasha or anyone else had anything to do with creating or spreading the journal. It had no address, no masthead or bylines. Even if some issues of the *Chronicle* seemed to come from Natasha's typewriter, that was still not proof that she herself had typed it. The circle of people using that machine had never been established.

The court took no time to come to its judgment. It found her guilty, but of "unsound mind." She would be placed in a "psychiatric hospital of special type for compulsory treatment." The period of time was left undefined.

In the months that followed, while Natasha awaited her transfer, she was placed in the hospital wing of Butyrka prison. "I'll try to say briefly what's most important," she wrote in a letter to her mother in November. "I think that all I did was right and justified, but it is terrible to feel that you and the children have to pay for the right things I did. The weight that has fallen on you—that weight I have felt fully only in prison. . . . I miss the children terribly. Do they remember me?"

It was in early January that she sat chained to a seat on a train chugging its way through a barren, snowy landscape. Natasha knew where she was going, knew too much in fact about the prison for the mentally ill set up under Stalin, five hundred miles east of Moscow on a bend in the Volga River. Only a year before, in Issue No. 10 of the *Chronicle,* she had compiled a report on the Special Psychiatric Hospital in Kazan. She enumerated its horrors in a sparse style, exactly as they were conveyed to her by former inmates: "If the patients commit offences—refuse to take medicine, quarrel with the doctors, or fight, they are strapped into their beds for three days, sometimes more. With this form of punishment, the elementary rules of hygiene are ignored: the patients are not allowed to go to the lavatory, and bedpans are not provided." She also knew the general layout of the psychiatric hospital, what would be expected of her and the other patient-prisoners during their three-and-a-half-hour workdays (sew aprons and sheets), and even the name of the antipsychotic medication the doctors would soon force her to take.

Natasha remembered the words of a poem she had written for her friend Yuri Galanskov, who had been similarly locked up in a psychiatric ward in 1966 and drugged: "In the madhouse / Wring your hands, / Press your pale forehead against the wall / Like a face into a snowdrift." Now it would be her face, pressed and vanishing.

The *Chronicle,* though, continued. There was a new editor, and there would be another and another after that until the early 1980s, when a fierce crackdown finally killed the journal. And yet the dissidents' relentless focus on glasnost—what Lyudmila Alexeyeva called a "process of justice or governance, being conducted in the open"— would within a couple years become the signature policy of a new Soviet premier, an effort at transparency he felt he had no choice but to implement. It would soon undercut the totalitarian state and ultimately cause it to implode. The journal, which for so long had funneled and concentrated the dissidents' efforts, was the vessel for this process. In language crisp and unadorned, its insistence on truth had made it harder and harder to accept lies. The fate of the *Chronicle's* founder was treated no less clinically. In Issue No. 18, an item among others: "On 9 January 1971 Natalya Gorbanevskaya was transferred from Butyrka Prison to the Special Psychiatric Hospital on Sechenov Street in Kazan (postal address: building 148, block 6, postbox UE, Kazan-82), where a course of treatment with Haloperidol has been prescribed for her."

Chapter 6

CONTROL

————

THE HOMEMADE MAGAZINE—xeroxed, folded, and bound with staples—was called *Jigsaw,* and it was no ordinary publication. So said its creator. It was an anti-publication: "JIGSAW IS NOT A CONSUMER PRODUCT. It is not a product at all. It is more of a process. A method. I'm starting to see that process is the key. read on. feel free to respond to anything that I've written or submit something you think is appropriate. Especially if you are a woman and/or want to write about that whole aspect of things."

Hardly punctuated, crowded with typewritten words and looping cursive and scattered, pasted-in images—of Chrissie Hynde fingering her electric guitar, of wide-eyed Bette Davis brandishing a gun in *Dead Ringer*—*Jigsaw* was a direct line into the mind of an outsider girl, a punk girl, pushed out of mainstream culture and creating a new one: "I want to be able to talk with my own words in my own way . . . to express real sentiment. But it's so hard to even have a conversation . . . a real conversation that actually deals with conflict. Everything seems so manufactured, so oppressive."

This was not just a public airing of teen angst. Tobi Vail, who began creating *Jigsaw* in her bedroom in 1989 with scissors and a glue stick, was a drummer in an all-girl punk band in Olympia, Washington. The promise of punk—and her subsequent disillusionment—had brought her to this point. In its early years, in the 1970s, in the days of the Ramones and the Sex Pistols, punk was about freedom, anti-authoritarianism, and laying waste to societal norms, and plenty of women on the scene felt empowered by it as well. But the music and the culture by the late 1980s had gone hardcore and hyper-masculine, all shaved heads and leather jackets. The quintessential punk venue was the mosh pit, a mass of sweating, heaving bodies slamming against each other. A writer, venturing into the pit for *The New York Times* in the early 1990s, like an anthropologist sneaking up on an Amazon tribe, described a scene of great violence in which everyone seemed to be trying, he wrote, "to kill one another."

Young women were shoved to the edges, literally, relegated to the role of "coat hangers," as they were sometimes called, standing around holding their moshing boyfriends' leather jackets. Tobi hated this. And she wasn't alone. *Chainsaw*, another zine by an alienated punk girl, lamented how far the culture had drifted from its origins, "from the GEEKS who decided or realized (or something) to 'turn the tables' so to speak, and take control of their (our) lives and form a Real under-ground."

And so her zine was a way to re-create an underground. An alternative to the alternative. The mosh pit wasn't the only problem. Tobi felt as if she were standing on the edge of society itself and all its conceptions about femininity, the unspoken rules for how a woman ought to look, how a woman ought to be. Every time she came across big hair and shoulder pads on the glossy cover of *Cosmo* or *Vogue*, she felt the burden of societal expectation. Not only was the pathway through girlhood constraining—a maze with many ways in yet only one way out—but the problems that did concern girls, the secrets they whispered to each other in their bedrooms, about eating disorders and rape and sexual identity, had zero outlet.

Zines had existed since the 1930s, when science fiction nerds shared their obsessive fandom with each other through homemade booklets of their own short stories and reviews. But in the 1970s and into the 1980s, it was the punk scene that made full use of this DIY form, perfect for a subculture that screamed about wanting nothing to do with capitalism. The attraction of the zine in the past was what turned Tobi on to it as well: the ability to create your own medium, to produce, and not just be limited to what you could buy on a magazine rack. For samizdat, too, it was crucial to control your means of production (and distribution)—in the dissidents' case to evade censorship and repression. Here the control gave the girls a chance to talk back by creating their own thing.

But first Tobi needed to hear some echoes. Zines always sought out other zines. And to that end she included in her second issue of *Jigsaw* a list of the few other self-published titles being written by girls, like *Bitch* and *Incite,* along with their addresses, and a letters section with reader responses to inspire others. By her third issue she was more explicit: "I am making a fanzine not to entertain or distract or exclude or because I don't have anything better to do but because if I didn't write these things no one else would either."

IN EARLY 1990, the second issue of *Jigsaw* fell into the hands of a couple of young women who also felt the need for a place to put their anger and let it grow.

Molly Neuman and Allison Wolfe, freshmen at the University of Oregon, picked up a copy of the zine at an Olympia show that featured Nirvana, whose skinny, besweatered front man, Kurt Cobain, was Tobi's then boyfriend. They saw in *Jigsaw* a reflection of their own frustrations not just with punk but also with the feminism they had inherited, the hand-me-down 1970s dream of their mothers, which was supposed to be the answer to all their problems. They were overwhelmed by *Jigsaw.* Its very existence, its heart-pouring, earnest tone, seemed to offer an answer to a question they couldn't even really articulate yet. They wrote to Tobi, who responded right away. "It's really inspiring to find out there are actually people in the world who are thinking about the same sort of things I am," Tobi wrote. "Sometimes I feel kind of ISOLATED I guess." She suggested that they trade tapes of bands they liked or that Molly review "some stuff" for *Jigsaw*. And then closed with a P.S. that listed other girl zines.

For Allison, in particular, feminism felt stale. Her mother, who had come out as a lesbian after a divorce, worked as a nurse and had opened up the first women's health clinic in Olympia. Her home was often targeted by antiabortion activists, who sent death threats and would throw rocks at their windows. For her mother, feminism was a lifestyle—Joan Baez's album *Diamonds & Rust* was on the record player, a long row of books about women's bodies and self-discovery sat on their shelves—but the incense-thick air of feminist bookstores had little relevance or interest for Allison. It felt fusty. In the women's studies classes she took that first year of college, she'd get annoyed when professors would correct her use of the word "girl" ("we say 'women,'" they would tell her) because it pointed to a feminist ortho-doxy that didn't reflect her life *as* a girl.

Molly was more intense and internal, bottling up what Allison, a nonstop talker, let explode. She had grown up in Washington, D.C., in a family in which politics was always present, her father part of the communications shop at the Democratic National Committee. Just before moving to the West Coast, she had become interested in race and, as only a recent high school graduate could, believed she had an epiphany watching Spike Lee's *Do the Right Thing*. That summer she delved into the writings of the Black Panther leader Eldridge Cleaver.

The two met during their first week in the dorms when Allison overheard Molly on the hall's pay phone loudly breaking up with someone, screaming, "But . . . I love you!" They became fast friends, Molly soon cutting her bangs short like Allison's. They felt lucky to have found each other: two politically aware eccentrics who didn't fit in among the school's dominant hippieish aesthetic. They were both tough, emotive girls, looking to create their own style.

As soon as they read the second issue of *Jigsaw*, they started to get "that feeling in their heart," as they later described it, and they created their own zine: *Girl Germs*. They spent much of the fall of 1990 put-ting it together, interviewing bands like the all-female Portland grunge group Calamity Jane, and scouring yard sales for Barbie coloring books, Girl Scout guides, and old anatomy textbooks that they could cut and paste. Even though they went to school in Eugene, they spent more and more time in Olympia, where Allison had grown up. Home to the funky Evergreen State College, it was an island where punk seemed truer to its source. There were dozens of grassroots art galleries; music shows happened in people's basements and in alleyways. It was easier for anyone to pick up a guitar and play—even a girl. You could catch a show there by the rare punk bands led by women, like the Lunachicks, Babes in Toyland, L7, and Frightwig. Every coffee shop seemed to have at least one flyer with a female drummer advertising her skills.

Around this time, Kathleen Hanna also picked up a copy of *Jigsaw* and wrote to Tobi to tell her how much it meant to her. "I felt like we are/were trying to do similar type things and I felt validated. I know what it's like to have a girl tell me that she doesn't think it really means anything that she's a girl." Kathleen was a little infamous in Olympia. She was a student at Evergreen, lead singer in a band, Viva Knievel, and a poet known for her confrontational spoken word at the Capitol Theater, prose poems she then compiled into her own zine, *Fuck Me Blind,* using a pseudonym, Maggie Fingers. She had recently stood in front of a crowd at a party, stared hard at the men, and screamed, "I know what you did! I know what you did!" over and over again. People also whispered about how she worked as a stripper to make money. But what mattered to her most and what informed her evolving art was her internship at a domestic violence shelter, SafePlace, doing crisis counseling and giving talks on rape and sexual assault to teenage girls. She was moved by the small groups of survivors she would organize, the way they talked and listened to each other, the support they could give one another once they achieved some intimacy and privacy.

She wanted to tie this spirit to punk. Interviewed in 1990 by an amateur anthropologist of the scene, Kathleen explained her thinking. "I'm really interested in a punk-rock movement /angry-girl movement of sexual abuse survivors," she said. "And it's not just angry girls, it's everyone, because I've had so many people come up to me with their stories of sexual abuse, of being beaten up by their parents and stuff.

Even if it's not getting punched, it's the emotional violence and hier-archy of the family—which is the same hierarchy that puts man over woman, it's the same fucking shit that is white over black, human over animal, boss over worker."

Though she was reading a lot of feminist theory, some of the big ideological battles of the 1970s and 1980s—like whether pornography was a form of oppression—didn't speak to her. She resolved these is-sues in her own life matter-of-factly. Speaking of stripping, she said, it's "a job and like all jobs, it fucking sucks. I personally decided to be a sex trade worker 'cause I feel a lot less exploited making $20 an hour for dancing around naked than I do getting paid $4.25 an hour (and being physically, psychically, and sometimes sexually exploited) as a waitress or burger-slinger. Why do certain feminists want to penalize me for choosing an obvious form of exploitation instead of a subtle lower-paying one?"

Kathleen and Tobi had such kismet that they bonded in the ulti-mate way: by forming a band, one they decided to call Bikini Kill (shades of a 1960s B movie about killer girls in bikinis and Bikini Atoll, site of the nuclear tests in the 1940s and 1950s). They rented rooms across the hall from each other in Olympia and almost imme-diately began performing while also swapping books by bell hooks and Judith Butler. When Kathleen took the stage to front Bikini Kill (with Tobi on drums, Kathi Wilcox on bass), her appearance—short leopard-print skirt, her hair a black bob against pale skin—was, like everything she did, a well-thought-out act of provocation. "Dare you to do what you want!" she screeched. "Dare you to be who you will!"

Tobi began calling the gathering number of girls producing zines and starting bands that year "Revolution Girl Style Now," and Molly and Allison felt themselves part of it. Their zine was ready in Decem-ber, the winter break of their sophomore year, and Molly, home for the holidays, decided to "publish" *Girl Germs*. In high school she had spent one summer working as an intern for Morris K. Udall, a congressman from Arizona, and used her access to his Capitol Hill office to run off several hundred copies on his Xerox machine. When a storm hit the city that evening, she was snowed in alone in the deserted building, munching on candy bars and potato chips to keep herself awake, copying and stapling all night.

She returned to Oregon at the beginning of 1991, with a few hundred copies of *Girl Germs* No. 1 in her suitcase, ready to distribute. The zine was everything she and Allison hoped it would be, punk and aware. "My brother who is two and a half got a toy rock'n'roll drum set for Christmas this year," Molly wrote. "I got a guitar when I turned 18. I had this idea that I might want to be in a band. But nobody told me I could or encouraged me to. There's a fundamental difference in the way I was socialized and the way my brother is being socialized. He is being given the tools to create. I must seek out those tools."

BESIDES OLYMPIA, THERE WAS one other city where punk retained a socially conscious flavor: Molly's home, Washington, D.C. The capital had experienced renewed vigor as a punk scene ten years after Minor Threat and Bad Brains had turned it into an epicenter of the music. Now a few bands, like Fugazi and Nation of Ulysses, were attempting something blatantly ideological with their songs, offering a further twist on what it meant to be punk, promoting clean living, independence, and anti-consumerism. During their spring break in 1991, Molly and Allison had followed the advice of some friends and made their way to the Embassy, the three-story row house in the Mount Pleasant neighborhood that also doubled as the headquarters for Nation of Ulysses. The place was alive. There was a practice space and a recording studio in the basement. It was there that they grew more confident about the band they had started a few months before, called Bratmobile, and even found another guitarist.

At first Bratmobile was largely aspirational, a few a cappella numbers and some bad covers. But with the starkness (just two chords on Molly's guitar, repeated again and again) they created their own sound, brave and heartfelt. Allison sang in a childish lilt, not Kathleen's primal scream, but as if she were rewiring childhood melodies: "You're too cozy in your all-boy clubhouse / To even consider having kool-aid at my house." As Bratmobile gained a small following that year, Molly defended their unvarnished act as a conscious choice: "I think it's really good for bands to go out when they're not ready. Because, then, as you do get a grasp on your instrument, people see you in a continuum, as opposed to just you jumped out of nowhere, which is what I always thought: The boy comes out of the womb with a screaming Led Zeppelin guitar, and I feel like I'll never know how to do that." The aesthetic was similar to the zines; the messiness and lack of finish were a rebuke to polished patriarchal society.

Kathleen saw what was building in D.C. a few months later at a show that was almost instantly legendary. It was June 27, and Bikini Kill had played in Kentucky the night before and Alabama the night before that. They had been met almost everywhere with a mix of jeers and insults from men (and a few thrown beer bottles) and always a small clutch of girls trying to move closer to the stage, a few who would thrust their own zines at them. Mostly, though, there was confusion: Were they trying to be sexy? Why were they so angry? But now they were at dc space, a club at Seventh and E streets NW, and the crowd was completely theirs. Kathleen, with her back to the audience, ripped off her T-shirt so that when she turned around, the word "SLUT" sloppily scrawled across her stomach could be seen under her black bra. She jumped and screamed and yelled out her lyrics, and the crowd, women and men, were mesmerized. After the show, Ian Mac-Kaye, the lead singer of Fugazi and a key impresario of punk music at the time, immediately offered to record them for free.

The band decided to stay in the city, everyone scraping by, with Kathleen stripping at the Royal Palace, a club just north of Dupont Circle. In 1991, D.C. was in bad shape, with the murder rate reaching a record 482 homicides, including the killing of a young woman who lived alone in a basement apartment just down the street from where Kathleen was renting. And on Cinco de Mayo, there had even been a riot a few blocks from the Embassy. After a Salvadoran immigrant was shot by the police, rumors spread that he was handcuffed at the time. Protesters threw bricks and bottles at the cops, and the melee ended with tear gas. One of Allison's friends who witnessed it all wrote to her that what was needed that summer was a "girl riot."

Molly and Allison came back to D.C. in July. One night, hanging out with Kathleen and a few other women, they pulled out a typewriter and some glue sticks and decided to transcribe the feminist revolutionary spirit they were feeling. They assembled a zine, a mini-zine, just one page folded into quarters—something they could hand out at shows. Molly then commandeered another Capitol Hill copy machine. They called it *Riot Grrrl,* a riff on "girl riot" and a slight jab at "womyn" and "womban" and all the other inventive feminist spellings of the word "woman." Also, it looked like a growl.

On the cover was Madonna with her fists in the air and the logo for Utz potato chips, with a little girl looking mischievous, modified with a Sharpie to read "slutz." Inside, the girls declared the beginning of a movement: "There has been a proliferation of angry grrrl zines in recent months, mainly due to the queezy feeling we girls get in our stomachs when we contemplate the general lack of girl power in society as a whole, and in the punk rock underground specifically. In this long hot summer we are presently experiencing, some of us girls thought it was time we put our collective angry heads together and do a mini-zine, and put it out as often as possible. Hey, there's also a sale at kinko's now, if you know anyone who would want one of these, it would only cost 6 cents to copy it for them." As Sara Marcus, who wrote the definitive book on Riot Grrrl, put it, the new zine's title "created its audience of girls by naming them, radicalized them by addressing them as already radical." The girls started handing out the *Riot Grrrl* zine at a barbecue that Fourth of July.

By the second issue, the zine had doubled, to eight quarter-sheet pages filled with information about upcoming gigs and parties, as well as musings by Kathleen like "Be as vulnerable as you possibly can" and "Commit to the revolution as a method of psychological and physical survival." Were there like-minded girls who wanted to shake complacency and talk about difficult subjects? On the back cover of that second issue of *Riot Grrrl,* the call was made clear, even plaintive: "We don't know all that many angry grrrls, although we know you are out there."

———

THE WOMEN WHO made *Riot Grrrl* would be loath to pinpoint what exactly their revolution was for. But they knew what it was against. They could see the gains of their mothers' generation, but they weren't enough. During the 1980s feminism had headed in two directions, but neither felt useful to them. On the one hand, talk about sexism had become all too academic, chewed up and turned into abstract theorizing about power (largely impenetrable to a lay audience and absent a direct political agenda). The other path felt soft and meaningless, with its highly solicitous tones of self-help (see Gloria Steinem's 1992 book, *Revolution from Within: A Book of Self-Esteem*). These girls still felt sexism in their lives—in small ways, like the persistence of pink and blue stereotypes, and large, like the degrading way rape survivors were treated. But they didn't want to ignore the trauma and just succeed like the men. They wanted to reckon with these realities by holding on to that pain, the individual experience of it, and building a politics that came out of the hurt. For Kathleen it was the victims of sexual assault she had worked with in Olympia who were her audience. And zines met their needs. "Zines are profoundly personal expressions, yet as a medium of participatory communication they depend upon and help create community," wrote Stephen Duncombe, a New York University professor who studied the form. "The contradiction is never resolved." That was fine. The contradiction was the point.

Kathleen called a real-life meeting of Riot Grrrl in Issue No. 3 of the mini-zine. It took place on the evening of July 24, 1991, at Positive Force, another punk group house, this one in Arlington, Virginia, just outside D.C., where kids in torn jeans and T-shirts covered in black Sharpie volunteered at homeless shelters, brought food to poor seniors, or took part in anti-apartheid marches. About twenty young women showed up, including Molly and Allison, and they just talked, going around the circle. It lasted hours, reminiscent of the consciousness-raising meetings their mothers had taken part in decades earlier. They wanted to express the way they saw the world, as girls, the way they were sexualized, not taken seriously, physically assaulted, and just made to feel bad about themselves. After their second meeting, Kathleen, Allison, and Molly sat down for an interview with Mark Andersen, one of the founders of Positive Force, who was then trying to write a book about the D.C. punk scene. "I seriously believe the majority of people in this country have stories to tell that they aren't telling for some reason," Kathleen said. "I mean, with all of that energy and anger, if we could unify it in some way . . ."

The meetings continued, though never drew more than a handful of girls who were based in and around D.C. It was rather the zines that produced the community. More and more were popping up and identifying openly with Riot Grrrl. It was a medium they felt belonged to them, and the swapping and sharing that resulted allowed them to coalesce naturally around certain themes without needing to define their aims.

"Well I'm a riot grrrl—that's the coolest thing in my life right now," wrote a contributor to *Fantastic Fanzine,* a zine put together by Erika Reinstein, an eighteen-year-old living in the D.C. area. "Well yeah . . . basically the coolest. I love myself, well not always. I mean I try and love myself. Because I know it's important. Except the thing is I still have all these feelings like about myself. And there are things I just don't talk about. Even though I know that I can talk about anything at Riot Grrrl. Like my weight is one of those things. I mean it helps a lot that I am in an environment that is generally very accepting. It helps a lot because I'm learning. I'm trying to really accept myself. But still it's kind of like this secret that I have, you know that I don't think I'm really pretty or attractive."

They wanted to own their vulnerability and give it room to be discussed on their terms. "BECAUSE we girls want to create mediums that speak to US," Erika wrote in one issue. "BECAUSE in every form of media I see us/myself slapped, decapitated, laughed at, trivialized, pushed, ignored, stereotyped, kicked, scorned, molested, silenced, invalidated, knifed, shot, choked, and killed."

The number of zines grew throughout 1991. Girls would seek out readers, asking that a dollar be sent to the address provided in exchange for a copy. A crisscrossing dialogue ensued, with zines referencing each other, writers copying and pasting one another's words.

And they also began to partake in a kind of shared visual vocabulary. There was joy in being your own editor and art director and publisher that was evident in the final product, even when the subject matter turned dark, as it often did. Beyond their DIY quality, their photocopied and stapled-together look, the zines all reflected a desire to subvert and undermine and mock popular culture, to draw a great big mustache on it. It was an aesthetic of bubbly, girly handwriting, but also smeared red paint. In one zine, *I ♥ Amy Carter*, ironically but lovingly dedicated to the former first daughter, stories from the *National Enquirer* on Madonna's rumored lesbian lover sat next to solicitations for information on a female serial killer. There was a reclamation of all the impossible images of women that advertising produced and that weighed on the consciousness of girls. By taking the photo of an impossibly skinny blonde in a shampoo ad and then adding a thought bubble that had her wondering about whether she would be raped tonight, the zine makers were desecrating a poisonous culture while also trying to remake it. And the scrapbook look, of cut-up magazines, bubbly hearts, and stickers, also captured adolescence, the moment of transition from innocence to sarcasm and dark humor. As Kathleen succinctly put it, "We are turning cursive letters into knives."

In their third issue of *Girl Germs*, Molly and Allison expressed an incipient anxiety that anyone might try to claim some ownership over this creative burst. They wanted it made very clear: all you needed to participate were scissors and a glue stick and maybe a typewriter. "Riot Grrrl is so much. It will end up being so much more I am sure. Right now it isn't anything concrete, it's not a fanzine or a group or anything specific, although it is also all of these things. As of now, it has been a mini fanzine, and there have been some girls who met once a week calling themselves riot grrrls, talking about issues in and outside of punk rock that are important to us. But I know, and I'm sure some of you know that it's going to be something BIG. . . . There's no copyright on the name so if you are sitting there reading this and you feel like you might be a riot grrrl then you probably are, so call yourself one."

Zines were now everywhere. *Psychobitch* from Martinsville, Indiana; *Riottemptresses* from Lexington, Kentucky; *Growing Pains* from Chicago; *Girl Fiend* from Amherst, Massachusetts; and many more, each one pushing another into existence. Though always at least partly diaristic, the zines circled around the same set of taboo issues: rape, eating disorders, body image, sexual assault.

Most of the zine creators were white and upper-middle-class, girls like Molly and Allison, but there were a few zines, too, that tried to capture inequities beyond sexism. Nomy Lamm, who grew up in Olympia, had lived with a handicap since the age of three, when her leg was amputated because of a bone growth disorder. She started a zine, *I'm So Fucking Beautiful,* to talk about fat discrimination. The writing was bracingly forthright and unlikely to appear anywhere else: it was the scribblings of a teenage girl who didn't want to feel so ashamed anymore. "I know I'm never gonna be thin and don't want to be thin (usually), but I still have this thing like 'well maybe if I were just a little bit smaller then not only would I just be able to accept my body, I'd be able to really, really love it!' and no matter how much I say that fat is totally awesome and that we should revel in our fatness, I don't think I'd want to be fatter than I am now. So what if I do get fatter?" Her zine also had a sense of humor, with Lamm giving her readers permission to laugh and break through the silence around these hard issues. In a list of "fun things about fat," number one is "fat floats, so I don't have to worry as much about drowning!"

Another zine from far afield was *Gunk,* from Ramdasha Bikceem, who was a fifteen-year-old New Jersey skater girl when she put out her first issue. As a Black girl, she was an unusual participant in Riot Grrrl and wrote about her status as an outsider among outsiders. In the fourth issue of *Gunk*—an issue that had a childhood photo of her face, looking furious, below the words cut out from the side of a milk cartoon "Have You Seen Me?"—she recounted her experience at a gathering of Riot Grrrls in D.C.: "I think I was one of only 3 black kids there I mean Riot Grrrl calls for a change, but I question who it's including. . . . I see Riot Grrrl growing very closed to a very chosen few, i.e. White middle class punk girls. It's like it's some secret society, but then again there are some who feel that a secret society is what we need."

The multiplying zines signaled to Kathleen and Allison and Molly that there were other angry girls out there. The music they were producing was also getting more recognition. In late August of that year, 1991, Olympia's Capitol Theater held a six-day music festival called the International Pop Underground Convention, and a special Girl Night brought together all the bands who were the musical corollary to the zine scene—Bikini Kill, Bratmobile, Heavens to Betsy, 7 Year Bitch, and many others. It was momentous for the women who just a year earlier hadn't thought there was a place for them in punk. Reporting on the evening in the next issue of *Girl Germs,* one girl who had been in the audience described the feeling: "Girl's night will always be precious to me because, believe it or not, it was the first time I saw women stand on a stage as though they truly belonged there. The first time I had ever heard the voice of a sister proudly singing the rage so shamefully locked in my own heart. Until girl's night, I never knew that punk rock was anything but a phallic extension of the white middle class male's frustrations." Allison and Molly invented a shorthand to memorialize this moment: "prdct," or "punk rock dream come true."

There was something special in this emotive Northwest brand of punk, and America at large was soon introduced to it through Tobi Vail's now-former boyfriend, Kurt Cobain, and his band, Nirvana. Their album *Nevermind* was released a few weeks after Girl Night, and by November it had gone gold and then platinum. By January 1992 it had knocked Michael Jackson's latest album off the top of the *Billboard* charts and was selling about 300,000 copies a week. Capitalism was always looking to conquer a cool subculture, and the quick commodification for a mass audience could have scary consequences. The terror in Cobain's eyes told the story. You lose the power to set your own direction.

IN JULY 1992, Riot Grrrl saw itself, for the first time, covered in the pages of a mainstream publication (in a magazine not produced in someone's bedroom, that is). Only a year had passed since that first real-world meeting in D.C. The network of girls now regularly communicating through swapped zines had expanded, but it still felt like a private project; it was still burgeoning. When a young journalist from *LA Weekly,* the city's independent paper, asked to sit in on the inaugural meeting of the Olympia chapter of Riot Grrrl, Molly and Allison, the organizers, saw no problem. It seemed strange to imagine anyone would want to write about them. "This meeting is really figuring out what we want Riot Grrrl to be here," Allison told the group of about seventeen girls sitting cross-legged on the floor of a basement laundry room. As the journalist jotted down their words, the group brainstormed an idea to create pocket-sized zines about sexism and rape and planned a concert for the following week, Riot Grrrl Extravaganza, at which admittance for girls and any boys who showed up in dresses and bras would be two dollars. All other boys would pay three dollars.

The resulting article, appearing a few months later, took its headline from their motto: "Revolution Girl Style Now." Floodlights were now shining, hot, through their bedroom windows. So much so that the first sentence seems ironic in retrospect: "Maybe the girl revolution won't take shape in the public world, the world of men. It certainly won't happen out on the street, where girls aren't safe. Maybe it will begin in a private, enclosed space men never enter, a generic space women enter and leave, often together, writing messages for each other on the wall: a restroom." Women's restrooms at many universities were indeed where students could anonymously scribble the names of men who had sexually assaulted them, as a warning to others. Zines were now this "private, enclosed space." They were "time bombs disguised as thick letters," as Emily White, the author of the piece, wrote. "All across the country, girls wait to hear from the fanzine network, a phantom community they belong to but never see—it's an underground with no nucleus, built of paper."

The article was thoughtful and not cheap, a sincere attempt to make sense of what Riot Grrrl's inchoate energy represented. But it was also quick to draft the girls as the perfect frontline soldiers in the then raging culture wars. Anita Hill had made her accusations against Clarence Thomas during his Supreme Court nomination hearings in the fall of 1991, dividing the country over the issue of sexual harassment. In June of the following year the Supreme Court announced its decision in *Planned Parenthood of Southeastern Pennsylvania v. Casey*, a case that reaffirmed *Roe v. Wade* all while making it more difficult for a woman to get a legal abortion, in part by upholding the state's parental consent provisions for minors. Then there were the high-profile rape trials of William Kennedy Smith and Mike Tyson, in which women's accounts of rape were framed as dubious. This was also an election year, and by the summer of 1992 its contours were clear: a Republican Party backed by the Christian Right against a Democratic candidate whose wife, Hillary Rodham Clinton, provoked contempt by saying her career had saved her from a life in which she would have "stayed home, baked cookies and had teas."

Second-wave feminism, which had opened up workplaces for women and won battles over reproductive rights, seemed unprepared for the moment, for what Susan Faludi had called a "backlash" (her book of that title spent thirty-five weeks on the bestseller lists in 1992). But maybe there was a younger cohort who was ready to join the fray. The piece declared, "The Riot Girls have the right kind of rhetoric with which to face this dark hour because, like many teenage girls, they phrase every setback, every dream, in the language of crisis."

This was a lot to put on their shoulders. But the article thoughtfully approached the Riot Grrrls on their own terms and was so sensitively written that it did not make them wary of the media. Further evidence of just how interesting they had become to the grown-up world emerged when the first Riot Grrrl convention took place on the last weekend of July in Washington, D.C. The gathering brought together more than a hundred girls. It was a weekend full of shows and dance parties, workshops and themed discussions, on "everything from self defense, to how to run a soundboard, to how to lay out a zine"— and one meeting simply called "Rape." It was a meaningful if chaotic gathering, with many large circles in which girls passed around boxes of Kleenex and told their stories. The rough, unfinished, and undefined quality of the activism was evident too. At one session organized by Kathleen, "Un-learning Racism," cliquish tendencies alluded to in the *LA Weekly* piece came out into the open. Most of the girls rejected the notion that they might be complicit in a culture of tacit white supremacy. *They* were supposed to be the victims here. The few participants of color were upset and felt excluded, while the white girls claimed reverse racism was at work. It was all very jumbled (and it was, of course, precisely here, navigating the shoals of class and race, that second-wave feminism had had its own crisis two decades earlier). The confrontation would eventually find its way into zines like Mimi Thi Nguyen's *Race Riot*, entirely concerned with the unique problems of girls of color in the movement.

Suddenly they were being watched. One woman who showed up at the convention said she was writing an article for *Spin* magazine. Another was researching a piece for the *Washington City Paper*. An amateur filmmaker was trying to interview girls for a documentary. And one woman announced at a workshop, "I'm from *USA Today*."

IT WAS THE ARTICLE from that newspaper, published a week after the convention's end, that made the Riot Grrrls begin to feel that their movement—was it a movement?—was slipping out of their hands. "Better watch out, boys," it opened. "From hundreds of once pink, frilly bedrooms, comes the young feminist revolution. And it's not pretty. But it doesn't wanna be. So there!" The girls were belittled, all "hairy legs, army boots and tattoos," and any bigger political ideas were presented as nothing more than irrational aggression. In one scene from the convention, describing a concert by the group Cheesecake, a "scrawny boy" yells something derogatory, only to be "surrounded by an angry mob of girls, hopping and slam-dancing in a frenzy. He bolts to safety, chased by their jeers." The girls come off as simultaneously naïve and reactionary: "Another woman says that if you ask a man to touch your left breast and he touches your right, 'that's rape.'" There was no explanation given for why the Riot Grrrls did what they did, besides condescending sketches of their conversations as "strictly, like, girl talk. Insightful, honest, often touching." They were "teen angsters, searching for their sexual and social identity."

It had been only a year since the zine network had started to branch out. But the sudden onslaught of cartoonish coverage short-circuited everything, and just at the moment, following their first convention, when they were beginning to think about where to go next.

It felt relentless. Someone from *Newsweek* called Allison's house three times in a week. Requests came in from the major daytime talk shows, from Sally Jessy Raphael and Maury Povich. The girls felt misunderstood and mischaracterized, frustrated that their bedroom-grown subculture was being stripped of deeper meaning and reduced to just another passing trend. The *USA Today* article was accompanied by a sidebar breaking down the "in-your-face fashion" of the Riot Grrrl look: "fishnet stockings and garter belts under baggy army shorts." Even seemingly positive forms of attention felt oppressive. *Sassy* magazine, a publication for young women that did a better job of presenting the lived reality of teenage girls than any other glossy, embraced the zine phenomena and in early 1992 began featuring a "zine of the month." This went out to their readership of hundreds of thousands. When Molly and Allison's *Girl Germs* was highlighted and their address given out, they got an overwhelming amount of mail, and demand for their zine exceeded their ability to deliver.

Feeling pinned down and exploited, turned into a product, Kathleen vented her annoyance in the D.C.-based feminist publication *Off Our Backs:* "Interview magazine called us yesterday. Maria Shriver wants us on her show. That's scary as shit. I know that we are tokens. I have no fucking illusions that these people give a shit what I have to say for real. I do think that people want to stare at my tits, want to see me put my foot in my mouth, to see us fuck up. They can control what we're doing by labeling it and ghettoizing it and putting it in some weird box. I won't let that happen."

If the zines documented the unfiltered collective conscience of this group of young women, then they revealed that by the fall of 1992 the skewed public attention had become a crisis, making them want to push back even harder against the image projected onto them. "I feel like I have so little control of my life as it is without some reporter saying who I am," Erika Reinstein wrote in her zine. "I feel marginalized enough as it is without the corporate media making matters worse." Erika's annoyance was also at the reporters' unwillingness to grasp "the idea of a movement of individuals working together without some kind of map or chart or set of rules." The prefabricated narratives imposed on Riot Grrrl missed what was so special about all that was unfolding through the zines—the tension the medium permitted. Everyone's zine was their own, but they were also intertwined. A set of common concerns was emerging over time and possibly even an agenda, but no one was going to tell anyone what they could or couldn't write about, or what it all meant or could add up to.

Ananda La Vita, who was living in the Positive Force group house in Arlington and fielding many of the media requests, captured what was so frustrating and destructive about the coverage. "One thing I am particularly upset about is how they take something that has no actual definition, and they attempt to define it," she wrote in a typewritten screed for other Riot Grrrls. "Riot Grrrl is about destroying boundaries, not creating them. But these mags make us look like we're one 'thing,' that you have to look a certain way or be into a certain type of music or believe certain things in order to be a Riot Grrrl, when there are no such requirements.... Seeing ourselves described by these mainstream writers puts boundaries in our minds. I think this is really dangerous. We can counteract it by keeping alive the 'underground' aspect of Riot Grrrl—keeping alive our communication with each other. We can't let these papers dominate our image of each other."

The article appearing in *Spin* that November, "Teenage Riot," represented a low. It was illustrated by a thin, sulking fashion model posing with the words "Riot Grrrls" painted on her flawless skin. A group of actual Riot Grrrls in D.C. had a solution: they would put in place a "media blackout," simply refuse to cooperate with any journalist or publication. They would ignore calls, not allow their photos to be taken or words quoted without permission. Their zines had given them a sense of power and self-worth. To hold on to that, they had to refuse to be consumed.

———

ALLISON AND MOLLY toured with Bratmobile during the summer of 1992, and it wasn't good. Their close friendship felt the strain of their nights playing shows throughout the Midwest, from Chicago to Madison to Bloomington and Dayton. Partly this was the pressure of being a band, of young egos colliding, not knowing how to compromise. But they also carried the burden of representing Riot Grrrl at a moment when the movement was getting more attention than anyone knew how to handle. By the fall, there was little left of Bratmobile.

The media blitz had taken a toll. Now they were spending more time responding to false depictions of themselves than expanding the network they had formed. And that wasn't the only problem. The groups in Olympia and D.C. who had conceived of Riot Grrrl in their bedrooms not even two years earlier didn't recognize it anymore. Even Tobi, whose *Jigsaw* had kicked things off, sat down in early 1993 to write a new zine, lamenting "how something that was once mine and genuinely meaningful to me has been taken from me and has been made into something quite else than was initially intended."

The coverage had brought an entirely new generation of girls to the movement, a lot of them, and all at once. The new arrivals had learned about Riot Grrrl in the pages of *Sassy* or *Newsweek* or through Bikini Kill's growing fame, rather than through zines or by meeting other girls at shows. It was not always clear what was drawing them to meetings or making them want to get out their scissors and glue sticks—was it part of that original desire to create a new culture, or because the superficial elements of it were now trendy? Tobi was exasperated by these "posers or maybe just well intentioned and hopelessly enthusiastic extremely isolated young girls living in small town america who read dumb articles in dumb magazines written by dumb people." The D.C. group, still working out of the Positive Force house, was inundated with mail—lots of flowery stationery—with girls begging to start their own local groups, asking for permission, as if Riot Grrrl was like the Girl Scouts. In response, some of the girls put together a zine they mailed back, containing the only instructions for starting a chapter: "If you want to start one, you've already begun, all that's left to be done, is to do it."

The movement was being diluted, and so a decision was made to write a zine together answering the question, for themselves more than anyone else, "What is Riot Grrrl, anyway?" Instead of offering one collective answer to their central question, each of them, twenty Riot Grrrls in all who took on the new zine, would contribute a mini essay defining the movement for herself. The overlapping and contradictory voices would provide the answer. It wasn't one thing. It was a conversation. Angelique, who dotted the *i* in her name with a heart, wrote, "We are coming together in full force because we know the world treats us like littlegirlsdumbslutsstupidwhoresuglybitchesold-maidshelplesscreaturesPROPERTY. and we know what we really are. (sometimes)."

The limited ways they saw their lives reflected back to them from these hip magazines reminded the girls exactly why they had found zines so attractive to begin with. They had felt ignored by the wider culture. Zines had given them the chance to build up the confidence to say something back. But now they were little more than the cut-and-paste look of their zines or their Doc Martens; the most superficial elements had been scraped and repurposed. And it made them feel even further silenced. "The media has made us into a fad so that we can easily be put in the back of people's closets with the macrame and parachute pants when we aren't 'the next big thing' anymore," wrote another contributor. After making the zine, the D.C. chapter took one further step: they formed a media working group, to try to shape their own image, though many of the girls dissented. Some felt it would undermine exactly what had made Riot Grrrl so special to start now passing down diktats.

The outside attention persisted all through the end of 1992 and into 1993. "Mean, Mad, and Definitely Underground" was the headline in the *Los Angeles Times*, "Feminist Fury" in *The Seattle Times*. Even *Cosmo*, defender of the very femininity that felt most oppressive to the girls, ran an article that spring: "The New Activists: Fearless,

Funny, Fighting Mad." These pieces portrayed the Riot Grrrls as aggressive, almost domineering, in their anger. No longer passively surrounding the mosh pit as coat hangers, now they were scaring the boys away. In one article in *Seventeen* magazine, "It's a Grrrl Thing," the "crowd of girls with chopped-off hair in plaid vintage dresses" were menacing and confused, "condemning the Y chromosome as the root of all evil," alienating everyone with their "militant slant." The internal debate over media coverage was presented as just a frivolous catfight: "Will Riot Grrrl refocus feminism or fry in its own fury?" The article, of course, completely ignored the hard issues that the Riot Grrrls actually used their zines to discuss. Ironically, elsewhere in the same issue of *Seventeen* were the results of a national survey about sexual harassment that found that 40 percent of the readers endured catcalls and handsy men every day.

The number of zines was meanwhile exploding, from a few dozen to thousands by 1993. With more families buying personal computers and new easy-to-use desktop publishing software, the bar to taking part was now much lower. Alienated teenage girls everywhere joined in the homespun, confessional writing. In one of the last organized moves of the original group of Riot Grrrls, meant to reassert the centrality of zines to their way of communicating and coming together, a couple of girls launched Riot Grrrl Press in 1993. Kathleen and Allison first had the idea: to create a distribution service and a catalog that one could order from by sending in fifty cents for a requested zine. But it was Erika Reinstein, the D.C.-based Riot Grrrl, who took on the task with May Summer Farnsworth, the two of them turning their apartment into a blizzard of paper. Girls would send in their own zines, and sometimes even their thick original copies still curling at the edges and smelling of rubber cement (May, who worked at a copy shop, would secretly use the photocopy machine to create flat masters when her supervisor wasn't looking). Then the orders for zines poured in, dozens of letters piling up every day.

It was a lot of work. In the initial call for zines, Erika and May listed six reasons why the press was "important RIGHT NOW." The first was "self-representation, we need to make ourselves visible without using mainstream media as a tool." The other reasons were "networking" and "taking the burden off (usually) young women who can't afford to distribute their zines, or whose zines aren't well known." This would "create another vehicle of communication for women." They would be a "central place." As if their point weren't clear enough, when their first catalog came out in July, it included a P.S.: "We still say if you are a reporter FUCK OFF RIGHT NOW." Among the nearly ninety titles listed were zines about body image (*Girl Trouble, Cherub*), about queer identity (*Luna, Party Mix*), and about sexual health (*Clitoris*). Kathleen, who had turned much of her attention to Bikini Kill—then about to release their first album, *Pussy Whipped*—was excited to see the press come to life, a wresting back of control. Girls sent her lots of mail. Now she could send back a catalog, jotting on each one, "Here is a list of girl powered zines that you might be interested in getting." The implication was always this: now go out and make your own.

The catalog was a clever way to reel Riot Grrrl back in, to make it once again an incubator of a new type of feminism, one that was being described even in *Ms.* magazine, the foundational publication of the second wave, as an emerging third wave. In early January 1992, Rebecca Walker, daughter of the novelist Alice Walker, wrote a short essay in the magazine's pages that read like something out of a zine. It started with her own anger while watching the Clarence Thomas hearings, then described an experience she had on a train with an aggressive group of men, and finally burst into a need to act, "to push beyond my rage and articulate an agenda." But, like much of what appeared in the zines, the tight focus on women's lived experience—what nearly two decades later would blow up under the hashtag #MeToo—had yet to cohere into a political program.

There was work to do to translate the rage, and the zines were where it was most likely to happen. But for the Riot Grrrls, it was already too late. On the surface the movement had heft: at an April 1993 gay rights march in Washington, the Riot Grrrl contingent was three times bigger than their showing at a similar protest the year before. But their message, their plan, was still diffuse. And when they found a microphone shoved in their faces, as it had been almost since their start, they offered a yell and spoke generally about "girl power."

No greater omen foretold the demise of Riot Grrrl than the rise of the Spice Girls, a girl group from England that started climbing to the top of the music charts in the mid-1990s. Looking like a variety pack of Barbie dolls, all in crop tops and tight skirts—an image the original Riot Grrrls would have mocked and abhorred—the Spice Girls claimed "girl power" as their own motto. The liner notes to their first album declared, "The Future Is Female," and called their legion of teenage girl fans "Freedom Fighters." "We're freshening up feminism for the nineties," they told *The Guardian*. "Feminism has become a dirty word. Girl Power is just a nineties way of saying it." Within a few short years Revolution Girl Style Now and its messy DIY creativity, its attempt to turn trauma into change, its uncompromising attention to individual experience, had transmogrified into a capitalist dream, an easily digestible, catchy pop anthem about consumption masquerading as empowerment, played again and again on the radio: "I'll tell you what I want, what I really, really want. . . ."

A few young women did try to keep the zine scene alive, but soon, in homes everywhere, the scratchy sound of a modem connecting to AOL could be heard. If girls wanted to reach out to one another, to commiserate and try to upend the status quo, they didn't need to reinvent their own medium to do so. There was now a much faster way: just log on to the internet.

Interlude

CYBERSPACE

—————

SOCIAL MEDIA AS we know it was born in a wooden shack in a shipyard in Sausalito. More precisely, it was born in the closet of that shack. Just north of the Golden Gate Bridge, not far from the rickety houseboats floating on the edge of the bay, sat a humming and vibrating VAX computer, the size of a small refrigerator, connected to a dozen modems. And in 1985, an eclectic group of Bay Area professors, engineers, freelance writers, and self-proclaimed futurists began dialing into those modems and talking by typing, at all hours of the day and night, about all manner of things: the worsening AIDS epidemic, their favorite Grateful Dead songs, the ethics of circumcision, the most useful UNIX commands. No one had done this before, engaged in this sort of disembodied, nearly instantaneous communication through writing. They soon began calling themselves a "virtual community."

The description could easily apply to Peiresc's web of correspondents or the links in the chain of the samizdat underground or the Riot Grrrls and their network of zines. These, too, were communities brought and held together through writing that allowed them to replicate, virtually, the warmth and energy that is generated when huddling together in a corner. What was different and suddenly completely new was the speed and scale of it.

The few hundred people who dialed into that VAX computer were not aiming to start a movement; they had no status quo they were aching to shatter. They just wanted to chat. In that sense, including them here represents a detour of sorts. But they saw themselves as just the first to test out these tools, and they were soon convinced that the tools themselves had revolutionary potential. Their ability to converse in this way mesmerized them as they watched the flickering green letters on a black screen accumulate, expressing personality, wit, genuine friendship, affinity for the same eccentric hobbies. It led to some big dreaming about what this space that was no real physical space at all—cyberspace—could be for, what it could achieve, what capacities it could offer its users, whether it had the ability as a medium to improve on all those petitions and local newspapers and manifestos of the past.

Inside that shack, a few feet from the VAX, sat John Coate, the hippie put in charge of managing this new community. He asked himself this question all the time, especially as his hours logged online grew: Was he witnessing the birth of a new source of power for anybody who wanted to upend the world? And his answer was always yes, but also no.

ALL YOU'D HAVE to do is spend a minute with Coate to appreciate the idealism that was there from the beginning. In 1986, when he started at the WELL—which is what this conversation exchange was called—he was in his early thirties, tall and thin with feathered blond hair and a style of speaking that was so slow and sticky that he had earned the nickname Tex (which we'll call him as well). He also really liked cowboy shirts. Tex had never used a computer before in his life when he showed up for his first day of work. His most obvious skill was knowing how to fix cars. But he had spent the past decade living on a commune in Tennessee called the Farm. This seemed to be the common denominator among the first employees of the WELL: they were former communards. They had all experienced the 1970s off the grid, forming new families and connections based on what they felt was more honest stuff.

People had been using networked computers to communicate for a little more than a decade by that point, but the existing forums were limited and lacked much imagination. ARPANET, the proto-internet, was open only to a small group of academics and researchers. For anyone else with the technical know-how, a small nerd archipelago of what were known as bulletin board servers existed, spots for local teenagers to discuss *Star Trek*. The WELL, as conceived, was to be capacious, embracing anyone who cared to enter and hang out and stay awhile. It would be as independent and quirky as a commune, its clearest antecedent, though one held together by telephone wires.

Its co-creator was Stewart Brand, well known in the Bay Area as a sort of new age impresario, who, in the words of the cultural historian Fred Turner, had become the hub of an idiosyncratic but auspicious network that "spanned the worlds of scientific research, hippie homesteading, ecology, and mainstream consumer culture." Where others saw in computers a bureaucratized future of punch cards and soullessness, Brand saw liberation, a tool for creativity and personal growth that could allow the individual to push beyond society's constraints. He was best known for creating the *Whole Earth Catalog* in 1968, a Sears, Roebuck for back-to-the-landers, which sold composting toilets, plans for geodesic domes, solar ovens, and a way of life that put great hope in technology. Brand was also, in his bones, an entrepreneur. If he had already seen himself as outfitting pioneers for the frontier, he was now looking to expand those boundaries beyond the physical, and maybe make some money doing so.

In 1984, Brand met a businessman named Larry Brilliant, who owned a company that sold a computer conferencing system called PicoSpan. Brilliant wanted to test out this new system, and he knew he could get a jump start if he handed the tools over to an established network. That's what Brand had to offer. By the mid-1980s the *Whole Earth Catalog* had become the *Whole Earth Review*, a magazine produced on that dock in Sausalito. Together they decided to create the WELL; Brand, who had a knack for branding, got to the name after

doodling for a few minutes. It was an acronym for Whole Earth 'Lec-
tronic Link (a name Tom Wolfe could love). Brilliant would supply
the $100,000 VAX computer and the software, and Brand, for bring-
ing his *Whole Earth* cachet and his people, would be half owner and
responsible for creating an electronic petri dish, an experiment to see
if authenticity could grow through computers.

And this is how Tex got to be there: he knew how communes
worked, and he knew how they could fail.

Tex had grown up in a prominent San Francisco family, but his life
had swerved away from middle-class respectability in the fall of 1970,
when he joined a group traveling the country like nomads in a caravan
of converted school buses. They were following their spiritual guru,
Stephen Gaskin, a man with a cultish hold on his flock. Gaskin's
philosophy was a mash-up of Zen Buddhism and countercultural
pieties like veganism. He stressed the importance of marriage and
childbearing—his wife was Ina May Gaskin, a pioneer of the home
birth movement—but he also encouraged his followers to be in what
he called "four marriage," in which two couples committed themselves
to each other as a form of egalitarian polygamy. Tex first got hooked
on Gaskin when he saw him speak at a dilapidated theater in San
Francisco, sitting cross-legged and blowing a ram's horn to indicate
that his lecture for the day was done.

The caravan experience was formative. The ten people on Tex's bus,
mostly strangers to one another, had to learn to live together. It wasn't
just a practical necessity. They believed they were remaking society.
When a problem arose, they would have a session of "sorting it out."
These would be group confrontations, in which people were completely blunt about one another's most minor faults. "We spent night
after night talking to each other," Tex told me. "We were going to tell
the truth. We were going to be emotionally honest. Be open and see
where that led. The idea was to try to have kindness when you tell
people about their habits that you find annoying. It's not enough to be
okay with a process like that. You have to thrive on it. You have to be
willing to hear things and change according to each other's feedback.
People who didn't want it left."

Behind this way of thinking and being was a kind of free speech absolutism. You let it all out, and the society that would emerge from this unfiltered directness would be stronger. Gaskin eventually led the group of three hundred that was part of the caravan to settle together on a plot of land, a 1,014-acre farm south of Nashville. They were building a new civilization—diverting water, building latrines, but also freezing in tents while constructing houses out of plywood and dealing with the occasional bouts of hepatitis. The Farm grew, and by the mid-1970s it had passed five hundred members, with many dirty children toddling around everywhere.

The same rules about total openness applied, but it got harder at scale. Gaskin allowed anyone to stop by and visit, and soon there seemed to be an endless stream of vagrant hippies, draft dodgers, and even mentally ill people showing up. One year there were twenty thousand visitors. This was an exercise in extreme tolerance, and Tex learned it well. All voices were welcome, even if it took patience to listen and stick it out and cut everyone slack. When the Farm set up satellite projects in the late 1970s, Tex threw himself into newer situations requiring these monk-like abilities, moving first to the South Bronx to help run an ambulance service, squatting in an abandoned building heated by burning old pallets and packing wood he found in defunct factories. Then he moved to Washington, D.C., to start a group home for Native Americans. All in all he calculated that throughout the 1970s and early 1980s, he had lived in fifteen different households with somewhere around two hundred people.

WHAT TEX BROUGHT to the WELL was a faith that communication itself could be redemptive. He believed that this was the key to self-government, to making this new virtual community work. But he'd also learned what almost anyone learns when they dabble in such a human experiment: that success rests on the fragile balance between the needs of the individual and those of the collective, a balance that had to be monitored, calibrated, and recalibrated daily. It could be exhausting. But without that vigilance, without those rules,

without a structure that pointed people toward productive deliberation, things could quickly go off the rails. He'd seen it. And when he
left the Farm in 1982, it was largely because Gaskin, their leader, had
turned into an authoritarian, demanding too much for the collective at
the expense of the individual.

At the WELL, Tex found an environment seemingly built to with-
stand this tension. Some of it was intentional and some a happy accident. PicoSpan, the conferencing software, gave the WELL its basic
form. It was created by an Ann Arbor programmer at the University
of Michigan who infused it with his libertarian tendencies—a bias
toward the free flow of talk—but also lent it the orderliness of an academic gathering. The WELL was divided into a series of "conferences," each watched over by a "host," and then further carved up into
specific "topics." The conversations were categorized, segmented, and
supervised, but there was also room to continually shift the direction
as every comment nudged the group along: the structure helped delin-
eate and allow for focus, but within was freedom and individual initiative.

Brand also made a few crucial decisions. He had set the subscription fee low but not too low—eight dollars a month and then two
dollars per hour to log on. If it was too expensive, users might write
long, log on, deposit their posts, and then log off, preventing a more
dynamic back-and-forth. It would result in competing and unreadable
screeds—not a chat. But if it was too cheap, those who had time to
stay online and banter all day would dominate, tying up the phone
lines and annoying everyone.

The other inadvertently consequential choice Brand made was visible every time a user logged on to the VAX computer. A cryptic message would appear: "You own your own words." This was a way to
protect Brand from any liability. Its literal meaning was that you, the
user, had copyright over every sentence you produced. But the disclaimer also became a kind of ethos: you were accountable, a citizen
here with both rights and responsibilities. So seriously was this ownership taken that even three decades later Tex wouldn't share old WELL
archives until I promised not to quote them without getting permis-

sion from the authors—amazing to consider in our age of perpetual retweets. There was also no anonymity allowed. You could have a playful ID in parentheses, but your real name would be listed right next to it. If you wanted to delete your posts after they were written, there was a command for that, called a "scribble," but it left a trace, showing you had eaten your own words. Just like in real life, you couldn't pretend they had never existed.

To successfully participate in this community, you had to offer an interesting personal anecdote, make a provocative interjection, or expand the discussion in some way. The stars of the WELL understood this. They were good writers who could translate a quick spoken repartee into text. But they were also conversationalists—demonstrably interested in what others had to say, acknowledging their contributions, and prodding the talk along. You got attention not by saying something that would silence all chatter and turn others in your direction but by contributing in an amusing or thoughtful or useful way to the flow.

Maybe the most distinctive feature of the WELL from our perspective today was the role of the host—"fair witness" was the original title as dictated by the creator of PicoSpan, and coincidentally the same term used on the Farm for people who brokered peace when interpersonal matters got messy. "Host" was ultimately chosen in order to stick with the model of a French salon that Brand imagined. He had George Sand in mind. For every conference, there was one person, remunerated with a free subscription, who oversaw the various strands of conversation. As Howard Rheingold, an early and avid WELL devotee and popularizer of the phrase "virtual community," put it, hosts on the WELL had the same role as party hosts in real life: "to welcome newcomers, introduce people to one another, clean up after the guests, provoke discussion, and break up fights if necessary." Rheingold, a Bay Area writer with a Groucho Marx mustache and a thing for colorful Balinese shirts and panama hats, was a good example of the kind of person drawn to the WELL. He had taken a special interest in how computers could expand knowledge and human experience, and on the WELL, where he would spend countless hours, he discovered what he called "a group mind, where questions are answered, support is given, inspiration is provided, by people I may have never heard from before, and whom I may never meet face to face." He had fiddled around with other bulletin board servers, but nothing quite replicated the transcendence and camaraderie he found on the WELL.

THE CONFERENCES on the WELL became intense little places for people to obsess together. In 1986, there was an influx of Deadheads, the tie-dyed, tripping tribe of groupies who followed the Grateful Dead, one of the last authentic remnants of the 1960s counterculture. They had been led to the WELL by David Gans, a musician who hosted a weekly hour of radio devoted to their jams (a show he has continued to host for decades). It was a ready-made virtual community that constituted itself in parking lots outside concert venues, and many of the band's original followers, hitting middle age, were professionals with access to computers. Now they could hang out together all the time. "The community just dug itself," Gans told me. I spoke to him in Albany, New York, while he was on tour with a Dead cover band, Gratefully Yours. "We became this giant thing. We'd argue over set lists, we'd complain about the repetition of songs, we'd worry about Jerry Garcia's health. Everything a community does with the object of its affections and with itself, we did."

Tex's job, he learned, was to oversee it all, provide the guardrails so the conversation could keep moving forward without interruption or bad feeling. It demanded a near-constant gauging of civility. The WELL even had a special private conference, called Backstage, where the hosts could talk with Tex and the other admins about any issues that might come up, a talk-it-all-out approach borrowed from the commune. Topic #103 from Backstage, in February 1998, "Temperatures Are Rising," is a good example. One host worried, in post 33, that "responses to controversial statements, like (rag)'s use of 'girl,' or the capital punishment discussion in mind, are getting more and more assertive." But he wasn't too concerned. He said he read this more confrontational tone as "a sign that our mutual trust has built up to the point where we no longer feel the need to coddle . . . we are more free to express our feelings in somewhat forceful terms." The following post, 34, disagreed. "The heat can put off people who don't have the same background we do," the host noted. "For example, (shibumi) remarked this evening that the recent brouhaha in tru has made him reluctant to post there." (In this exchange, "mind" and "tru" are two different conferences; quoting from the WELL is tricky, because each post was embedded in long streams of chatting, full of callbacks and inside jokes.)

When he started the WELL, Stewart Brand said, "the theory going in was that everybody plays until we find out what is unplayable behavior." But it was not always easy to determine what counted as productive conversation and what was a distraction or even a form of sabotage. And as Tex was learning, the fact that it was a faceless medium made things even harder: in order to reap the benefits, it took an enormous amount of work and supervision.

Tex even found himself kicking out a troll, though that term wasn't being used outside fairy tales yet. Mark Ethan Smith, who went by the username (grandma) and had a gender-fluid identity, preferring not to use any identifying pronouns, became a domineering and vitriolic force on a number of conferences. Smith's hobbyhorse was the inherent evil of all men, posting thousands of rageful words a day, attacking and biting. If anyone responded to the provocations, Smith would only grow more incensed and then claim to be the victim. Tex, after spending hours on the phone trying to talk to Smith and then to others who had been offended by the barrage of anger, made a decision to bar Smith from the WELL. This was the corollary to all the idealism, one that would be forgotten once people began getting nostalgic about the early online world. Back then, too, the realization came quick: cyberspace needed bouncers.

When things got confrontational on the WELL—moments of "thrash," in their lingo—what helped, in addition to Tex's watchful eye, was the architecture: flow mattered here more than anything else. There was always an incentive to reach equilibrium again, to keep lengthening the thread, inspiring a new topic. The prize didn't go to the person blasting the largest flame, delivering the biggest insult. It went to the person who could move things along. "Mostly everyone tried to get at the truth of whatever a particular thrash was about," wrote John Seabrook, a *New Yorker* writer who joined the WELL first as a silent lurker and then got swept up in the community, to sum it all up in a way that would "set everything right again."

As time went on, adjustments were made to account for the dislocation that came from communicating virtually. Starting in 1986, for example, many of the participants began meeting up regularly in person; with long-distance calls to the modem still too pricey, almost everyone was local to the Bay Area. These gatherings, given the unpleasant name "fleshmeets," started with a few regulars who wanted to buy coffee for Tex and the other admins. Some just longed to lay their hands on the mysterious VAX computer, the home for all their conversations, and listen to its hum. Soon there was a chili cook-off, meetings in Golden Gate Park, or once even a group trip to the circus. Words detached from physical form created opportunities for wild projection, as we well know, and it was odd at first to encounter someone you had sparred with online or whose wit had been a source of awe. But seeing everyone's utter normalcy had the effect of bringing it all back down to a human scale. People learned, for example, that Tex was a close talker who usually gripped your shoulder to tell you what he had to say from three inches away. If they wanted to build an intimate, open connection online, they were learning, it helped to have a corresponding one in the real world.

But there was also a growing awareness that in certain cases what was needed was increased privacy. One conference, Women on the WELL, limited its admittance. The personal discussions here, about domestic violence, eating disorders, the struggles of balancing a career and a family, these could only happen away from the gaze and typing fingers of men. This adaptation, too, was critical—how inclusive or exclusive to be, what kind of talk could develop only in quiet spaces, and what needed the bustle of a crowd. For women, this concession made the WELL a particularly welcoming place. By the late 1980s, while women made up only 10 percent of people going online, they constituted 40 percent of the population of the WELL.

Anyone who entertained the idea of a virtual community in those very early days came eventually to the same understanding: there was the dream of it and the reality. If it helped people connect in new and wondrous ways, it could also detach people from social norms so completely that it undermined all the benefits of communing as a group. Stacy Horn, a recent graduate of New York University's Interactive Telecommunications Program, built her own sister site to the WELL called Echo (East Coast Hang Out), filling her fifth-floor walk-up in Greenwich Village with rows of stacked modems and a mess of telephone wires. She loved her forum, and it became a vibrant place, one for chatting about local politics, sharing dating stories, and arguing about plays or the city's best pizza. But it also required constant moderation. Communicating in cyberspace, she wrote a few years later, "wasn't going to bring peace and understanding throughout the world, tra-la-la-la. Cyberspace does not have the power to make us anything other than what we already are. . . . It is a revealing, not a transforming, medium."

MARSHALL MCLUHAN, the media theorist, had a useful shorthand for describing what people tend to do when confronted with a new technology: "rear-view mirror thinking." Faced with novelty, "we tend always to attach ourselves to the objects, to the flavor of the most recent past. We look at the present through a rear-view mirror. We march backwards into the future."

If you asked Tex and his fellow members of the WELL back then to describe the space they were inhabiting with their typing, they would draw on what they saw in that rearview mirror. In just one short article from 1988, Tex pointed to a number of different ways the WELL was imagined: as a "neighborhood pub," "an electronic Greenwich Village," "the electronic equivalent of the French salons during the Enlightenment period," and "the kind of things coffee shops were supposed to be about." But in the same way that a car was never really just a faster horse, talking online was not just a virtual café. No metaphor could really grasp what it was. And yet metaphor is perhaps the WELL's greatest legacy.

The work it took to make the WELL a community was soon forgotten, lessons like the one Tex conveyed in that 1988 article: "It is possible to be more concerned with grabbing and holding the attention of the group rather than concentrating on the content of what is said." Amnesia set in as the size of online talking grew. What was remembered and propagated instead was the ideal version of it, the fantasy of the always-open coffee shop with a table available for each and every interest and concern. And—crucial for our purposes—a place where people with radical notions could easily find others to join with them and imagine a new reality.

This was the vision of John Perry Barlow, sometime Grateful Dead lyricist, writer, thinker, and one of the founders of the Electronic Frontier Foundation, an early organization established to defend free speech online. It was on a post on the WELL that he first used "cyberspace" to describe their virtual gathering place, borrowing a phrase from the science fiction writer William Gibson. And a few years later, in 1996, Barlow wrote "A Declaration of the Independence of Cyberspace," which remains the purest distillation of the dream, one that grew out of his own experience on the WELL. There was no mention of Brand's design choices or the hosts or Tex's guiding hand (and kicking foot, when people needed to be thrown out). Instead, for Barlow cyberspace consisted of "transactions, relationships, and thought itself, arrayed like a standing wave in the web of our communications"— a pure community built through talking, what the Farm, too, was supposed to be. It was an "act of nature," one that "grows itself through our collective actions," a "world where anyone, anywhere may express his or her beliefs, no matter how singular, without fear of being coerced into silence or conformity."

Just like the hopes of those hippie homesteaders looking for a better, more democratic society, Barlow's fantasia ignored all the exertion and interventions necessary to make any of it even close to possible—

the responsibility that on the WELL was always understood as the necessary flip side of freedom. It soon became all freedom. Eric Schmidt, the then executive chairman of Google, pointed lovingly to Barlow's declaration as a dream that "has been realized" in a 2015 op-ed in *The New York Times.* As he saw it, "The Internet has created safe spaces for communities to connect, communicate, organize and mobilize, and it has helped many people to find their place and their voice." Whether this is really true is the question we will turn to next. But what Schmidt seemed to miss was that these spaces were purposefully designed and that how they were built and how they were managed would determine how useful they could actually be and for what. "It's just a tool," he wrote, as flippantly as someone who would call a hammer and a saw the same thing. "We are the ones who harness its power."

As for the WELL itself, it couldn't keep up. By 1991, it had reached five thousand users. Service wasn't great. Every day seemed to bring a new technical problem, with the system periodically crashing or modems stalling. Tex still oversaw a rich Backstage conversation, and by his count in his five years there he had hosted sixty-one WELL parties and spent thousands of hours on the phone talking people out of quitting, smoothing out hurt feelings, or just listening to rants. Users continued to be passionate. At one point, in 1988, the sluggish VAX had to be replaced, and they collected money themselves to acquire a new Sequent computer, "like switching from a Schwinn to a Rolls," Rheingold said. It was a striking moment. They set the rules for their own governance, possessed their own words, and now even had a stake in the silicon body that contained, as Rheingold put it, "the beating heart of the community."

But there was constant pressure to figure out how to make this work as a business. A subscriber service for playing interactive games, first started in the mid-1980s and renamed America Online in 1991, already had tens of thousands of users. Its founder, Steve Case, had been hanging out on the WELL, picking up ideas, and by the mid-1990s, AOL, now complete with "chat rooms," would see its subscribers jump into the millions. The WELL, which had loomed so large in those early years as a model for the future, became a tinier and tinier island, soon microscopic in size. In 1994, the World Wide Web suddenly took off. In January of that year, there were roughly seven hundred websites in existence. At the end of that year, there were just over ten thousand.

By then, Tex had decided to quit. Managing this whole community alone, even with its relatively small size, had become exhausting. "I was so tangled up with everybody I was kind of losing my bearings a little bit," Tex said. "On our commune we were kind of quasi Buddhists, and the objective was always to get unattached, to rise above things, to not get too caught up in praise and blame. And suddenly I'm enmeshed in a system where there was some kind of praise and blame coming my way, every day. I would go to bed at night after a while almost in a fetal position. It was socially exhausting. I was absorbing a great deal from people, and it was expected of me that I would not lose it."

But that was only part of it. Those users most invested in the uniqueness of the WELL could see what was coming. It was difficult to imagine scaling it up in size and maintaining the intimacy and the many mechanisms that had allowed it to flourish. But getting bigger was necessary to keep it viable in the crazily commodifying web. "The odds are always good that big power and big money will find a way to control access to virtual communities," Rheingold prophesied in 1993. "What we know and do now is important because it is still possible for people around the world to make sure this new sphere of vital human discourse remains open to the citizens of the planet before the political and economic big boys seize it, censor it, meter it, and sell it back to us."

These days Tex lives on a couple of acres of land in Mendocino County in Northern California. He's had a career in local media, helping the *San Francisco Chronicle* start its first website and then running a community radio station. He is still wistful about the WELL. But he has no illusions that there was any magic at work back then. He knows what it took. "Flower children that we were," he told me, "we believed we could bend technology to our will."

Chapter 7

THE SQUARE

CAIRO, 2011

THE PHOTOGRAPH THAT started it all was of a broken face, an image so stomach churning, so terrible in its implications, that you had to either look away or gasp in terror. The face belonged to Khaled Said, a young computer programmer from Alexandria, Egypt, picked up by policemen in a cybercafe one day in the early summer of 2010 and then beaten to death in a nearby stairwell. Though the authorities alleged Said was a big-time thug and drug dealer who died by choking on marijuana he was trying to conceal, his middle-class roots and education made the claim immediately suspicious. Why the police stopped him that day is still unclear; his parents later said he had in his possession incriminating video evidence of corruption. Whatever the reason, nothing could explain his face.

At first Wael Ghonim couldn't believe what he was looking at—and then he began to cry. "His lower lip had been ripped in half, and his jaw was seemingly dislocated," was how he described what he saw in the photo, which had been taken at the morgue by Said's brother. "His front teeth appeared to be missing, and it looked as if they had been beaten right out of his mouth." Ghonim was a twenty-nine-year-old marketing director for Google who had grown up in Egypt but was then living in Dubai as part of the company's efforts to branch out in the Middle East. What he saw in that photo was the most visceral, bloody illustration of what he had come to resent and fear about his homeland: the arbitrariness with which power was wielded. That someone, someone very much like him, could just be picked up off the street and beaten to death with total impunity was horrifying.

From his faraway office, he had already tapped into the growing dissatisfaction of a minuscule Egyptian dissident movement contending with a stagnant economy and a forever president whose "temporary" Emergency Law—suspending due process while emboldening the police—had been in place for thirty years. But this was different. This was a face. He knew there was a whole class of Egyptians who would also see themselves in Khaled Said. As Susan Sontag wrote in *Regarding the Pain of Others,* an image of violence inflicted was "an invitation to pay attention, to reflect, to learn, to examine the rationalizations for mass suffering offered by established powers. Who caused what the picture shows? Who is responsible? Is it excusable? Was it inevitable? Is there some state of affairs which we have accepted up to now that ought to be challenged?"

These were the questions that gnawed at Ghonim. And he decided to use his particular skill set to respond: he started a Facebook page. He had been spending a lot of time that summer on the site, which just the year before had introduced its Arabic interface. Seemingly overnight, the number of Egyptian users had jumped from 900,000 to 5 million. Ghonim gave the new Facebook page a simple, blunt name: "We Are All Khaled Said." Familiar with the site's functionality, he chose to make it a "page," rather than a "group," so that any future posts would automatically show up in the feeds of those who had "liked" it. He also decided to remain anonymous. His first post was a rat-a-tat of anguish: "Today they killed Khaled. If I don't act for his sake, tomorrow they will kill me."

GHONIM NEVER SET OUT to be a revolutionary. He had no more fervent dream as a teenager than to one day work for Google, a company that, as he put it, "embodied who I was as a person." His family was part of a wave of middle-class Egyptians who couldn't afford to stay in their own country during the 1980s, and so Ghonim spent part of his youth in Saudi Arabia, where his father worked as a doctor. In college back in Egypt he was drawn to two worlds that he would try for a time to combine: Islam and the internet. He had briefly joined the Muslim Brotherhood, an Islamist movement, officially outlawed for decades, that acted as a vast secret society and offered a sense of belonging. The internet, Ghonim first encountered in a cousin's bedroom in 1997 (excitedly clicking on the website of the Library of Congress, of all places). The moment was "magical." He liked the control it gave him. "I find virtual life in cyberspace quite appealing," he would later write. "I prefer it to being visible in public life. It is quite convenient to conceal your identity and write whatever you please in whatever way you choose."

An ambitious young man, with the rectangular glasses of an architect and a mess of curly black hair, he graduated with a degree in computer engineering and then an MBA in marketing and sales from the American University in Cairo. A series of start-ups followed, including one called IslamWay that collected audio recordings of religious sermons and recitals of the Koran. And by 2010 he had fulfilled his dream and was working for Google, running marketing outreach to the Arab world.

In just the first day, 36,000 people followed the new We Are All Khaled Said page, and 1,800 commented. Within a week, it would eclipse all of Egyptian Facebook. Ghonim had started an emotional feedback loop, and he kept stoking it. "The day they went and killed Khaled, I didn't stand by him," read one of his posts. "Tomorrow they will come to kill me and you won't stand by me." He used words like "blood" and "martyr" again and again and, most critically, "us" and "them." There was a sense of righteousness, a community rising up around the need for vengeance—Ghonim later said he was writing in "a language closer to my heart than to my mind." And those reading him then commented and liked and shared. It took only a few days for the page to reach 100,000 followers, many of whom started contacting the anonymous admin over email—he had set up an account for this—offering their own thoughts and pictures for him to post on the page. One woman emailed an ultrasound photo of her fetus with the words "My name is Khaled, and I'm coming to the world in three months. I will never forget Khaled Said and I will demand justice for his case."

Who were these people liking the page? Young, disaffected Egyptians like Abdelrahman Ayyash, who spoke to me from his exile in Istanbul. When he first saw We Are All Khaled Said, the tumult of emotion from so many directions felt to him like a "game changer," he said. Even if Facebook was a recent development for Egyptians, the internet was not new for people like Ayyash. And it was his experience talking online that had primed him and so many others for this moment. His family, from the Nile delta city of Mansoura, were members of the Muslim Brotherhood, and it was on the Brotherhood's primitive online forums that Ayyash first explored the new medium. These were, it should be said, closely monitored, and any mention of the Brotherhood itself was immediately deleted. Ayyash soon lost interest.

But from there, he stumbled upon the blogosphere. By the mid-2000s, blogs were a craze among the cosmopolitan youth of Cairo and Alexandria who used tools like the Google-owned Blogger or WordPress to make their own personal newsletters, sharing their every thought. Ayyash hungrily read the often overlong and self-indulgent public journals of Copts, Baha'is, gays and lesbians, Salafis, Communists, and the woman whose blog was simply titled "I Want to Be a Bride." Class and religious divisions that had become so calcified in Egypt seemed to break down, and the blogs gave young people a chance to peer into the minds of others. Ayyash started his own in 2006, teasingly questioning some of the Brotherhood's diktats. A typical post was titled "I'm a Muslim Brother and I Watch Movies." His blog even earned him a scolding in 2007 from the head of the Brotherhood's political department, Mohammed Morsi, the man who would go on to briefly become Egypt's first and so far only freely elected president.

Blogging in those years became synonymous with dissidence. One Muslim Brotherhood website wondered in 2006, "Would you marry a girl who blogs?" The first modern protest movement in Egypt against autocracy fermented among bloggers who eventually gathered on the steps of the High Court in Cairo in 2004, their mouths covered by yellow tape scrawled with the word *Kefaya* (Enough). In 2007, the Mubarak regime even sentenced a blogger to four years in jail for his posts.

And then came Facebook. By 2010, everyone seemed to abandon their blogs en masse. Facebook reached a wider audience and offered more immediate gratification. While blogs called for longer pieces structured around an argument or narrative, Facebook posts were shorter bursts of information and feeling. They also felt ephemeral. Less care was taken with the craft of writing them and the cultivation of a voice or unique perspective that might draw readers back. What mattered now was adding an utterance to the scrollable feed that might stand out. Ayyash summed up the switch to social media this way: "The blogs were more of an intellectual space; Facebook was a personal one."

But it did bring all those bloggers into a single noisy room, increasing the cross-pollination and sense of shared grievance. The political talk didn't end; it just got snappier—more reductive but also more entertaining. Ayyash continued to drift from the Muslim Brotherhood, openly questioning its antagonism to women and Christians, and even started a Facebook page to register his offense at the group's rigged internal elections. The April 6 Youth Movement began in 2008 when a couple of activists posted an event on Facebook, a general strike to support textile workers in the Nile delta city of Al-Mahalla al-Kubra. It quickly gained seventy thousand followers.

We Are All Khaled Said, when it went viral in June 2010, felt like another level of dissent. Facebook was churning with voices of discontent, and now they weren't just on the same platform, they were all on one page. After Ayyash clicked to follow, he himself posted a comment: "If the people don't do something about this, I will leave the country for good."

———

GHONIM, SITTING IN DUBAI, watched stupefied as the number of people following the page metastasized. He had recruited another admin he'd met online—a nineteen-year-old activist in Egypt named Abdelrahman Mansour—and together they were updating nonstop. But Ghonim knew he would have to escalate if he wanted to maintain momentum. He turned to his marketing background. It wouldn't be too different, he figured, from the "sales tunnel" approach that he had learned at school. The first phase would involve dramatic posts, violent images and videos of police brutality, to pull in readers. He needed to provide a steady supply of emotional content, including posts written in the voice of Khaled Said imploring the living to take action. The second phase, he said, was to harvest more "likes" and comments, ramping up engagement. The third phase was to get those active on the page to produce their own content, essentially turning it into "a product being marketed by its loyal users." The fourth and final phase would occur "when people decided to take the activism onto the street."

All four phases happened very fast, practically in the span of a week. Ghonim received a message from one of the page's followers, Mohammed, identified only as a twenty-six-year-old from Alexandria, and promptly posted it: "How about if we all gather along the Alexandria coast on Friday?" The idea was to carry out what they decided to call a "Silent Stand." It was the newly formed group's way of venturing out into the real world of protest. A few thousand young people, dressed in black, standing quietly or softly praying from the Koran, stood along the corniche facing the dark waters of the sea in Alexandria and along the Nile in Cairo. Mindful not to provoke or look unruly, they did not shout or chant, just gathered in mournful silence. The dramatic staging of it also served to feed Facebook, because photos and videos from the protests were posted on the page, gaining more "likes" and emboldening others. "It was amazing," Ayyash remembered. "You cannot imagine how powerful it was to see those images of people from Alexandria and Cairo lining the beach or on the highway wearing black and staying silent. It was chilling for me. And that was the moment that I thought, yeah, Khaled Said is different from anything we have seen before."

After the Silent Stand, the number of followers on the page grew, eventually topping 200,000 that summer. It became a creative environment, developing "its own culture," Ghonim said. Ideas were proposed and critiqued. Even the Silent Stand, repeated a number of times in the weeks after the first one, became a subject of open debate. The few seasoned activists in the group complained it was too passive a political act. Others thought it was smart to avoid direct confrontation with the state. Ghonim himself saw value in the gentle approach, which allowed more and more seemingly apolitical young Egyptians to scale what he called "the barrier of fear" and express their anger on an issue as unambiguous as police violence. No one was talking about regime change, but the subtext, Ghonim knew, was clear: "These people are not zombies. They are real. And given the right time, the right call, they will act."

But as the months went by and summer turned to fall, he also came to recognize the trap of organizing on Facebook. It demanded a fresh event, a novel focal point around which to rally the page's followers. He tried to keep the collective fury going with videos of police torturing their victims. Then, when the first round of a parliamentary election took place in November, he put out a request to monitor polling stations and report back on instances of vote rigging, which he then posted. (Mubarak's party, unsurprisingly, won 95 percent of the seats.) But the Khaled Said page was a restless place, now primed to expect a new high every few days. This was not a space for conversation and lengthy threads. It was a space where a particular, unyielding human desire for intensity and action could be satisfied. The number of followers, after reaching 250,000 by September, began to plateau.

Ghonim was still anonymous and living in Dubai, not exactly sure how to harness the page's growing energy. He even ran opinion surveys to elicit some metrics on what everyone wanted to do next. Ironically, in this lull, before external events overtook them, a nascent opposition movement was beginning to form. Even given where Facebook wanted them to go—its penchant for performance above all else, privileging emotion over reasoned argument (all qualities that had worked to Ghonim's advantage so far)—the comments became more thoughtful. They were wondering aloud together about the big questions: What was fundamentally wrong with Mubarak's regime? What would be the best methods for attacking it? What were their own principles and aims? There was an ongoing exchange about economics and how any change in the country had to involve reducing poverty. At one point the issue of martyrdom came up, and there were differing opinions on whether suicide was an ethical protest tactic. One indication that this was turning into a community was the strong interest in learning the identity of the admin—much like the frenzy that surrounded Mabel Dove's columns in *The African Morning Post* or even the desire to buy a coffee for Tex and the other WELL admins. Ghonim's anonymity was something of a marketing gimmick—he loved the 2006 movie *V for Vendetta*, in which a renegade in a Guy Fawkes mask starts a revolution in a dystopian England, and he would teasingly post clips from the film on the page. But remaining anonymous also hid the fact that he was actually hundreds of miles away, safe in Dubai. Instead, he created a persona for the admin, an Egyptian everyman: "I do not wish to start a revolution or a coup . . . and I do not consider myself a political leader of any sort. . . . I'm an ordinary Egyptian who cheers the Ahly team, sits at the local café, and eats pumpkin seeds."

The question of how aggressively to protest and where to direct their anger was never fully resolved. It remained a regularly flaring tension. At one point during the Silent Stands a few demonstrators began chanting, "Down, down with Hosni Mubarak," and it was captured on video. Ghonim thought it a step too far, fearing that public support would disintegrate if their message became overly political and deviated too far from a concern with the rule of law and human rights. But a counterpoint—which Ghonim, to his credit, also posted—called the admin himself naïve. Our problem *is* political, the dissenter commented. This opinion, Ghonim noticed, gained far more "likes" than his own moderate stance. The community he had prodded into existence was looking for a confrontation.

IT'S HARD TO KNOW what would have happened next if the spark that set off Tunisia's shocking revolution had not turned into a conflagration. The self-immolation of a fruit seller, Mohamed Bouazizi, which quickly led to the fall of Zine al-Abidine Ben Ali, the country's ruler, kicked the feedback loop into overdrive. No longer was it a fantasy to believe that an authoritarian leader could be deposed by his people, could be forced to apologize and flee in fear. Besides respect for those who took to the streets in Tunisia, the dominant feeling on the We Are All Khaled Said page was shame. "If Bouazizi had burned himself in Egypt," read one comment, "admin would have organized a silent stand." A decision had already been made to mark January 25 with a protest. That was Police Day, the annual holiday meant to honor the country's security services. Now, after the fall of Ben Ali, they had to do more. Despite all the *V for Vendetta* playacting, Ghonim didn't want to put anyone in harm's way. But his younger, more radical co-admin, Mansour, convinced him that this was the moment. On January 15, Ghonim changed the name of the event to "January 25: Revolution Against Torture, Poverty, Corruption, and Unemployment." An uprising was now scheduled on Facebook.

It wasn't exactly inevitable. Tunisia provided the push, but there were only two possible roads for a movement that had been built on social media: either We Are All Khaled Said would soon fizzle out, incapable of sheltering a nuanced assessment of means and ends, or it would rally at a massive event—one that, ideally, could be captured on film and fed back to the page. Despite the name of the planned revolution, there was no real consensus yet about the way forward. Ghonim did post a long message titled "I Wish" that was a list of his own desires, some political ("I wish I had a real voice in my own country"), but most so dreamy as to be practically meaningless ("I wish teachers would establish in the hearts and minds of students a genuine love for knowledge and learning" and "I wish we could love one another"). Another document posted on the page written by a more hardened group of leftist activists made explicit their four objectives for the protest: ending the Emergency Law, confronting the problems of poverty in Egypt, firing the hated interior minister, and putting a two-term limit on the presidency. These were specific, concrete demands, but there was no time to discuss them or gain support for them because the scheduled revolution was hurtling toward a single overarching goal: the ousting of Mubarak.

For Ghonim, the stakes of what he had set in motion were suddenly apparent. Like so many others who had proclaimed as much on the page, he now felt ready to die for the change he was seeking. He booked his ticket for Cairo. The invitation to what quickly became known as #Jan25 was seen by more than half a million Egyptians in a single day, with 27,000 confirming immediately that they would attend. Traffic to the page itself reached 9,125,380 hits, and the number of followers jumped to 382,740. There was off-line organizing too, person to person and on photocopied flyers. Taxi drivers relayed the details of the protest to their passengers. But the momentum began and was sustained on Facebook.

What happened over the next eighteen days has been well documented. The young people who met on the internet marched through tear gas to Tahrir Square, the epicenter of Cairo, chanting about "bread, freedom, human dignity" and were joined by hundreds of thousands. And it's not an exaggeration to say that what they created there, in the square, was, very briefly, a utopia. A world glimpsed only virtually, on blogs or through comments on the Facebook page, burst into reality. During those days there was a sense of common purpose that surpassed anything seen before in Egypt. The protesters risked their lives together, facing the army that surrounded Tahrir and the marauding thugs on camelback who at one point charged through the encampment. The young revolutionaries, which is what they were now, spoke of liberating one little patch of Egypt where they hoped to plant a democratic country, guided justly. They hugged spontaneously, wrapped themselves in Egyptian flags, sang protest songs, and organized massive operations to feed and house one another in the square. Young Islamists like Ayyash chatted with committed socialists and recently radicalized college students; Christians and Muslims guarded each other while they prayed.

Social media ceased to be a determining factor in this moment. On the third day of the standoff, Mubarak pulled the plug on the internet, and from then on it was just the insistent physical presence of a mass of people refusing to leave until Mubarak stepped down. In retrospect this goal would appear too narrow, cutting the head off a body that didn't intend to stop moving, but it brought solidarity and quieted, for the moment, any debate about what would come next.

Ghonim never saw much of Tahrir. He was arrested shortly after the occupation began. On January 27 he was walking out of a restaurant when he was stopped by the police. He had made the mistake of having dinner with two Google executives, one of them being Jared Cohen, a former State Department employee who had worked on spreading digital tools to dissidents. Ghonim was assumed to be a CIA spy and Cohen his handler. He was blindfolded, handcuffed, and thrown into an underground cell, where he would remain for eleven days. He tracked time by the muezzins' calls to prayer. In his dreams his hands were free, but he would wake to find himself restrained and aching. After a week, stuck in darkness, his clothes and body stinking, he grew suicidal.

When he was finally released, blinking in the bright light, he was both disoriented and psychologically taut—and suddenly, strangely, also a celebrity. He had no sense of what had taken place in his absence: in an attempt to help save him, his identity as the admin of We Are All Khaled Said had been revealed. And within hours of being let go, he found himself on live television. Ghonim insisted that he was not a leader. He kept repeating those words, "I'm not a hero," in that interview and in days to come. About Tahrir, he said, "I was just a loudspeaker. I just made some noise and urged people to go down." When the interviewer displayed the images of all those who had lost their lives in the square, news to Ghonim, he broke down, weeping uncontrollably in front of tens of millions before getting up and walking off the set. In the humility he showed, the pure emotion, and in the absence of anyone else who seemed to be representing the revolutionary forces in Tahrir, he was thrust forward.

This was celebrity of the sort social media loves: an ordinary person unexpectedly finding himself on an enormous stage, like an *American Idol* contestant. His tearful television appearance went viral. A Facebook page called "I Nominate Wael Ghonim to Speak on Behalf of Egypt's Protesters" drew about 250,000 followers in forty-eight hours. He stood in front of tens of thousands in Tahrir and later even negotiated with the Interior Ministry. The feedback loop he had built was now swirling around him. He was the thing people were having strong reactions to and posting categorically about, just as they had about the photo of Khaled Said. Almost immediately, he felt flattened and misunderstood, but also panicked, desperate to take advantage of his moment in the spotlight. It was around this time that even President Obama fantasized out loud that he hoped "the Google guy" would one day become president of his country.

Within a few days of Ghonim's release, the occupation of the square, the rolling protests and street battles, all ground to a halt. What had been impossible to imagine a few weeks earlier had come to pass: Mubarak had agreed to immediately resign. On the day after the news, the singing and hugging over and the tents dismantled, the Facebook page that had started it all, which by the end of the eighteen days had nearly 700,000 followers, coordinated the cleanup of Tahrir. This was an act of new citizenship—the country belongs to us now—but there was something naïve about it in retrospect, as if all that was left to do was pick up the trash and tidy up the square.

THE NEXT TWO AND A HALF YEARS—from that triumphant February in 2011 to the summer of 2013 when the army retook full control of the country, leveling and destroying until it was clear who was in charge—was a period of intense political drama, crowded with elections and protests and massacres. But with some distance now the story reduces in size: The young had led a revolution. In Tahrir, they punched opened a portal to an alternate future, but it was one that only the Muslim Brotherhood, with its long history and rigorous discipline, was capable of entering. And, for a brief moment, they did. But the army and the institutional forces that had always propped up Mubarak never intended to let the country get away from them. In the end, everyone got a chance to play for a bit, but that body without a head found one in General Abdel Fattah el-Sisi, and the old establishment rose again, labeling all of its detractors terrorists.

It's an open question whether any force in Egyptian society, let alone one as freshly constituted as the revolutionaries of Tahrir—an unlikely blend of moderate Islamists, socialists, and nationalists—could have really contended with the army. But that portal they opened up was meant to lead to somewhere better, to a more democratic future. Why this didn't happen is still a source of much hand-wringing and heartache among those who can even bring themselves to talk about it. But all the logistical might that Facebook had provided in the lead-up to Tahrir, in the overthrow of a dictator, proved useless when it came to organizing themselves into a true political opposition, a unified and coherent base that could stand up to both the Brotherhood and the army.

The first problem, it seems clear, was time. Hot-wired as it was by Tunisia, the revolution happened too fast. There was no chance to form what the Italian Marxist philosopher Antonio Gramsci called a "historic bloc," the negotiated web of alliances and relationships rooted in a shared ideology that he posited as the necessary first step to seizing state power. Facebook encouraged instead two other tendencies that countered the hard work of hashing out a new agenda: rejectionism and emotion. Ghonim spoke of the page as being guided by "Tahrir's pulse." In one post near the end of the eighteen days, he wrote that their success was due to the fact that "we do not understand politics, compromises, negotiations, and cheap tricks.... Victory will be ours because our tears are heartfelt."

Facebook *was* good for tears. But this next stage demanded precisely those skills and strategies Ghonim dismissed. The first test of the revolutionaries' ability to survive the fraught moment (let alone emerge victorious) came very quickly. Within a month of Mubarak's fall, the generals provisionally running the country put a series of constitutional amendments before the public, without offering any clear timeline for the transition to civilian rule. It was a feint toward democracy that actually tightened their authority and control over the process. The Tahrir coalition was largely opposed to this sequence of events, believing that elections for a new government should take place first. But they couldn't decide on the right way to articulate this position, how exactly to frame their argument, and small differences between them swelled. Instead of consensus building, infighting took over and something Ghonim came to think of as "mobocracy." He described to me a dynamic much influenced by social media's maximalism, in which a position had to be uncompromising or you would be "perceived as weak or neutral or irrelevant." This of course was no way to find commonalities among the groups that had come together in Tahrir and now had returned to their corners.

And it only got worse at every inflection point—when the first parliamentary elections took place, and then the presidential one, and then every time the Muslim Brotherhood lay claim to a revolution they had initially shunned, or the army committed atrocities and then seduced the people into thinking that it alone could bring about stability. Proving just how right you were wasn't enough; you also had to explain how wrong everyone else was, to make the one true point that would win the debate. Social media platforms tend to "favor declaration," wrote Siva Vaidhyanathan, a professor at the University of Virginia who has studied Facebook. "They do not allow for deep deliberation. They spark shallow reaction." Intense comment threads were the descendants of those "thrashes" on the WELL, except here there was no moderator to step in and calm things down, just a currency of "likes" that rewarded the statement that drew the most blood. The revolutionaries did meet off-line as well, in stuffy apartments clouded with cigarette smoke and yelling. Facebook alone was not responsible for all their failures. An established democratic political culture had never existed in Egypt; they were attempting something hard and unprecedented in their country. What they didn't need was a medium of incessant one-upmanship, which only helped turn the air acrid.

There was also no longer any interest in the guiding hand of an admin, let alone one seen to be a member of the elite. At one point the Muslim Brotherhood even created a competing page on Facebook called "We Are All Khaled Said—the Official Page," questioning the authenticity of the original instigators and their connection to what was happening on the ground. When I met Abdelrahman Mansour, Ghonim's co-admin, who was then into his sixth year of exile in the United States, he said that even he had begun to question the group's legitimacy. "Are we representing society or are we not?" he asked. "We kept talking and imagining initiatives on the internet without taking them into the streets or formulating a new party."

The closest Tahrir ever had to a governing body was the Revolutionary Youth Coalition, a group of organizers who had come together in the square and represented a range of temperaments and political persuasions. If there was a promise of a future that wasn't Islamist or junta rule, it began with them. But they struggled from the start with the ideological work of transforming what was a criticism of dictatorship into an articulation of the rights and responsibilities they wanted for themselves and their fellow Egyptians. What kind of compromise could be found between Islamist and secular Egypt? What freedoms were nonnegotiable for liberals like themselves? How could they sway fellow citizens who had never known voting rights and had long abandoned any expectation of transparency or accountability from their leaders? They couldn't arrive at answers. They had no forum for asking questions and working them out, so they ended up fixating on the immediate tactical problems, "like teenage boyfriends with noble intentions and truncated attention spans," wrote Thanassis Cambanis, a longtime Middle East correspondent who observed the aftermath of the revolution. Especially given the patchwork nature of the revolutionary coalition, it was necessary to choose certain battles while abandoning others. They were allergic to the practicalities of doing politics.

Social media never made it easier. It was only ever able to point them back to Tahrir Square, the tried-and-true method. When the moment clearly called for protest—when they demanded Mubarak be put on trial, or when the Justice Ministry proposed a law banning all demonstrations—they knew what to do. They could zero in on a point of outrage and motivate people to gather around it. It was as if social media had replaced their revolutionary project with a single instinct. Their greatest strength was the ability to resuscitate the magic and power of Tahrir, to pull off a *millionya*, a million-man march. But it was becoming a limited tool, a lever turned crutch. And while the activists did regularly return to the square, enamored with their own ability to quiet all the voices on Facebook for a day or two, the more politically savvy and deeply connected forces in the country, like the Muslim Brotherhood, did what they had long known how to do: set an agenda and impose order in their ranks. The revolutionaries never got quite organized enough. They lacked "the bloodthirsty hearts of the Bolsheviks who seized Russian factories, or the French who stormed the Bastille," Cambanis wrote.

Politics eventually became the only way to claim the rewards of the revolution. When it was time for elections, first of a new parliament and then of a president, the weakness of Tahrir's activists was exposed. They could not build a party. Those few revolutionaries who emerged as leaders did not seem interested in representing anyone but themselves, distracted by the lure of international conferences and speaking tours in the West. Ghonim received a reported $2.5 million book deal, which he announced on Twitter he was giving away to charity. But he was relentlessly attacked on social media as a hypocrite and an egomaniac, and even a spy. He feared increasingly for his safety.

One of the activists who did try to enter the political realm was Mahmoud Salem. I'd talked to him over the phone back in 2006 but hadn't known his real name then, only that he was the blogger who went by Sandmonkey. I was working on an article about Middle East bloggers and his pseudonymous blog, *Rantings of a Sandmonkey*, was smart and irreverent and written in eloquent English. In retrospect, it was also brave, especially given that his mother was a prominent official in Mubarak's ruling National Democratic Party. We talked about how blogs had broken down his preconceptions, even when it came to Jews, the ultimate other in Egyptian society.

Salem was widely read in the West by Egypt watchers, so when he unmasked himself as Sandmonkey in the middle of the eighteen days of Tahrir, after being detained and beaten by a crowd of pro-Mubarak supporters, it briefly became an international news story. Salem had as triumphalist an attitude as any other activist about the role of social media in tearing down the old regime: he was a proud adherent of the Khaled Said page. But his feelings changed once he decided to take the leap into politics and run for Parliament with the Free Egyptians Party, a newly constituted secular, liberal grouping, to represent the mostly middle-class Cairo district of Heliopolis. It was going to be hard, and Salem, ambling and with a guffawing laugh, stuffed into an ill-fitting suit, was not a natural politician. He posited his fifty thousand Twitter followers as one reason he had a chance—a bad sign. But, still, he wanted to embrace the new democratic world the revolution had opened up and not let it be monopolized by the Brotherhood or more established parties.

What he hadn't anticipated was that social media would actively undermine his political efforts. "Running for office meant you were a power-hungry sell-out," Salem would write in an essay for the *World Policy Journal.* "Voting meant you were participating in a charade and betraying the blood of those who had died protesting. Meanwhile, the dead were immortalized and turned into social media avatars before they were even buried." The only people who maintained legitimacy were the ones rushing headlong into a confrontation with the police, again and again, and gaining attention online as a result. "This means of mediated ascension was nothing short of disastrous," he wrote.

For him the revolution contracted into "a strange cultish religion," "group-think on steroids—an abomination of a monster with thousands of arms and no brain." What social media gave the revolution, the aspect that it seemed stuck on and could never outgrow, was "a spirit for destruction." It was an incessant rejectionism. No one seemed interested in building, he said.

Salem ran, he told me, because he knew that Egypt's future would be decided in secret back rooms. And he watched with anxiety as all the Tahrir activists disparaged the idea of trying to get inside. It was "imperative," he said, to at least try. He failed, miserably. The party he joined had formed late, just a few weeks before the first round of the parliamentary elections, and he had to somehow capture the hearts and minds of a million voters in his district. Being a candidate was no fun. Salem was made for strategizing and, after losing his own election, he turned right away to running political campaigns for others. What he learned from this work made him even more critical of social media. "The street has to trust you," he said. "Which means the people have to know you're fighting for them, not just to mobilize them in anger and lead them in chants."

ASTOUNDINGLY, ONLY THREE candidates associated with the revolutionary youth made it into Egypt's Parliament when the votes were finally counted in January 2012. Three out of 508 parliamentary seats. Just half of 1 percent. A year had passed since the utopia of Tahrir Square, and the people who had birthed it were now shut out of the new Egypt taking shape. The big winner was the Muslim Brotherhood, or so it seemed until six months later, when the judiciary annulled the whole election and the military issued decrees strengthening its power. But if the Brotherhood would have a more precipitous fall in the long run, the liberal activists appeared the more immediate losers, edged out completely from a historical process whose spark they had lit. The next president would not be the Google guy. He wouldn't even be sitting in Parliament, a body now dominated by men with beards and women in headscarves.

A week after Mohammed Morsi's inauguration in June 2012, the Revolutionary Youth Coalition announced at a news conference that it was dissolving. But first, its members wanted to conduct an open postmortem before the press. "Even though it is not standard operating procedure in Egypt, we believe it is necessary for every group to submit a clear and transparent account of what it has done, good and bad." The self-flagellation was both admirable and further indication of just how poorly suited they were for the cutthroat, zero-sum political environment that Mubarak's ouster opened up. They blamed themselves for being out of touch, for not having reached out enough to the established institutions and having been a little too enamored with their brief fame and the illusion it gave that they were actually representing a constituency—a problem social media surely did not mitigate. Then, in a final act of digital hari-kari, the Revolutionary Youth Coalition deleted its Facebook page.

The remnants of this lost vanguard would still make efforts over the next year to reach the wider public. At one point, they took to the streets, bypassing social media with a film program called "Kazeboon!" (Liars!) that they projected on the sides of buildings all over Cairo. The short films offered unambiguous proof of the army's increasing violence against protesters juxtaposed with generals smilingly explaining it away. The revolutionaries wanted the people to see this hypocrisy at a moment when the military was presenting itself as the only force that could restore order to the country. But if "Kazeboon!" felt comfortable as a form of activism, it was because it was still aimed at kicking up ire, not rallying people around a new ideology. The murderers needed to be called out and replaced, like Mubarak, but then what?

The walls were closing in, including on the Muslim Brotherhood, whose time in power was cut short after a year when a massive petition campaign that claimed to have collected twenty-two million signatures against Morsi's rule led everyone back to the square. It was as if the needle were set back in the groove, a song Egyptians knew well by now. Angered by Morsi's authoritarian direction, many of the Tahrir activists thought this was the right move and called for the army to step back in and remove him. A second revolution, they called it, a chance to rewind to 2011 and give true democracy another go.

But this was a counterrevolution in disguise. Within days, the defense minister, General Abdel Fattah el-Sisi, took charge. And in August came the denouement, when he aimed bulldozers and snipers at Muslim Brotherhood members and their families who had staged a massive sit-in in Rabaa Square. Some one thousand people were killed that day, according to Human Rights Watch. "What Tahrir ignited, Rabaa extinguished," wrote David Kirkpatrick, who was Cairo bureau chief for *The New York Times*. The Arab Spring was over. There would be no Islamic version of democracy; there would be no democracy at all. A paralyzing nihilism set in. "When you can kill a thousand people in broad daylight with no consequences, none whatsoever—that was the day the game changed," Mahmoud Salem told me from his exile in Berlin. "Nothing matters."

BY THE TIME of the Rabaa massacre, Wael Ghonim had left Egypt and was refashioning himself as a social media reformer. "I was wrong," he said, speaking into a headset microphone onstage at a TED event in Geneva in late 2015. This was the man who, more than any other, had become an avatar of the Arab Spring, and specifically social media's part in the uprising. He had embraced the role, heartily. In his 2012 book, *Revolution 2.0,* he insisted that only one ingredient was needed "to liberate a society": the internet. After Mubarak announced he was stepping down, with shouts of joy and fireworks filling the air behind him, Ghonim was interviewed on CNN and said he wished he could personally thank Mark Zuckerberg. (When he finally did, the behoodied Facebook CEO refused to let Ghonim snap a picture of the two of them together.)

But Ghonim now treated Facebook like a spurned lover. "The Arab Spring revealed social media's greatest potential, but it also exposed its greatest shortcomings," he said from the stage in Geneva. Facebook, he saw, was indeed a tool, but it was designed with a specific purpose, one that hadn't suited the needs of his vanguard.

On the WELL, even when the conversation involved only a couple thousand people and the stakes were much, much lower than replacing an entrenched regime, a great many guardrails were needed to keep it a productive space, a home for talk that could build and not just destroy. What happened when you scaled those numbers up into the millions, removed those guardrails, the guiding moderators, and then introduced algorithms that kept people on the platform longer by elevating the loudest, most emotional voices? What you got was an incredible amplification system that also proved extremely ineffective at allowing people to focus, to organize their thoughts, to become ideologically coherent, to strategize, to pick leaders, and to refine a message. In short, the revolutionaries were denied everything they needed if they were going to win the day—a tall order in any circumstance. Once the rubble was swept off Tahrir Square and the paving stones were put back in place, it was this reality, Ghonim told his audience, that hit him "like a punch in the gut."

When I spoke to him in 2016, after that remorseful TED Talk, he was living in Silicon Valley and running a start-up called Parlio with two Egyptian friends. Launched in 2014 with $1.68 million in seed funding from venture capitalists, the site was meant as an alternative form of social media, one whose algorithms would reward quality of engagement over quantity. It would prize "thoughtfulness and civility and substance." Users had to sign a social pledge to participate. There was even an algorithm for identifying fights so that moderators could intervene. "The belief that we had as we were starting Parlio is that public conversations could actually work, you just needed to build the right environment," Ghonim said.

He was earnest about this, believing he could fix all that had gone wrong with Facebook, exploit that knowledge in the creation of a better design. But it never really took off. In the internet ecosystem of the late 2010s, any new form of social media faced a problem known as the network effect: the bigger a network was, the more benefits to joining it, and nothing could come close to Facebook by that point. In 2016, Parlio was acquired by Quora, a site specializing in Q&As in which experts answered questions generated by users. Ghonim and his team were folded into the bigger company's operations. He soon fell into a depression, and when, in the summer of 2017, he found himself crying in a meeting room at the Quora offices, he decided it was time to quit.

What happened to Wael Ghonim after that was fodder for much rumor and concern when I began asking former Egyptian revolutionaries about him in 2019. They told me to look at his YouTube channel and Twitter. That's where I found the troubling videos. In the first of what would be dozens of increasingly bizarre clips posted every day, he shaved off all his hair and eyebrows. Then he began to appear shirtless, smoking thickly rolled blunts. He confessed that he had cheated on his wife and brought her on camera to tell his audience that she had asked for a divorce. Sometimes he would post videos of himself laughing maniacally or dancing. His friends and comrades said they tried to get in touch, worried that he was having a nervous breakdown. He cut them all off, even people he had been close to for years.

Everyone had theories. Maybe it had to do with his brother, who had just been detained in Egypt? Ghonim understood the effect he was having: half of his posts mocked those who were shocked. This was his true self, he screamed. When I reached out to him to see if we could speak (I'd interviewed him a number of times over the past few years), he left me a paranoid, badgering voice message, questioning my motives and wondering why he should talk to me. "Do you think I'm an attention whore, like the attention whores who are always driving for any kind of attention?" The saddest interpretation came from one former friend who believed Ghonim was actually manipulating his knowledge of social media in order to annihilate his previous image—he no longer wanted to be seen as a savior, someone who might have answers, about the future of Egypt or Silicon Valley. The videos were a kind of willed reboot. "This is not spontaneous," this friend told me. "When you work in the business, you fully understand when someone is using it." Maybe the most self-aware message was Ghonim's bio on Twitter, where he now had nearly three million followers: "I'm a character in my movie. It's a reality show that turned surreal."

As for Egypt, its reality, too, has turned surreal, or rather, nightmarish. Sisi's rule has proved repressive in ways no one could have imagined before the revolution. Even the slightest attempt at protest has been brutally suppressed. The few online outlets trying to cover the crackdowns and imprisonments are blocked in Egypt. The handful of activists who remain are embattled, devoid of hope, and not looking to social media for solutions.

Alaa Abd El Fattah, a computer programmer, leftist, and early blogger who is widely considered the most creative and tactical thinker of the revolution, has spent most of the past ten years in and out of prison. His physical state, whether he is on a hunger strike or recovering from having been beaten by his guards, is a constant preoccupation of the small band of dissidents and those outside the country still paying attention. His long curly hair and scruffy beard are now something of a symbol of continued resistance.

When Alaa was briefly released from prison in the spring of 2019, a video circulated online of him sitting on the floor against some pillows, chatting with an interviewer. The conversation turned to Facebook, which seemed a progressively stranger place to him every time he went back online after the forced absences. For those who still wanted to dream up a new politics, there had been "a regression," he said. "It's not the fault of Egyptians; it's the medium they are using. You're just swallowed up by Facebook. You have emotional discussions with your friends, because Facebook is made for that. This is a trap." He would be looking to analyze the current situation and instead find himself "in these circles of people sending GIFs and heart emojis." The platform was "stifling," Alaa said, yet people couldn't get off it, even now that they knew how "defective" it was. To break through the oppressive reality in Egypt, what was needed was a path toward "an alternate imagination," a space for theorizing, for allowing in complexity, for working toward action. "I don't know where or when it will emerge."

Chapter 8

THE TORCHES

CHARLOTTESVILLE, 2017

ON MAY 13, 2017, a small platoon of white supremacists—newly rebranded as the alt-right—shuffled around beneath a noonday sun. An outsider might have mistaken the three dozen men, mostly in their twenties and thirties and sweating through white polo shirts, for a gathering of golf caddies. They looked awkward, unaccustomed to so much light and so much company, as they began self-seriously marching to the beat of a snare drum on their way to the bronze foot of the Confederate general Stonewall Jackson. There they listened, enraptured, as Richard Spencer, their unofficial leader, explained through a bullhorn why they would make their stand in this place, Charlottesville, Virginia. Spencer looked, as always, well manicured, in a tan blazer, his hair in a Hitler Youth cut (sides shaved, top slicked back). "They are trying to take away our gods," he yelled. "They are trying to take away our ideals. They are trying to take away who we are. And instead of this monument, God knows what they are going to erect, some monument to death, some monument to slavery and the Holocaust, some monument to the black cloud that hangs over everybody's head." He offered a succinct summary of their cause: "What brings us together is that we are white, we are a people, we will not be replaced."

If this was all they could have publicly mustered that weekend, it would have seemed something less than frightening; pathetic, even. But what happened that same night sent tremors across the country. A group of about a hundred, larger than the afternoon crowd, paraded with blazing tiki torches to the statue of Robert E. Lee, one of the city's other tributes to its rebel past, loudly chanting, "You will not replace us!" and "Blood and soil!" (and, most bizarrely, "Russia is our friend!"). It didn't last very long—only about ten minutes before counterprotesters and then the police arrived—but the procession was captured through the fly's-eye perspective of a drone and shared again and again on social media and in the mainstream press. The torchlit faces, the spewed-out slogans, the shadows that elongated their shaved heads against the night—all of it brought to mind Nazi rallies, Klan meetings, open expressions of hate that most Americans thought existed only at the bottom of the ash heap of history. It's safe to assume this was the desired effect.

It was a success, in other words, and one the bigots badly needed. Spencer had spent years starting and running increasingly right-wing publications, including AlternativeRight.com, which he set up in 2010. He also headed a think tank called the National Policy Institute with a media savviness rare in a neo-Nazi. Spencer had felt emboldened by the election of Donald Trump, a man whose winking at racist and nativist forces had become something of a tic. This was the moment to announce the alt-right as a movement that no longer needed to cower in basements or on online message boards. But piggybacking on Trump's ascent had not been as easy as Spencer had imagined. Just a few months earlier, on the very day of Trump's inauguration, Spencer was being interviewed on a busy street corner in Washington, D.C., when a man in a black hood suddenly slammed a fist into his face, knocking Spencer to the ground. It was humiliating.

Before Trump, the alt-right had very little political influence. Limited to bottom-feeder social media sites like 4chan, the movement was a mismatched collection of white supremacists and self-proclaimed identitarians, and a bunch of bored and sexually frustrated young men, all pretty much anonymous. It was less a community than a paintball team. To the extent that there was any ideological common denominator, it was in their denigration of the "social justice warriors" of the Left, the progressive forces that were imposing their multicultural and gender-fluid values on everyone. What thrilled them about Trump's win, more than his populism or protectionism or even his embrace of white identity politics (the "forgotten men and women" he spoke to in his inaugural address), was his style, which seemed to borrow so much from their "own the libs" attitude. The objective was to get under the skin, to drive the "other side" crazy, and Trump did.

Given the hyper-masculinity that coursed through the online threads, seeing Spencer, one of their heroes, brought so low in the early hours of the Trump presidency was especially confusing. They were the rightmost flank of Trump's coalition, the makers of the memes, and this was supposed to be their time. Who were they if they couldn't even show their faces?

A few months later, in April, they finally got some satisfaction, and confirmation that being audacious was the only way to go. In Berkeley, enemy territory for the alt-right, a number of so-called white civil rights groups had organized a free speech rally that pretty quickly turned into a violent mess of thrown rocks and bottles and firecrackers. Antifascist counterprotesters had shown up, and it had become ugly, sloppy. At one point a large trash bin was used as a battering ram. But remembered most from the melee was a few seconds of video in which Nathan Damigo, the head of Identity Evropa, one of the many new alt-right groups, leaped into a crowd of brawling bodies and slammed his fist into the face of a dreadlocked activist named Emily Rose Marshall. The clip was uploaded endlessly on message boards, turned into a thousand memes: Damigo, with that same Hitler Youth haircut, dressed crisply in blue shirt and blue jeans, attacking Marshall, who looked like any right-winger's fantasy of a social justice warrior. The Daily Stormer, the neo-Nazi website, called Damigo a "true hero."

The members of Identity Evropa were unabashed, but also determined to use a vocabulary that would not alienate. Damigo himself was an ex-marine who had started his campaign while a student at California State University, Stanislaus. He wanted it to copy the nationalist movements then gaining traction in Europe. No white robes. No tattoos on faces, necks, or hands. Articles about Damigo always noted that instead of swearing, he used words like "gosh" or "golly." And his rhetoric centered on white people being denied the right to preserve their "heritage," appropriating the language that minorities had been using to make their own case for representation. "We don't want to be seen as overly threatening," Damigo told a reporter on the same day he'd punched the dreadlocked young woman.

An event like Berkeley was "transformative," wrote Bradley Dean Griffin, a prominent white nationalist who had been sharing his anti-Semitic and racist views on his blog, *Occidental Dissent*, since 2008. It created a spectacle that would draw in more recruits and redefine the image of white supremacists. It may be "fun to engage in troll storms, swarms and raids online," he wrote, but to grow, the movement needed to step outside. It was the only way, he insisted, to "summon the culture war that is going on online" and bring it to the surface, to make it "explode like a volcano."

By the spring, Charlottesville presented itself as the perfect such opportunity: geographically in the borderlands of American politics but a decidedly liberal college town (in the volatile days after Trump's inauguration, the mayor declared it a "capital of the Resistance," and nearly 80 percent of voters had gone for Hillary Clinton). It was a city that during the Civil War had a population of slaves that made up 52 percent of its residents and where the bronze statue of Robert E. Lee, sitting on his horse, Traveller, had dominated a small park in its downtown since 1924. It was a place primed for a fight. In early February, when the city council voted to remove the Lee statue, Spencer saw the galvanizing issue that he was seeking: a chance to tell a story about a reactionary, nihilistic Left looking to trample on their past, to erase their tradition.

The events in mid-May helped remove the memory of that sucker punch. Spencer posted a photo on Twitter of his face aglow in the light of a tiki torch. But he wanted more. He wanted to return to Charlottesville and show the full power of a newly emboldened movement. He would need Jason Kessler. The torchlit rally had happened largely because of Kessler, a self-styled independent journalist and blogger from Charlottesville who, like Spencer, was a graduate of the University of Virginia. Kessler's path had been a bit meandering; a sometime truck driver and handyman, he had only recently begun expounding on the threat of "white genocide." (Among other things he had written a book of poetry and a novel called *Badland Blues,* which, according to its jacket, featured "a homeless dwarf madly in unrequited love with a local waitress.") He took to the statue battle. "Every generation has a fight, and our fight is this," he had yelled outside the city council meeting deciding the monument's fate. It was his newly formed group, Unity & Security for America, along with some of Damigo's people, who had made up much of the crowd. And after the success of the May rally, it was Kessler who filed an application for a permit to hold a demonstration that summer, on August 12, at the small park where the Lee statue was located (its name would soon be changed from Lee Park to Emancipation Park). He called the event "Unite the Right" on social media, a bit of wishful thinking on his part because there was nothing particularly united about the Right's various strands.

It was a start, but both Kessler and Spencer knew they needed many more allies. And to assemble them, to do the hard work of aligning and getting a large enough group of people to agree on tactics and objectives, they required a space of their own, one with particular features. Sites like Reddit and 4chan, so popular with the alt-right, were too full of snark and towel snapping, just memes trying to outdo memes. So, in June, they turned to Discord, an online platform meant for gamers, and opened up what was known on the site as a "server," a self-administered chat room. They called it Charlottesville 2.0.

I KNOW WHAT happened next, thanks to a group of leftist hackers who run a website called Unicorn Riot. They managed that summer to gain access to the constellation of white supremacist servers on Discord—tens of thousands of posts from June through August. This was a chance to eavesdrop on a conversation that was not meant to be public in any way. And for all that was sickening about spending this much time with people whose idea of fun was arguing about whom they would send to the gas chamber first, it was deeply revealing. This is what it looked like when a nascent group had what the Arab Spring activists didn't have: somewhere to concentrate, to debate their differences and try to work them out. Among themselves, they were able to pat each other on the back and dream their twisted dreams together, and they got stronger.

Discord was a useful platform for them, but it was never intended to house their chatter. It was made for teenage boys who sat playing *World of Warcraft* late into the night and wanted to simultaneously gab with their friends as they slayed zombies and dragons. Its most popular function was the server, which was an invitation-only chat room (there was also a party line audio option). Each server had its own administrator who set the rules, could kick people out, and was responsible for keeping the members in line. Unlike Reddit, there was no upvoting to incentivize attention-grabbing posts, turning every exchange into a popularity contest or a purity spiral. It was just ongoing talk in a relatively small room on terms set by the participants. It resembled the WELL more than any other major social media platform. This was about huddling together as opposed to gaining followers.

The alt-right leaders liked the anonymity and privacy—though given the ease with which Unicorn Riot infiltrated their chats, they might have benefited from a little more paranoia. Among other secrecy benefits, you could run Discord straight off a web browser without downloading an application and never have to give your real name. By that summer of 2017, two years after it had started up, the site had about 45 million users and was increasing by 1.1 million every week. Discord's Jewish co-founder and CEO would later say he had been clueless about what a home for hate his site had become.

Keegan Hankes, the former research director of the Southern Poverty Law Center, the premier organization monitoring extremism in America, also spent a lot of time on Discord that summer. He told me how administrators of various alt-right servers would vet people before letting them in: they would video chat to make sure they saw white skin. Hankes once let a fellow researcher "borrow" his face for this purpose. What made Discord useful, Hankes said, was that each particular faction had its own server, which became a sort of "base camp" for them. They could strengthen identity in a more local way, each group building up its private convictions, but also check out what others were thinking and possibly join with them.

The Charlottesville 2.0 server, which I spent a couple of dark weeks combing through, was the main organizing hub. Spencer remained a figurehead, but in the server it was Kessler, going by the handle MadDimension, who seemed most in charge and was trying to keep the conversation centered on how to enlarge their base. "Please stop the fighting. I'm trying to work out security plans for our speakers and it's embarrassing to be bringing professionals in here while people are bickering," was a typical post.

Among the pool of disgruntled provocateurs who felt white men were America's true victims, there were still wide ideological gulfs. The Jewish Question, or JQ, was one. For some, Jews were the secret source of the diversity that was supposedly choking the country, the ones who had opened the gates and were controlling the narrative. Solving this particular problem was a central preoccupation of those who were "Hip to the JQ": KommieKillinKowboy suggested "a google maps plug in that would mark kike owned businesses with a star of david so white nationalists could avoid them." Some championed the idea of ethno-states, even Israel (where all Jews could supposedly be shipped). The crematorium, of course, was also popular.

Then there were individuals and groups who shared the general spirit of antifeminist, anti-globalist, anti–political correctness, but wanted to stay as far away as possible from the Hitler birthday parties and Sieg heils. This was the alt-light. They were slightly to the left of Damigo and his identitarians and certainly nowhere near the Klan or the more blatantly neo-Nazi groups like the Atomwaffen Division with its belief in accelerationism, the active fomenting of a cataclysmic race war. The alt-light's online universe of grievance included the manosphere, where men's rights were defended against the tyranny of a feminized culture. Groups like the Proud Boys, led by the hipstery co-founder of VICE Media, Gavin McInnes, led a "pro-Western" and "pro-male" fight club, hiding their racism and misogyny behind nostalgia for a world where boys could just be boys. There was a lot of time spent dissecting this difference between the alt-right and the alt-light—Greg Johnson, a prominent white supremacist thinker, described it this way: "The alt-light is defined by civic nationalism as opposed to racial nationalism."

Whatever the definition, getting Gavin McInnes and his enlightened frat boys in the same room as followers of the KKK grand wizard David Duke would not be simple. But it's the task Kessler and Spencer had set for themselves, and if there was any place to plan these marriages of convenience, to figure out how they would work, to court and lobby, it would be on Discord. If they wanted to go bigger, this would offer the best space to make it happen. As ManWithTheHand noted not long after the Charlottesville 2.0 server was set up, unlike the earlier spontaneous protest, this time they were giving themselves time to gather their forces: "Lightning represents our first event, quick, fast, and all of a sudden. This second event is the thunder, they will hear us rolling in, we will be loud and fearful, and they will know it's coming because thunder always follows lightning."

ALMOST AS SOON AS the server was created, one of the most popular topics, returned to nearly every day, was "optics." This was shorthand for thinking through exactly how their protest might appear to the mainstream. For most of the alt-right groups, like Damigo's Identity Evropa, their entire reason for being was that they envisioned a way to advocate for their ultimate goal—a white, Christian America—without alarming the people who they imagined were their natural constituency. They saw no benefit in outdated symbols, like swastikas, or showing up heavily armed or wearing hoods. At the same time, they didn't want to turn away those who already supported their ideas but were not quite ready to put on suits and ties.

This negotiation was what they meant by "optics." The endless banter about how best to present themselves ("Thoughts on these shoes?" "Are we gonna do armbands?" "White shirts with army green pants or army green shirts with black pants?") landed on the blandest of the bland: white shirts and khakis. This seems trivial, but it also represented the first of several small victories enabled by the platform. What else but white shirts and khakis could occupy the overlapping center of the Venn diagram? What everyone agreed upon is that they should look like nice young men. Not only would this make their movement more accessible and respectable, but it would signal their commonality of purpose. "Optics are very important," wrote bainbjorn. "If everyone shows up with their own versions of things we look disorganized and like common rabble. If everyone wears a white shirt and khakis and our security has the exact same shield and helmets then we look legitimate. We don't need to reinvent the wheel here. We have to have uniformity in everything we do if we are serious, no rogues no lone wolfs no individJEWals."

The other concern was over what they should carry. "I like the aesthetic of shields, in general," wrote Kurt14Lipper. "Optics saying that we are about defense. All of this is in our own defense. Until we're pushed too far." They wanted to do torches again. But then which ones and would they be a fire hazard? "If we're doing real torches, which we should, we gotta be very safety conscious," wrote HipToTheJQ. "I do think for aesthetic purposes, if we do torches again, they need to be actual torches," wrote Erika, an Identity Evropa activist from Florida who was also Charlottesville 2.0's moderator and one of its handful of women members. "The only reservation I have against walking around with fire on sticks this time is that we'll have potentially very violent opposition waiting for us. I really don't want our people getting burned if a brawl breaks out while we're marching with torches." Kristall.night asked, "Is there a cleaner burning oil that can be used in the torches instead of the tiki crap?" Someone suggested citronella.

It was hard not to find these palavers at least slightly amusing. They had none of the swagger associated with the public-facing side of the alt-right, the trolling on Twitter, where vicious, scary things were said and then covered up with a sneering attitude of "just kidding" or "why are you getting so upset?" There was plenty of taunting and teasing on Discord, and the occasional pile on, but there was also sincerity among the "fam," as they often referred to each other. I read one conversation in which the group consoled one of their own, Hand Banana, with genuine locker room affection after he admitted that a woman he went on a date with turned out to be half-Jewish—"Second Jew this year for me. Sad!" "We need to both feel bad for you and simultaneously give you a hard time for it," wrote Tyrone. There was not much showing off. Even if they didn't agree about certain strategies, they were among their own people, those who had already been "red pilled," alt-right lingo for having been converted to the cause. They would be horrified by the term, but this was a "safe space" for them. In one of the few audio chats that Unicorn Riot had managed to access, the leaders of three hard-core white supremacist groups talked about the joys of baking sourdough bread.

But there were real debates about the finer points: swastikas, for example. When one of the members in the server complained about not being able to wear Nazi paraphernalia, a discussion broke out about why they needed to keep it hidden. "Because telling a 85 IQ boomer they shouldn't want to live in a country full of muslims and violent mexican gang members is relatable and agreeable whereas slapping a swastika on and worshipping a dead german politician isn't," wrote one participant in the server who went by the handle Wyatt and took up the "optics will always matter" side of the debate. Challenged by a few members (as one put it, "Hitler and the Swastika are awesome"), Wyatt made clear he had no problem "using 3rd reich nostalgia in the culture war and breaking down welded shut doors of cultural taboo," but that this was no way, he wrote, "to win any hearts and minds." The goal of their coming together was not to start a political party or raise an army; they had a much more limited but strategically important objective: "getting a majority of white people on board with white identity itself." To this, Stormer DC added, "You're not gonna be able to secure a future for white children if you are unwilling to go through the pain of destroying the Nazi stigma."

Most of the server backed this position, but the conversation opened out into a wider argument: swastikas and the blatant Nazism they represent as being a more authentic and braver way to "shock the system," as one member put it, versus an incrementalism that Wyatt and others were championing ("you guys think it's going to be some massive revolution. It's not. Day by day. More and more white people are going to wake up. And soon within the next 5–10 years there will be enough to initiate a massive shift in culture and politics"). They also discussed the failure of white supremacists of the past to make much of an impact, especially when compared with the rapidly increasing visibility of an alt-right group like Identity Evropa. "I didn't want to say this because it's rude but in A YEAR Identity Evropa eclipsed every white nationalist movement in the past 50 years," Wyatt wrote. "They succeed because of how they look. How they act. and how they CARE about how they look and act." As the back-and-forth got more contentious, there was also a reminder, by one member, that this particular protest was about the Lee statue, that this was their unifying issue. "I think we all agree that the removal of that statue is an affront to all of us. . . . Let's keep it about that," wrote SpencerReesh. The debates often worked toward this search for commonality. "Many of us are National Socialists, on both sides of this disagreement," wrote Gavius Corvus in a kind of summation. "We want the same thing, it's just a differing on the best course of action to get there. Like Wyatt said, it's good that we can have these discussions. In the past, our movement has let itself be torn apart by these relatively petty disagreements. I think it's a fantastic sign that we can have these disagreements now, and still stand together when it counts."

Optics was clearly more than just a matter of aesthetics. It was a conversation about building a larger base. What were their priorities? Which principles were essential and which could be discarded? Another argument broke out at one point when Jason Kessler asked for any volunteers who wanted to burn the Pride flag, the rainbow emblem of the LGBTQ movement. He immediately got pushback from a few members who thought this wouldn't be a good look. But most surprising was the response from Erika, the server's moderator. "Gays are a small minority," she wrote. "Burn a communist or anarchist flag." Kessler tried to clarify: "It's not about gays. I don't care about gays. That damn flag has become the de-facto symbol for Cultural Marxism," by which he meant an emblem "of Silicon Valley, of the Democrat Party, of our ethnic and cultural replacement. . . . It is a multiculturalism flag at this point." Erika tagged Kessler in her response using his handle. "@MadDimension it's not about what you and all of us see. It's about how the rest of the world will perceive it," she wrote. "People will exclude whatever speech you make before burning the flag, and it'll just be 'NAZIS WANT TO GENOCIDE FAGS.'" Kessler insisted that the flag had greater significance than just being about gay pride, that it signaled to white people another set of values than their own: "I think the greatest strength of the Right wing is that we convey truths and secret emotions that people suppress because of social stigma. I think the heartland of America is sick and tired of that fucking flag." Erika kept repeating that it didn't matter what he thought it symbolized. To most of the world, it simply meant gay pride. Burning it would be a distraction, and they needed to focus. "Burning a fag flag is a terrible idea," Jack "Ajax" Richardson chimed in. "We have a winning combo of good optics, clean appearance, intelligent and level reasoning, and civilized manner. Flag burning goes against all of that. We can't try to change our formula mid-stream." Kessler ended up quietly backing down, and Erika didn't make an issue of his retreat. "Please have some patience guys," Kessler wrote. "You can talk about flag burning or whatever you want and no one has a right to tell you that you can't. This should be a place where people can openly debate ideas."

These moments of friction almost always resolved themselves. To Athena Marie's question, "Why can't we organize a book burning after the event?" Stormer DC wisely responded, "Because it will accomplish nothing other than making us look like we're scared of literature." The tension was often broken by vile jokes or the sharing of stupid and racist memes. "I just think that a more subtle hand is required to make people see the light," wrote Soy Goy.

———

AS THE WEEKS progressed and the chatter on Charlottesville 2.0 grew (by the time Unicorn Riot downloaded the whole server in August, there were more than twenty-one thousand posts), Kessler began sharing information about logistics—who would be speaking at their rally and what other groups they were trying to pull in. Finding a way to integrate Gavin McInnes's Proud Boys was a major topic.

From the server's start, Erika had policed who could and couldn't join and made it clear that at least for the moment she and the others were keeping it exclusively alt-right, if only for security reasons. But Kessler was eager to expand. At one point he proposed inviting a local group of Proud Boys for a drink in a downtown Charlottesville bar. He figured it was likely that antifa, the black-clad antifascist activists, would attack them and that the experience would move the Proud Boys further into his camp. Kessler shared the plan on the server. "I understand the goal," wrote AltRightVa. "Get PB out there to fully understand that no matter how they try to distinguish themselves from us they will be grouped in with us and may as well join us. It makes sense." But others thought this was deceptive and could alienate the potential recruits. "There has to be trust between the different organizations if this thing has any chance," countered atthias. Kessler went ahead anyway; as he had predicted, there was a scuffle, and they were all kicked out of the bar. "The guys who came with us are jacked for August 12th," he then reported back.

Getting old Klan members to join simply meant cleaning up Grandpa and persuading him to keep his swastikas in the closet. The alt-light, and Proud Boys in particular, were a more complicated matter, forcing the members of the server to decide how loose they were willing to get with their own ideological commitments. Some Proud Boys were not even white. They had a much more glib and slippery attitude about what they believed. But they were also undeniably potential bridges to the mainstream. "The biggest difference between the right and left right now is that the right refuses to work with 'ideologically impure' groups while the left adopts a big tent strategy much to their advantage," wrote Hand Banana. Kessler kept pushing everyone to be open. (He even subjected himself to a Proud Boys initiation ritual: three stages, the second of which involved sustaining a beating while calling out the names of breakfast cereals.) But there was resistance and suspicion as the list of participants got longer. "I never said I wasn't willing to work with ppl that are not 100% in step with us," argued ManWithTheHand. "I don't see why we shouldn't absorb alt light ppl. But the main issue is we are making all the compromises here. Why do we have to throw everything we stand for aside while dealing with 'Ideologically Impure' groups? They need to meet us at the very LEAST halfway. And I don't think asking alt light ppl to endorse white nationalism is too much to ask for."

The antagonism between the alt-right and the alt-light became public on June 25, when Richard Spencer and Nathan Damigo put on a "Rally for Free Speech" near the Lincoln Memorial. It included a number of figures who had spoken in Charlottesville the month before, waving the banners of Identity Evropa and another new group called Vanguard America. On the same day, a rival demonstration "against political violence" was taking place near the White House, organized by figures in the alt-light, including Mike Cernovich and Jack Posobiec, two rabid conspiracy theorists. Posobiec was supposed to appear at the alt-right event but changed his mind when he learned Spencer would also be speaking. Both rallies were pretty sparsely attended, no more than a hundred people, but the dividing line was evident. It had mostly to do with how brazenly anti-Semitic they were willing to be. At the "free speech" rally, Kessler spoke about nefarious Jewish influence, directing himself at the cameras. "All you guys out here tell me who is in charge of the global conglomerates that own you, that own CBS and NBC?" At the other gathering the speakers were more concerned with pointing out the ways liberals and Democrats were evil incarnate.

For the members of the server, who analyzed the dueling demonstrations for the lessons they might draw for their own planned event, it was an illustration of just how hard "uniting the Right" would be. But they also noticed that Proud Boys appeared at both rallies, which only reinforced the sense that they would be the easiest recruits. One Proud Boys member, Kyle Chapman, who had taken to referring to himself as "Based Stickman" after he hit a counterprotester in the head with a stick at a pro-Trump rally in Berkeley, had started a paramilitary offshoot of the group called the Fraternal Order of Alt-Knights. "I am not afraid to speak out about the atrocities that whites and people of European descent face not only here in this country," Chapman told a crowd in July at something called the Unite America First Peace Rally in Sacramento. Even Gavin McInnes, after initially waffling, ended up encouraging those who felt "compelled" to go to Charlottesville. All of this information was churned over in the server. "I don't like Gavin or chopstick man, either, but many of the young white men who listen to Gavin and chopstick man right now will no doubt see the flaws in their logic and will be on our side by the end of the year," Erika wrote. "We should be open to having them at our events."

If they were wary about including people who showed some hesitancy on the Jewish Question, they were also guarding against being sucked toward the most violent end of the extreme Right. Kessler set the list of speakers, and it included plenty of openly anti-Semitic characters like Mike Enoch, who co-hosted one of the most popular alt-right podcasts, *The Daily Shoah*, which regularly and joyfully mocked Jewish suffering. He created the anti-Semitic (((echo))) meme, based on the reverb sound effect he used whenever mentioning Jewish people on his show. Members of the alt-right began to affix three sets of parentheses around names to indicate Jewish influence—most commonly on social media. (In January 2017, Enoch also infamously confessed that his wife was Jewish, an absolute scandal in the alt-right universe that almost got him ostracized for life.)

Despite giving a platform to Enoch, Kessler drew the line at including anyone from the Daily Stormer, the biggest neo-Nazi site on the internet. It was run by Andrew Anglin, the godfather of the alt-right, who was the first to start thinking about how to make racism and anti-Semitism modern and tech savvy. Anglin himself was pretty much in hiding, but one of his collaborators, Robert Warren Ray, better known by his nom de guerre, Azzmador, was one of the site's writers and podcast hosts. Azzmador, out of East Texas, was bearded, beer-bellied, and older than most of the alt-right. This was not great optics. When it got out that the organizers had denied him a speaking spot, there was some pushback on the server over why exactly Azzmador should be seen as untouchable. WhiteTrash wrote, "Azzmador should be speaking . . . someone needs to represent the most popular alt right site." Tyrone broadened the sentiment: "Everyone from Aryan Nation clover tatted felons or recovering degenerates to Proud Boys has a place. They are tools in the tool box." But this was another instance where the server became useful for smoothing things over. Kessler explained himself and started to win support from others who thought Azzmador might not be best at helping them gain wider acceptance. As HouseboatMedic put it, "As much as I fucking love Azzmador, not many normies are going to be swayed by an angry old bearded guy screaming at kikes that he's going to kick them into an oven."

WE THINK ABOUT the dark corners of the internet as places of danger and radicalization, where the absence of shame allows terrible notions to fester. And it's true. But there is another way of conceiving of what happens when a self-selecting group retreats to a quieter, slower, more private, and less performative space to have conversation: it breeds imagination. What I saw on the Discord servers from that summer reminded me of the Futurist manifestos, the relay of each man's maniacal aspirations for society providing a slap on the back for another man to take it further, to propose something even more bombastic. In this way, they all came to believe something impossible was actually possible: that their ideas could find a place in the sun.

The platform they used was already built around the fantasizing of gamers. Their dreams of eliminating Jews, of massacring Black people, took place next to other sorts of playacting, some the benign fun of a Dungeons & Dragons session and others that involved killing and maiming dozens of people at a time. Megan Condis, a professor at Texas Tech University who has studied Discord and masculinity, told me how being disembodied online, without any obvious markers of identity like gender or skin color, could yield a kind of creativity, using words alone to prove one's manliness, one's whiteness, one's commitment to a common goal, all to an exaggerated degree. "Everything has to be built from scratch," she said.

I saw servers where members spent most of their time designing together the flag that would represent their group, essentially building an avatar. They would make suggestions about colors and symbols, critiquing one another's drafts, bringing up examples of flags from the past to emulate. "I think if you are trying to make a flag that represents a Nation, you should copy the Northern European design and just make a simple tricolor," wrote blackhat 16 about one idea. "If you're trying to make a flag for a patriotic fascist organization within the Nation, you should add the symbolism and be more liberal with color placement." Commenting on another design, Australopithecus Jordan wrote, "The black sun in the top corner is appealing. It's subtle but attractive to our kin specifically." They would go on and on like this for hours, often late into the night, ostensibly workshopping but really reinforcing their dreaming in the same direction ("I really value your guys' feedback and hope we can find a . . . 'final' solution," wrote Wehrmacht).

Of course this dreaming was often less innocuous than the color scheme on a flag. One conversation centered on the question of how to create geographic enclaves for nonwhite people. "There may be the necessity of a restructuring of national borders for new nations to come to sovereignty," wrote AltRightVa. From this post spun out a series of proposals. He suggested carving out an area of Mississippi: "Make it a black nation and incentivize the exodus by giving all blacks who would want to move there some money and a dwelling. We could clear out Baltimore mostly through voluntary migration." Others warmed to this thought exercise. "If all went to plan and you were going to designate an area of the country for a black state, which area would it be?" 80D asked. "I say something like North Dakota but idk there's actually a lot of beauty there."

They spent a lot of time preoccupied with the role of women in their future all-white America. What began as a recurring concern about whether women should be allowed at "Unite the Right" veered into a more general sifting through of their values. Unsurprisingly, the consensus was that women should be in a "supportive role," as one member put it, doing the cooking and cleaning and childbearing. They were fairly explicit about this: women in the movement should be "forming the sewing circles," Johnny McFashy wrote. There was even a sick joke about "white sharia," the notion that they would be better off if they implemented traditional Muslim laws regarding women ("We respect women, only if they don't act like total degenerate sluts, are traditional, are with a man, and respects the will of said man, and is fertile, and is also not going out without her male partner because this is WHITE SHARIA motherfuckers!").

On the Charlottesville 2.0 server there was some tension around this fantasy of male domination precisely because of who their moderator was. Erika, who had the power to kick members out, showed herself unafraid to object when degrading comments were made about women. The men often didn't know what to make of her. They tried to put her in her place, asserting the rules of the world they hoped to create. This, even though she was the only one with any real authority. Erika was eventually revealed to be Erica Joy Alduino, who in selfies all over social media wore bright red lipstick and had a tattoo in cursive script just beneath her clavicle that read, "I will never be silenced." She was a central organizer of the rally, working closely with Kessler, who seemed to trust her. Being admin of the server was an important role. She set the limits. "I ban people who don't respect some basic rules regarding discussion on this server/optics going forward, and who keep escalating things," she wrote after a member used a derogatory phrase to refer to women. "Kinda like you." This drove the rest of the server crazy. One member, SchoolShooterRecruiter, summed it up, "A right wing movement should not have a female mod and it's ridiculous we even have to discuss this." Erika did have her defenders, though. When members got upset after she reminded them of Kessler's rule about not carrying guns openly at the event, Goldstein Riots stepped in: "Look, all erika did was point out rules that everyone else already knows, if you don't like it tough. Jason said no open carry, don't get your panties in a bunch because a girl pointed that out to you."

It might seem absurd to read too much into this vile, misogynistic bullying, but they were building and reinforcing shared values through these moments of conflict. The intense imagining was exactly what Andrew Anglin, founder of the Daily Stormer, had been prescribing for a long time. His own website's message board was also meant for creating a community. Only then, he figured, could they begin to take over the world.

In "A Normie's Guide to the Alt-Right," an essay he published two months before the 2016 presidential election, Anglin explained the unusual source of his ideas. "Of particular importance to me was the book 'Rules for Radicals' by the Jew Saul Alinsky, given that he codified the strategy used by the Jews to tear down the entire ancient body of European traditions and social norms and replace it with something the Jews felt more comfortable with," Anglin wrote. He wanted to apply the lessons he had learned from Alinsky about the stages of a movement. "The end goal of the Alt-Right is to first solidify a stable and self-sustaining counter-culture, and then eventually push this into becoming the dominant culture, in the same way that the Jewish-led revolutionary counter-culture of the 1960s has now become the dominant culture of the West." Whether the alt-right had spent enough time quietly steeping in their Discord servers to emerge and challenge the dominant culture was a question about to be answered.

AS THE WEEKEND of August 12 approached, the server became busy with logistics. ("Can I bring my Rottweiler?" "People better learn Dixie. We'll look and feel real lame if only like 10 people can make it through the whole song.") With less than a week to go, Kessler encountered some trouble with his permit for the rally. He was told by the city that a decision had been made to move them from Emancipation Park (the former Lee Park), a small square in the middle of Charlottesville and not easily secured, to McIntire Park, a much larger grassy expanse north of downtown. Kessler resisted, and then on August 10, two days before the demonstration, he filed suit against the city in federal court with the help of the ACLU. "Let the blood of your ancestors boil in your soul. We shall NOT be shoved to the back of the bus. That's what this is. Being shoved into a corner," SpencerReesh wrote. "A loosely dispersed crowd looks like a state fair, not a political rally." There was a lot of frustration and commiseration about what felt like a major setback on the "optics" front—the thing they cared most about. "The whole POINT was to be at the LEE STATUE," another member wrote.

The day before the rally, Friday, August 11, the court sided with Kessler and the ACLU, ordering the city to allow the original permit (putting the white supremacists in the strange position of praising their "kike lawyers"). After all those weeks of imagining and building themselves up, they were finally going to do it. The server became an emotional place. You could tell how bonded they had become through their conversations because even some vulnerability crept in. "All we have is each other," Mack Albion wrote. "We need to be reminded of that sometimes." The night before, another member, junker, admitted, "I'm scared." But mostly they were pumping each other up. "In all seriousness, circa 2012 I was reading transcripts of Hitler's speeches thinking that I was the only one pondering a new 'Eurocentric consciousness,'" wrote Beeravon. "Five years later, I am about to lie down to the last sleep before I witness that become a reality with the gathering of hundreds of men all who have it in them to strive for greatness. This shall be overwhelming, and undeniable change is coming our way."

People who were not sympathetic to the cause, including antifascist activists, were pouring into the city, and businesses like Airbnb were taking a stand against the alt-right's presence by refusing to serve them. They needed to fortify themselves, and Discord was where they could do it. "If anyone's feeling shaky or discouraged after reading about the hordes of people coming to protest us, AirBnB's bullshit, businesses flaking out on us, and the problems with the permit, remember: it's never easy being the tip of the spear," wrote AshBrighton—AL. "We are the start of something really big, and our courage will always be remembered when we win."

On Friday night, after nightfall, they surprised the authorities and the city by repeating what had worked for them so well in May: a torchlit procession. This time they marched through the University of Virginia campus to the school's statue of Thomas Jefferson. There were many more of them now, hundreds, and they were louder. "You will not replace us!" quickly turned into "Jews will not replace us!" It was the same angry red-faced shouts, the khakis and white polos and Hitler Youth haircuts, the arms raised in a Nazi salute, a line of flames. With the press already in Charlottesville, the image of fire cutting through the night circulated rapidly, displaying their defiance for the world to see. It was the lack of fear or shame that shocked. They seemed liberated. "Guys this looks beautiful," wrote queenarchitect, one of a few members of the server who was posting in real time. The police largely stayed on the sidelines and did little when a fight broke out with a small group of counterprotesters. A few people got maced, but the biggest harm was psychological. It was the reanimation of an American monster most people wanted to believe had been killed off. It was like a zombie invasion.

The server was quiet the next day. They were living the dream instead of working to bring it about. And things got ugly very quickly. Discord and the torchlit rally had lent them a sensation of strength; they had bolstered and unified them. The alt-right's favorite metaphor is the Overton window, which represents the range of acceptable political views at any given historical moment. The heat conducted on those servers made them feel as if they could open the window just a crack more if they acted together. It hadn't, however, changed a few basic realities: most everyone thought their worldview abhorrent and worth opposing, their numbers were still few, and despite their attempts to impose discipline ("Please do not salute during the rally," Kessler begged that morning), there were more than a few violent, deranged people in their midst. These were the unavoidable truths that converged on the streets of downtown Charlottesville on August 12.

That morning, the alt-right and those they'd managed to bring along with them—from David Duke to the League of the South, a neo-Confederate group—began making their way from their staging ground in McIntire Park to Emancipation Park and the Lee statue, where they now had a permit to hold their event. At the same time a broad coalition of counterprotesters, local ministers and rabbis, and antifascist forces who were ready to rumble (some of them armed with balloons filled with pink paint) were on their way there as well, marching from St. Paul's Memorial Church. It didn't take very long before these two contingents clashed and street fighting broke out everywhere, flagpoles turning into makeshift weapons. Many of the white supremacists came dressed as if they were in a video game, as if the helmets and body armor that bulked them up still gave them the same distance from reality they had on Discord. They rushed into crowds swinging their large plastic shields covered in the insignias they had designed together, red crosses against white. It was vicious. And the police stood by, watching as people slammed their bodies into each other. An independent report later commissioned by the city was scathing: "When violence was most prevalent, C.P.D. commanders pulled officers back to a protected area of the park, where they remained for over an hour as people in the large crowd fought on Market Street." Finally, at 11:28, a state of emergency was declared and then, soon after, "unlawful assembly," at which point police started making arrests, trying to clear everyone out.

Richard Spencer was struggling to reach the Lee statue when he was maced—first, he said, by counterprotesters and then by the police, who had an order of dispersal. He started livestreaming on Twitter, his face dripping wet and his eyes bloodshot. "This is an absolute outrage," Spencer said. "This is a peaceful assembly." Police in full riot gear moved in to push everyone out of the park, and Spencer kept filming— "I'm not moving, sir, I won't attack you, but I'm not moving"—until he was finally shoved back by riot shields. He tweeted to his followers, "My recommendation: Disperse. Get out of Charlottesville city limits."

The clashes continued into the early afternoon, when a large group of counterprotesters took to the center of downtown. It was then, around 1:45, that James Alex Fields Jr., who had driven from Ohio to attend the rally and earlier had wielded a Vanguard America shield, plowed his Dodge Challenger into the crowd and then quickly reversed down the narrow street, with bodies horrifically tossed every which way. The attack left dozens of people injured, and then, a few hours later, came the news that one woman had been killed: Heather Heyer, a thirty-two-year-old paralegal.

On the Charlottesville 2.0 server they cycled through denial ("Please just tell me it wasn't one of our guys") and anger ("Fucking caused more damage to our movement than 100 antifa") to resignation ("People, please use your heads. Cut back on the rage for just a second and think about how to articulate a message that stands by our cause without sounding like knuckle-dragging idiots"). Kessler seemed genuinely scared by the implications. "The fact that someone died is not a joke," he wrote. "If you're going to keep making those jokes leave the fucking server." They were desperate to integrate what had happened into their own narrative. "She died by being on the wrong side of history," Beeravon wrote. James Brower then added, "One person being a bad Apple doesn't represent the whole movement." Still, their optics had been ruined. "The best way to take control of this situation is to raise money for the family of the woman that died," suggested Stan—PA. "The leadership should start a fundraiser." They landed on blaming the city and the police and the governor for prematurely shutting down the event. "This man was clearly outraged that his civil rights were trampled on and his only outlet to let his frustration out was taken from him," wrote Mr. Bulldops.

They had stepped out into the light. And even with the death of Heather Heyer and the enormous and instantaneous backlash that would ultimately catapult them back into the shadows, they still felt a little victorious. The fact that they were dominating the news that weekend, that the alt-right had made itself known and appeared unafraid, seemed like an achievement. It had been a moment that, as Kessler told them, "shook the rafters of the entire political establishment."

Discord was a big part of that success. Dan Feidt, one of the Unicorn Riot hackers who cracked open the server, thought a lot about the platform in the days after Charlottesville. The big advantage, as he saw it, was the number of closed rooms it gave them to work together but also apart. "I know that some of the groups moved on to different messaging platforms like Signal. But that doesn't really help you create a lobby. When Discord was in its heyday, it had a front area, kind of a back area, different servers serving different functions, crossover areas, cross-pollinating areas." It made them feel as if they were "mentally in a whole subculture."

Within days of the rally, that subculture was under siege. A number of internet service providers made an aggressive show of shutting down any white supremacist presence. The fate of the Daily Stormer, the neo-Nazi flagship website, was emblematic. On August 13, GoDaddy, the web hosting company, informed Andrew Anglin that he had twenty-four hours to register his domain somewhere else. The site moved to Google the next day and was promptly kicked off; it was finally forced into the Dark Web, where it can be accessed only with special software. As for Discord, whether they had been aware of what was happening on their platform or not, the founders claimed to be disgusted. They immediately deleted more than a hundred alt-right servers and soon put in place a Trust and Safety unit to research and stamp out any hate groups who might use their site. This was the deplatforming of the alt-right, forcing them to scurry for cover and to search out even more covert places where they could converse. Jason Kessler experienced perhaps the most ignominious version of this. Saddled with legal fees from all the lawsuits brought against him by those injured in the attack, he was forced to move back into his parents' house. Once while Kessler was being interviewed on an alt-right livestream, his father's voice could be heard off camera, yelling at his son, "Hey, get out of my room! Jason, this is my room!" For Kessler, at least, there was truly nowhere left to go.

And yet, if the alt-right had been looking to bring their ideas into the mainstream, they were rewarded with the equivocating words of the president in the days following the rally when he held an impromptu news conference in the marbled lobby of Trump Tower. "I think there is blame on both sides," he told reporters. When he was asked again whether neo-Nazis weren't at fault for being the ones to organize the event in Charlottesville, he went even further. "Excuse me, they didn't put themselves down as neo-Nazis, and you had some very bad people in that group. But you also had people that were very fine people on both sides." And if there was one thing they kept telling themselves on the server, one concept they hoped would break through, it was just that: that they were very fine people.

Chapter 9

THE VIRUS

New York City, 2020

EVA LEE CAN SEE VIRUSES, and not in the way an epidemiologist or a virologist or an ER doctor might. She can see them before they manifest themselves in a cough or as red blotches on a face. An applied mathematician with a specialty in disaster, Lee has an ability to plot the path of contagion and then design systems for disseminating cures. She's been much in demand over the past fifteen years, deployed by the Centers for Disease Control and Prevention and the Food and Drug Administration, and as a consultant to both George W. Bush's and Barack Obama's administrations. She was in Japan after the Fukushima nuclear disaster in 2011 and with the marines in West Africa in 2014 for Ebola. When the H1N1 pandemic hit the United States in 2009, it was Lee who was called to Washington, D.C., to figure out a delivery system for the vaccine.

She loves algorithms and the two hundred modeling computers in her lab at Georgia Tech, but also calls herself "highly emotional." It was her sister's death by stomach cancer and her mother's suffering with sclerosis that turned her attention to solving public health problems. The cold abstraction and deep empathy can be a combustible mix. It makes her seem sometimes on the verge of bursting out of her skin—her two favorite adverbs, generously sprinkled, are "crazily" and "beautifully." She is petite and speaks quickly in an accent inflected by her youth in Hong Kong, flitting rapidly from topic to topic. There is an incongruousness to her, pieces that don't seem to fit, like her girlishly curly locks. Even though she specializes in the fine-tuning of large-scale operations—her best-known course when she taught at Columbia University was Facility Layout and Design—she is easily overwhelmed by the practical matters of daily life. Her emails are riddled with typos because she uses only one finger on each hand to peck out messages. She once optimized FedEx's worldwide system of courier delivery, but she's never come close to driving a car.

All of which is to say that when Lee began picking up bits of information in January 2020 about a new coronavirus spreading through the Chinese city of Wuhan, she was primed, in skill and personality, for a single-minded crusade.

Not long after January 21, when the CDC confirmed its first American case, Lee received an email with an unusually dramatic subject line: "Red Dawn." The reference was to a 1984 movie starring a young Patrick Swayze and Charlie Sheen. In an imagined America under Soviet occupation, a rambunctious group of high school students, who call themselves the Wolverines, mount a resistance to the Evil Empire. The playful subject line signaled a very informal chat, even if Lee could see immediately that it was a serious bunch assembled there—about a dozen infectious disease doctors, medical experts, and a few local public health officers. Among them, too, though they remained quiet and were sometimes left off the emails, were high-profile figures like Robert Redfield, then the head of the CDC, and Anthony Fauci, director of the National Institute of Allergy and Infectious Diseases, along with a bevy of second- and third-tier administration officials mostly from the Department of Health and Human Services. This all gave the distinct impression that whatever the group discussed would find a way up the chain of command. It was just the sort of outlet Lee was looking for.

The official who initiated Red Dawn was Duane Caneva, the chief medical officer at the Department of Homeland Security, who in an early email described the group's purpose as an "opportunity to provide thoughts, concerns, raise issues, share information." But as the threads grew longer, split off, and became more dire—"Red Dawn Rising" and then "Red Dawn Raging"—a few of the participants came to find in this private channel more than just casual conversation among peers. It was a refuge where they could size up the virus coming into view and begin furiously planning while the rest of the world seemed to continue spinning unfazed. There were no filters here. Lee, like many in the group, knew some of the others from real life and past emergencies. It was, as one participant in the chain put it, like "a large group of friends cleared to carpool confidential level."

Lee immediately took to it. "We were able to talk about facts, talk about what was going on without thinking about politics at all, which I don't have any head for," she told me. "It allowed us to be quite blunt." She assumed that there were at least an equal number of Democrats and Republicans, if perhaps even more Republicans, appointees in the Trump administration, but the messages were nonpartisan. What the group shared was a faith in public health as a discipline and a sober attitude when it came to the virus.

Familiar as they all were with outbreaks, they began to collectively read the sparse data that was available. On January 23, China began locking down the province of Hubei, where fifty-seven million people lived, creating what would be a massive quarantine. This was a pretty big warning sign, and in one of the earliest emails a participant began spitballing the possibilities. "Am going through an interesting exercise now of the 'what will you wish you would have done if . . . .'." They considered two scenarios. Could this be just like "a bad flu year," as someone else wondered, more like H1N1 of a few years earlier, or would it be like the 1918 pandemic, which ended up taking the lives of fifty million people worldwide? One of the most active members on the email chain, aside from Lee, was Carter Mecher, a senior medical adviser at the Department of Veterans Affairs who described himself to the group as "certainly no public health expert (just a dufus from the VA)." "I wish there was some better way of figuring this out quicker," Mecher wrote on January 29. "I just am not smart enough to see how. The uncertainty and the fog are like the air around us—it is just a part of it all."

The privacy and intensity of the email chain—Lee said she would stay up until three or four in the morning tapping out message after message—were made for this level of uncertainty. It allowed the Wolverines to be vulnerable together in their lack of hard data or much other information from inside China. They all knew that this was the moment, before they could really see the pandemic, that demanded they seek out the faintest signs of its progression. It was helpful to share a space with like-minded people who also knew how to look for those signs.

What made the fog clear a bit in early February was the story of the *Diamond Princess* cruise ship. After one passenger fell ill with the virus, the ship docked in the port of Yokohama, Japan, and over the next two weeks 691 others on board would come down with it as well, turning it into a floating petri dish—and a useful case study. The rate of infection was "unbelievable," as one participant put it. Carter Mecher did some simple math, using the 1,045 crew aboard the ship as "a proxy for a young healthy population" and the 2,666 passengers as a proxy for "the population we see in a nursing home or residential care facility." One of the concerns, he wrote, was "how a 'remake of this movie' could play out in similarly confined populations of elderly frail Americans." Lee was doing her own extrapolations. The cruise ship was "the worst form of social gathering," she wrote. But these conditions were not unique. "Why would it be so different than a mall with everyone walking around for 3–6 hours, eating, drinking, touching everything? Or at school enclosed in classrooms for multiple hours? Or at work enclosed in cubicles for 8 hours?" She was thinking like a modeler: "The health system burden can not be overemphasized. Just think about 1% infection in Georgia, and out of that 20% requires medical attention. That is over 18,000 people. Can we handle these extra people in the hospitals?"

ALL THEY NEEDED was the *Diamond Princess* to understand what they were facing, and this at a time, in mid-February, when President Trump was saying about the coronavirus, "Looks like by April, you know in theory when it gets a little warmer, it miraculously goes away!" There was something else, too. They were beginning to see the virus's stealthiness. On February 23, Lee reported to the group that a study by the American Medical Association found that a twenty-year-old woman from Wuhan managed to infect five family members without ever getting sick herself and even testing negative at first. "So spreading and its wide scope is unavoidable because there exists these very healthy individuals who can spread effectively—even during incubation period." The implications were enormous. If asymptomatic people could be contagious, then stamping the virus out quickly would be nearly impossible. This ominous insight led to one of the few times an official with the president's ear chimed in. Robert Kadlec, the head of the virus response effort at the Department of Health and Human Services, seemed genuinely shocked by what he was learning on Red Dawn. "Eva is this true?!" he asked Lee, in an email to the group. "If so we have a huge whole [*sic*] on our screening and quarantining effort."

The emails coalesced around a single imperative: start the interventions and *now*. For all the uncertainties about this particular virus, a well-established playbook existed. With no vaccine in sight, there would have to be widespread testing, contact tracing, and then quarantining. Because the CDC had made major mistakes in February in developing its testing kit, the country would have to go maximal in its preemptive measures, spreading an enormous net: shutting down schools and businesses, wearing masks, and socially distancing. In the language of public health, these are called NPIs—non-pharmaceutical interventions—and as soon as the shape of COVID-19 became clear to the Red Dawn group, there was consensus that every one of them had to be applied at once. "We cannot prepare for the future by acting in the future, we must be rolling it out now," Lee wrote as early as February 10. "There's no harm in doing it, but there will be a lot of regret if we don't."

This was the hardest part. It demanded not just scientific knowledge. It demanded imagination. No leader wants to shut down parts of the economy or mandate extreme changes in behavior when no one is dying, when the disease is effectively invisible. The extent of this particular challenge, the fact that their sense of urgency might not be appreciated, was evident to them by the end of February, when Nancy Messonnier, the then director of the CDC's National Center for Immunization and Respiratory Diseases, faced serious blowback simply for warning, in a briefing to journalists, that "we will see community spread," and that it was only a question of "how many people in the country will have severe illnesses." She relayed a conversation with her family she'd had that morning: "I told my children that while I didn't think that they were at risk right now, we as a family need to be preparing for significant disruption of our lives." The stock market dropped precipitously, and President Trump, who was returning that day from an overseas trip to India, was furious. From that point on, the CDC, which would normally speak for the government in a health crisis, was effectively muzzled.

Beginning with their earliest emails, the members of Red Dawn proceeded as if they had some authority—as if they could make things happen. They came up with proposals for how to organize what were sure to be overcrowded hospitals weeks before anyone wanted to consider this eventuality. They dreamed up a potential triage protocol. They debated when exactly the trigger should be pulled on closing schools or businesses. How many days after the first case was detected? They devised ideas for messaging. Lee described in detail how to persuade foreign students returning to the United States from abroad to get tested. "My feeling is that we can frame the message in a positive way (as a means to protect their health)." Another participant wondered if they could use the cruise ship statistics to drive the point home: "It might be eye opening for Seattle to simply overlay the cruise ship data atop their population age >60 and assume everyone under 60 has mild disease and even use an attack rate of 20%. Easy enough to do that for them."

As the administration continued to sideline the CDC and play down the virus's possible impact, the gulf separating what the group felt needed to be done and what was actually being done grew wider. "The unknown is what we've been planning for all these years," Lee wrote on February 28. "Everyone has to step up now." The inaction, the basic failure to see, despite Red Dawn's best efforts to show exactly what would happen—what was indeed happening "by the book," as Lee put it in one email—drove her mad.

THE MOST DESPERATE VOICES on the chain were those of local public health officials, people who respected the science and whose job it was to prepare their cities or states for what was coming. They wanted help conjuring the problem for their superiors. David Gruber, who was managing Texas's response, pleaded, "As a state public health official who is in agreement that NPIs must be strongly enacted early, I'm looking for help from this group that makes the case for NPIs. The target audience is those outside health." Another official, Eric McDonald, the medical director of San Diego County, complained that he needed more data to understand what he should be doing to prepare. "Frustrating doesn't capture it."

The Red Dawn members scrambled for solutions. "Maybe we should use a hurricane analogy that many understand," wrote one. Another suggested, "We should be treating this like we treat stroke and acute coronary syndromes where time = tissue. In this case time = transmission." Lee had her own visual aid for convincing decision makers. As she wrote on March 5, "I think a tree with the contact rate would be great to show the policy makers so they know how many of the elderly infected would end up in hospital beds and we can even show the queues!"

They were becoming the resistance to an occupation, just as their silly name implied, but it was an occupation of science by politics. Misinformation was invading reality just as the virus was finally revealing itself. On February 29 came the first announced death in the United States, a Washington State man in his fifties. The following day, New York State had its first positive case. Shutting down was really the only option. Red Dawn continued to be a space for thinking seriously about the implications. "I ran a few models for school closures and business tele-work for Santa Clara and King County and I want to share some graphs here," Lee wrote on March 3. Data about the accumulating American cases was coming in at a faster pace now. They had more to work with. "I really learn a lot from all of you," Lee wrote. "I found that you are all very mathematical:). Now I will go back to my equations again to see which cities are still in good shape to contain successfully."

By the middle of March, the World Health Organization made it official: this was a pandemic. The number of daily cases in the United States began to climb over five hundred, and ten deaths quickly became a hundred a day and more. A national emergency was declared on March 13. In a last attempt to be heard beyond their closed circle, the members of Red Dawn rehearsed for each other what they would say to political leaders, imagining these messages might somehow still reach them. "I notice a lot of HHS email addresses on this email group and you all have been quiet for most of the discussion over the past several weeks," one member of the chain whose name has been redacted wrote. "History will long remember what we do and what we don't do at this critical moment. It is the time to act, and it is past the time to remain silent. This outbreak isn't going to magically disappear on its own. If that is the conclusion some are taking, they are misinformed and dead wrong." Mecher from the VA wrote, "I don't think it would be prudent to play it cute and try to play chicken with this virus and hold out to the last moment to pull the trigger. It is like thinking you can time the market. You don't do that when thousands of lives potentially hang in the balance. That is what I would tell my mayor, or my governor, or my President."

But by then the hurricane had made landfall. The stroke was in progress. The tree was sprouting branches. Eva Lee kept a constant vigil at a laptop in her kitchen, surrounded by her many giant ficus plants and cages filled with dozens of birds she and her husband had rescued and raised over the years. She began to lose hope that anyone was listening. "Those were private emails, so I had no problem being direct," she said. "I always asked, 'Why is it that nobody's doing anything? Why is it that there's no action? And who is in charge?'" But the group also acknowledged just how hard it was to persuade political leaders and the public "to take action before the storm arrived and when the sun was shining," as Mecher put it. They were left to watch as the virus began thrashing its way from city to city—a story, he wrote, that was "unfolding and writing itself in real time."

In the beginning, the Red Dawn participants had pictured themselves as an early warning system, but now there was a shift: they knew they had to monitor and analyze and digest the data and make recommendations, even if no one was drawing on their knowledge—they acted "as if." And doing it together, in addition to making them more productive, allowed them to feel as though they weren't alone in their total commitment to science. The email chain provided the conditions for this feeling, for this work, in much the same way the *Chronicle* had allowed Soviet dissidents to document human rights abuses that would never be redressed. One of the more active Red Dawn participants was James Lawler, an infectious disease doctor at the University of Nebraska who had served in the White House under George W. Bush and as an adviser to Obama. He had even gone to Japan in February to help repatriate American passengers from the *Diamond Princess*. "We all used to be in a position where we could have had more direct influence," Lawler told me. "And now we no longer were. So we were using what tools we had."

RED DAWN WAS a sanctuary at a moment of confusion and dread—a place to talk honestly and away from the public, to prepare a strategy, a battle plan. But it was not the only such forum. Many channels opened up in those spring weeks when COVID first struck, when the virus could be felt in New York City hospital wards filled with the rhythmic sucking sound of ventilators. In the absence of much official guidance or a national plan, these private networks activated like new radio frequencies, suddenly crackling with concern and advice. The experts used apps like Signal for highly encrypted group chatting, or

WhatsApp, or even the direct message function of Twitter, which could allow multiple participants to sneak away together from the speed and noise of the public feed. The quiet felt necessary and useful because, just as for the Red Dawn participants, so much was unsure and they needed a way to develop their thinking.

Excerpts of the Red Dawn emails, meant to be kept confidential, were published by a handful of newspapers in April 2020, the result of a Freedom of Information Act request initiated by Kaiser Health News. When Esther Choo, an ER doctor in Portland, Oregon, read through the exchanges from just a month earlier, in March, it felt to her as if she were looking at a transcript of her own online chats. "I was like, I totally see what's happening here," she told me. "This feeling of knowing it's coming and you almost don't know how to express it to the public, that helplessness and increasingly a feeling that, with all haste, we have to communicate this. I know this well, how they sorted through the data and expressed frustration. That's exactly what we sounded like behind the scenes."

For ER doctors like Choo, who were heading into battle every day in respirators and plastic shields and surgical gowns to care for patients who were reduced to wheezing and coughing alone in hospital rooms, these online chats became a way to speak with others who might understand, who could offer practical tips and empathy after soul-sapping twenty-four-hour shifts in the company of death.

Craig Spencer, an ER doctor in New York City who began sharing information on a number of private WhatsApp groups, told me these became "a hotbed of activity": "Like, 'Hey, I've got this patient, with this, this, and this. What have you guys been doing that's been helping?'" From these group chats, he learned about early advances in care—like proning, or turning people over on their stomachs. "All of that stuff was coming in via my WhatsApp. That's where people I knew and trusted were."

Pretty soon, these doctors with social media presences were receiving dozens of daily requests to go on television and speak about what they were seeing in the ER. Someone had to be straight with the public about the knowns and the unknowns and provide some direct answers. The CDC seemed to be out of the picture. The nightly coronavirus updates, now dominated by the president, were driven not by the latest science but by a need to project blind optimism ("Just stay calm. It will go away," he said on March 10). So it was the doctors whose counsel was being sought out, often on cable news channels. "As the pandemic went on, we were asked so much more," Choo said. "Why is face mask wearing so important? What do we need in terms of personal protective equipment? It was much more than just 'Tell us anecdotally what is happening.'" The private groups took on a more important function: the doctors needed to band together even more tightly so they could coordinate their messaging.

Social media and the direct access it offered to an enormous audience made it only more urgent to navigate what could be said out loud. Craig Spencer, who worked the emergency room at Columbia University Medical Center, had about 580 followers on Twitter when he took to the site on March 23 to describe a day in his life. "The bright fluorescent lights of the ER reflect off everyone's protective goggles," he wrote. "There is a cacophony of coughing. You stop. Mask up. Walk in." It was a war zone. "You're notified of another really sick patient coming in. You rush over. They're also extremely sick, vomiting. They need to be put on life support as well. You bring them back. Two patients, in rooms right next to each other, both getting a breathing tube. It's not even 10am yet." And yet he emerged from the ER to find empty but otherwise seemingly normal streets. "Maybe people don't know???"

Spencer said his phone "had a seizure for two days" as the thread was shared by tens of thousands of people, including Barack Obama. Within a few months he had almost 200,000 followers. Esther Choo, the ER doctor who was working at Oregon Health & Science University's hospital in Portland, had also built an unlikely fan base on the platform. It began for her in 2017 after the Charlottesville protests when she tweeted about her experiences with patients who refused to be treated by her because of her race—she was born in Cleveland, the daughter of Korean immigrants—and what it felt like to cut open a patient's shirt on an operating table to discover a swastika tattoo. She had become an expert Twitter user, achieving that winning mix of earnest confession and witty repartee, with the occasional cute animal meme. She wore her black hair back in a sensible ponytail, and in on-camera interviews she was authoritative and in control—a feat in itself, considering her four young children were with her at home.

Choo and Spencer and about a dozen other doctors connected through Twitter DM groups—they called one of them the Brain Trust—and started to use them as their "back channel." As Spencer put it, "This is where we would develop a strategy for all the prime-time cable news programs so that we could tell people the truth at a time when the government was downplaying the virus." Mostly they conveyed to an anxious nation what the Red Dawn group had been saying privately since late January, that without widespread testing or a vaccine the only way to combat the virus was through methods that had proven useful since 1918. But if they agreed about listening to the science, there was still plenty they argued about.

One of the contentious issues in those first weeks was face masks. There was no doubt that these were effective for limiting the spread, but in March there was a shortage of masks, especially the N95 respirators that emergency rooms needed. The doctors worried that if they proclaimed masks a necessity, it would cause a run on what was a dangerously low supply. "We had many conversations behind the scenes about this," Choo said. "People were divided. And we went back and forth a ton. But that was certainly one where, after all that debate, when we decided to go for it, we went for it." Having agreed to promote masking—all while the CDC waffled in its recommendation—they then turned to language, how to distinguish between the kind of hospital-grade face covering that was needed for first responders and what people could make at home. They didn't have the vocabulary at first, so they workshopped, looking for the words that might stick. "Social distancing" was another example. It was a phrase they thought might confuse people and lead to mental health issues. What they really meant was "physical distancing," so that's the language they decided to promote, even though the term never stuck.

The doctors described this Twitter DM group to me as a "sounding board" or a "staging ground." "We fought a lot, which was why I think I valued the group," Choo said. But as the weeks went on and New York City in particular became a hot zone with hundreds of dead every day, it felt more and more important that they consult with one another before they went public. Choo estimated that three-quarters of their time was spent conferring on private networks. Only a fraction of their ideas would later appear on social media or cable news.

Among the biggest challenges they confronted, right away, was misinformation. The fact that the Trump administration was keeping public health officials from the microphones and CDC scientists from offering more full-throated recommendations meant that conspiratorial voices proliferated. Some insisted that the virus wasn't any more dangerous than the seasonal flu, that it was really a biological weapon deployed by the Chinese, that masks actually made you sick. It was endless, the amount of rampant fiction. And it came from the president as well. In late March, Trump started touting the antimalarial drug hydroxychloroquine as a miracle cure for COVID based on little more than, as he put it in a March 20 briefing, "a feeling." Then he took to Twitter and told his eighty-four million followers that the drug was "one of the biggest game changers in the history of medicine." By March 28, the FDA, at Trump's urging, had approved an emergency use authorization. Meanwhile, there was no real scientific evidence showing that hydroxychloroquine had any effect on COVID, and one man in Arizona even died after ingesting a form of chloroquine used to clean fish tanks (his wife recalled their reasoning: "Hey, isn't that the stuff they're talking about on TV?").

Twitter was a main vector for these speculative theories and outright lies. Looking at the platform's data from January 16 to March 15, one survey revealed that sites trafficking in fake news were shared at about the same rate as credible ones, like the CDC's. Another analysis examined 200 million tweets about the pandemic from January to May and discovered that 62 percent of the top 1,000 retweeters were bots, spreading more than a hundred different varieties of false information about the virus.

What had started as an ad hoc emergency response now became "a long-term project against disinformation," said Dara Kass, an ER doctor at Columbia University Medical Center and another member of the Brain Trust. They had to quickly separate what was useful from what was spurious. They spent two days, for example, deliberating about what to say when asked about a French study that suggested Motrin, the painkiller, wasn't safe to use for coronavirus sufferers—it was not worth listening to, they concluded. "You're asking me how does a bill become a law or how does an egg get fertilized and become a baby, I can give you this play-by-play without checking with anyone else," Kass told me. "If you're asking me whether or not the new trial on the Moderna vaccine, what does it mean for it to be 94.5 percent effective? A lot of these things had to be digested by our little focus group in order to come across with the best and most accurate talking points."

They weren't the only ones engaged in this effort. Scientists, too, had taken to Twitter to wage war against the fantasies and distortions. Some epidemiologists and virologists had acquired enormous platforms on the site, jumping from a couple hundred followers to tens of thousands over the course of the pandemic. It's strange to think a place so reductive and loud could be amenable to science, but it was, allowing these experts to explain the facts as they understood them, to unpack new studies in long tweet threads, and to offer recommendations. "It's a remarkable mismatch between medium and message," Carl Bergstrom told me. He's an evolutionary biologist at the University of Washington who in recent years has become an expert in the ways that misinformation and disinformation spread.

What people wanted in those first months was a binary certainty. Is it dangerous or not? Will I get sick or not? Should schools stay open or closed? And scientists do not work like this. The scientific method is about being wrong so that adjustments can be made. It's about tweaking a hypothesis by a few degrees. And the only way, many of these experts told me, to respect that process, while also providing useful information to the public, was to come together, like the ER doctors in their DM groups, in a closed network with people they trusted. "You do need the space apart to think through whether these strongly held positions are reasonable," Bergstrom said. "It allows you to question and develop your ideas, just finding out what you need to know." He could remember many times when he turned to these groups—when he wanted to question the CDC's recommendation to not test college students returning to school or when he wanted to propose that perhaps container laws should be dropped so that people could drink outside and not congregate in bars. "The audience that you're reaching is sizable, and you don't want to be giving bad advice for that reason," he said. "And there's such a deluge of information that's coming in, and it is easy to misread things or misinterpret things. And so it's really helpful to triangulate with a few other people that you trust."

In those first months of the pandemic, science was happening very publicly. Starting in the 1990s, in the field of physics, researchers in an increasing number of fields had been posting their papers to special online servers before they went through the peer-review process, which could take months. The pressures of a pandemic and the need to rapidly share new information made it even more necessary for research to get out before undergoing the strict vetting of a top-tier journal. And prestige publications like *Science* and *Nature* didn't want to look as if they were holding back important findings, so even they began asking their contributors to post on these online repositories first to give the public and other scientists immediate access. And still it didn't seem quick enough—there could be a week's lag time after submitting—so some scientists were just sharing their papers directly on Twitter. This is how, on February 29, the first sequencing of a COVID-19 genome in the United States came to be presented to the world: as a tweet.

All of this new research and the need to digest it only increased the demand for small groups that could exist alongside the larger Twitter conversation. Without peer review, scientists combed through the data together and decided what they could trust before they amplified it. This also led to cross-pollination, with experts from different but related fields checking each other. Angela Rasmussen, then a virologist at Columbia University whose following jumped from 200 in January 2020 to 180,000 by the end of that year, told me about her seven Twitter friends who have been on the same DM group since March. "There's been a ton of misinformation," she said. "But, you know, I'm a biologist, I'm not an epidemiologist, I'm not a statistician." Twitter had become a resource for meeting colleagues who did specialize in those areas. But they then needed their "staging area" to work through the new research and data on their own before making any pronouncements.

Esther Choo and Craig Spencer and their Brain Trust felt this burden many times over. Their platform was even bigger than Twitter. They were speaking to tens of millions of Americans on television every night. As March turned into April, New York City was like the set of a horror movie, with crematories now given permission to work around the clock, a fleet of forty-five new mobile morgues set up to handle the overflow. It was a city that was running out of body bags. These overworked doctors increasingly became the nation's advice givers. And they felt they had to rise to the challenge. "We didn't want to be the people who are like, let us crush your hopes and dreams, because people so needed hope," Choo said. "At the same time, it was so important to bring a measured voice."

The essence of their message—to take the virus seriously—seemed to be getting through. By the end of March, most of the country's 56.4 million school-age children and roughly 3 million teachers had moved to remote learning; on April 7, according to cellphone data, Americans stayed home for 93 percent of their day versus 72 percent on March 1. When a large-scale survey of new habits was conducted at the end of April, 96 percent of people claimed to be regularly and vigorously washing their hands, 88 percent were disinfecting surfaces, and 75 percent wore a mask when stepping outside—a major shift in norms.

But for every new helpful intervention imposed, there seemed to be another setback, like the president declaring that the pandemic would be over by Easter. And then there were moments like April 23, when Trump stood behind a lectern at the nightly coronavirus briefing and free styled, suggesting that the best way to fight the disease might just be to ingest or inject bleach. "I reached out to the group, and I was like, what are we gonna say about this?" Esther Choo remembered. "One of the doctors told me, 'Just bring your truest self to this, Choo. Don't overprocess this because your gut reaction is the right one.' So when I went on TV that day, I said, 'I don't even know how to react to this. It's such a ridiculous and horrible message that somebody is going to get hurt.'"

What was most disturbing to the members of the Brain Trust, the feeling they kept returning to among themselves, was the strange fact that this had become their responsibility, that they had to be the ones working out a message for the public. "When Ebola happened, nobody was asking Esther Choo, random doctor in the ER, for her opinion," she said. "Nobody needed that. Because there were experts doing it. And so it was completely shocking to be driving the conversation."

By the time the first wave of the virus peaked in the state of New York around mid-April, with nearly a thousand deaths a day, the wrung-out ER doctors had been intensely communicating with each other for weeks. After waiting for "the cavalry to arrive," as Choo put it, they had more or less accepted that they would have to take on this role, as representatives of science and public health, worriers for the collective who had to push against strong forces more interested in pretending the virus would just leave on its own. On their DM chats, they felt like "surprised and reluctant dissidents," Choo said. For months, they had told themselves they'd be able to stop once the government stepped in. "And it was one of the most sickening things for that never to happen."

UNLIKE THE DOCTORS, the Red Dawn group didn't have the ability to broadcast their opinions to a wider world. They watched helplessly as New York City was overtaken by the virus in March and April. Eva Lee found herself crying for hours when she saw it all come to pass. She said the chain even went quiet for a bit. "Everybody was silent; you could feel the mourning," she said. The United States hit a cumulative twenty thousand deaths on April 11, quickly surpassed by thirty thousand deaths four days later, and reaching fifty thousand on April 24.

When the Red Dawn chain was revealed to the public in April— Lee was mostly embarrassed by her typos; a reporter even asked her if she really knew English—the group switched to a more secure server, though pretty hurriedly reverted back to email as the most convenient way to talk and exchange information. Lee shared with me hundreds of these messages, picking up where the earlier, exposed back-and-forth had ended (she anonymized people's names before handing over the correspondence). The group had moved beyond frustration to resignation, finally accepting that no unified, federal response was forthcoming. Everything would be fragmentary, fractal even, dependent on the decision of each locality. States would inhabit wholly different realities. In South Dakota, the governor was announcing a "Back-to-Normal Plan" the same week that some counties in California were legally enforcing the wearing of masks.

Strangely, this created an opening for the group. Now that each municipality, each individual school, and each corner bar was desperate for specific guidelines, the ideas generated on the forum could prove useful. When Lee modeled what the impact of the virus would be with and without various interventions in a city of 3.3 million people—a number she chose because it represented 1 percent of the U.S. population—the emergency director of San Diego, also in the group, piped up and asked if he could use it, because that happened to be the exact population of his county. One participant on the chain prefaced his request "Questions for the Smart People." The focus shifted from national policy to local needs, which suited their detail-obsessed brains.

Lee hardly slept anymore, churning out dozens of responses every day. And the email chain gained extra significance for her because she was doubly isolated. Not only was she stuck at home like everyone else in lockdown, but she was coming to terms with the fact that she had just been convicted of a felony. It was her messiness that had gotten her into trouble. Lee was charged with falsifying information on a forty-thousand-dollar-a-year federal grant her lab had received from the National Science Foundation. Its terms demanded a certain level of financial participation from partnering institutes, and Lee says she had misunderstood how to calculate the contribution, putting down a uniform amount each year without checking. She then also lifted a signature of a Georgia Tech grants administrator from an earlier document so she could quickly finish up her paperwork. A federal investigation was launched, and in December 2019 Lee found herself in front of a judge tearfully pleading guilty. Her many defenders said this was simply a case of a person not well suited to or just uninterested in handling administrative tasks, whose only crime was her inattention (something she was never accused of in her work). In one article, her graduate school adviser testified that Lee had difficulty tying her own shoelaces or working a copier. She hadn't benefited personally from the fraud at all. But the mistake, if that's all it was, was a stain.

When Red Dawn's call to arms first arrived in her in-box, she was awaiting her sentencing—the U.S. attorney was looking for eight months of home confinement—but in the meantime Georgia Tech had suspended her as a professor. And now she was feeling the loss. The university had denied her remote access to her lab's many computers and the patented modeling software she had created for them. The solitude of the pandemic, compounded by the alienation from her academic community, was "painful," she said. And being separated from her tools had real consequences. "If I were not shut out, I would have written maybe ten times as many emails on Red Dawn because I could have done so much more analysis," she said. "My little laptop is so crazily slow and clearly can't model the entire United States rapidly."

But she was able to do a lot in those dazed spring months, when half the country worried that the worst was yet to come and the other half decided that the wearing of masks was a violation of their individual liberty. On Red Dawn, all that mattered, and had ever really mattered, was epistemology: What did they know about the virus, how did they know it, and what did it mean for actual communities? "Do you have any additional detail regarding hospital surge reorganization/facility layout guidance?" A barrage of emails would follow, with specific suggestions for setting up various zones and who should go in them. "Use notepad and stick them to the wall next to the patient indicating days since arrival. Big enough so you can see them from a distance." Another inquiry about pregnant women and how they could avoid contracting the virus once they entered the hospital to give birth developed into a whole set of protocols.

Lee was concerned early on that people with mild cases of the virus would be turned away from the hospital, only to infect family members and then possibly the other people in their apartment building. Before anyone thought to come up with solutions for these potential vectors of infection, the group was in the weeds with a range of practical proposals, including housing those with relatively mild symptoms in nearby colleges or sports stadiums. A specialist in optimizing space, Lee thought of repurposing hotels. "Eva makes a very good point," RH, one of the Red Dawn members, wrote. "We do have a lot of empty hotels right now." But then how should these hotels be set up? Everything from hygiene issues to airflow was discussed. One participant shared how hotels in Wuhan had been reorganized for safety: "We also now have a series of floor plans allowing for HVAC airflow from hall to room which reduced droplets." It's hard to tell if Red Dawn was the source, but by the end of April, New York City had put in place a program that looked very much like the one the group had envisioned.

They became a subterranean factory for producing this sort of precise advice. How many people should be allowed to sit at a restaurant table? "The 4-max model per table in Hong Kong seems to work rather well. We CANNOT afford to have 10 people at a table. Contact tracing is a 3-generation effort. So, 4x4x4 is a good size to track, but 10x10x10 is far too big." Should servers wear gloves? There was some debate about this. "One question I have in the note below is related to your mention of the use of gloves in restaurants," wrote WL. "That is becoming an expectation, but I don't see the science of it." There were suggestions about hair salons and tattoo parlors and the optimal way to stagger desks in a classroom. In one set of emails, Lee got into a protracted exchange about how to handle clothes once they had been tried on at a boutique: "I don't know what the current practice is, but as I model it, 30 minutes from one person to the next is a very bad idea," she wrote to the group.

Lee would run models, using the data at hand, and then deliver the numbers. Others would challenge them, or doubt the feasibility of a specific proposal, at which point modifications would be made. It's not that they always arrived at the truth (we now know, for example, that transmission via clothes is rare), but that was never really the objective. Esther Choo described a similar process among the ER doctors. "You have to unequivocally advocate for things where the data is equivocal," she said. This happens in public health all the time. If you stop smoking, no one can promise that you won't still get cancer, she said. Same with wearing a seat belt in a car. You could still die in a crash. But it is the job of experts to sift through the data and decide, on balance, what to recommend to keep people safe. Red Dawn was intent on doing this, meticulously, with what seemed at times like a blind faith that someone, somewhere, was listening.

ON THE FACE OF IT, there wouldn't appear to be anything subversive about the sorts of instructions that were bubbling up from the email chain, except that the CDC was being silenced for saying the very same things. On May 1, after their own internal deliberations, the agency was set to publish a seventeen-page report titled "Guidance for Implementing the Opening Up America Again Framework," a detailed checklist for business owners and local officials and religious leaders. The Trump administration quashed it. And when the Associated Press purloined a copy, their article ran with the words of an anonymous CDC scientist who said the White House told the agency that their booklet "would never see the light of day."

In the battle between science and politics—politics here meaning Trump's insistence that life and business would continue uninterrupted—science was outgunned. The CDC had no independent outlet for addressing the public. Its guidance, when not suppressed, was heavily edited. The agency's chief of staff, Kyle McGowan, later described how, for example, when the CDC wanted to recommend six feet of distance between restaurant diners, the White House budget director objected because it would be too economically onerous. The compromise—one that would have driven Lee and the Red Dawn experts insane in its vagueness—was to simply advise restaurants to implement "social distancing" without specifying what that meant. Months after he left the agency, McGowan concluded, "Every time that the science clashed with the messaging, messaging won."

Red Dawn persisted meanwhile with its tighter focus. "If asking for a national strategy is too much, then at least each county, each city, each jurisdiction . . . must have a strategy that is holistic where actions are all complementary to one another so that they can optimize the achievement of goals and the outcomes," Lee wrote to the group in July.

And this is where their impact began to be felt. The local leaders on the chain—the California deputy emergency response director, the Texas, San Diego, and Maryland COVID-19 incident commanders—took what was generated among the group and put it into practice. Lee would occasionally receive follow-up emails from local public health officials who had been sent her directives. She got a call from officials in New York in mid-April. The Maryland governor, Larry Hogan, announced that schools would be closed on March 12. His was one of the first states to take this step, and Lee later learned it was a direct result of Red Dawn's call for interventions. One congressman would email her "done" for every one of their suggestions his state had put in place.

Lee pointed me to Washington State, and King County, which includes Seattle, in particular, as a place that seemed to take Red Dawn's warnings seriously and reaped the benefits, avoiding the fate of New York City. The early blows of the coronavirus were felt in Washington—both the first confirmed case in the United States and the first announced death at the end of February. Until early April, when New York surged, Washington had the highest number of cases per capita of any state in the nation. But it quickly put in place extreme measures. On March 12, the state was one of the first to close schools and public venues. It limited gatherings to two hundred fifty people on March 11 and then fifty people a few days later. And on March 23, the governor ordered a strict lockdown. Like the leaders of a few other states that day, he prohibited people from "leaving their homes," even banning assembling for religious reasons. By early April, the decreased numbers told the story, as King County averted the escalation of cases seen in other metropolitan areas and the feared hospital overloads. Lee was in touch with local officials who told her that their decision-making had been shaped by Red Dawn and Lee's models. Even though I pressed Lee to give me evidence of Red Dawn's impact, she was not particularly interested in taking credit or drawing these causal lines. "People did listen, and they did take actions. I don't know everything, since I don't ever ask people about it. I just focused on the work, which is what I am good at."

They did what they could. No one was getting burned at the stake for delivering hard truths, but there were consequences for public health officials who dared to simply wonder out loud about the administration's priorities. In late April, Rick Bright, the official leading the federal effort to develop a vaccine, was removed from his job when he questioned Trump's endorsement of hydroxchloroquine. He gave testimony in Congress on May 14, imploring lawmakers to change their approach and warning that "our window of opportunity is closing," that the failure to put in place widespread testing and the absence of basic PPE in hospitals all had cost lives. Bright was attacked by the administration, and the president dismissed him in a tweet as "a disgruntled employee, not liked or respected by people I spoke to and who, with his attitude, should no longer be working for our government!"

This was the cost of speaking out when wishful thinking seemed to be the government's main strategy. Four hundred years after Peiresc had deployed his letters to nurture the development of the scientific method, there was still a need for a private space where this work could happen, where the pursuit of observable truth could proceed safely away from the centrifugal force of politicization and demagoguery.

Eva Lee continued to send a barrage of emails every day to the Red Dawn group through the spring and into the summer. And on August 12, she logged on to Zoom to attend her sentencing hearing in front of a U.S. district judge, Steve Jones. Dozens of public health officials had written letters of support, including Duane Caneva, the chief medical officer for the Department of Homeland Security, who had initiated the Red Dawn chain. Lee pleaded with the judge, weeping, worried that her inability to access her computers and chart potential infection rates would cost lives. "So my punishment means punishing all these people and it feels horrible to me," she said.

Rather than admonishing Lee for her crime, the judge heaped praise on her. "You are one of the most brilliant people I've ever read about," Jones told her. He couldn't bring himself to accept the government's sentencing recommendation if it would take her away from her work. "We need you in America for the next few months and the rest of your life to help us," Jones told Lee. "From what I've read and seen, you'll play a major part in how America will come out of this coronavirus." This was not how judges typically addressed convicted felons. He gave her sixty days of home confinement, but delayed its start until the spring of 2021, when the worst of the virus would hopefully be over.

Georgia Tech, on the other hand, refused to reinstate her as a professor. The university stuck with its original logic that unless Lee was involved in the official government response to the pandemic, there was no reason to make an exception for her. Her role seemed to be, as the university characterized it, contributing to "an ad hoc consortium of researchers via e-mail." Red Dawn was a little brain trust, they implied, but it was peripheral, just scientists, far from any podium, chatting together. Though that's precisely what made it so meaningful.

IN THE FALL OF 2020, as COVID deaths reached into the hundreds of thousands, I had a conversation with William Foege, who ran the CDC from 1977 to 1983. *The Lancet* once called Foege "the gentle giant of public health." He is six feet seven, which meant Obama practically had to stand on his tiptoes when he awarded him the Presidential Medal of Freedom. Foege was credited with the global eradication of smallpox in the 1970s ("2 million died each year of smallpox," his citation read, "a decade later, that number had dropped to zero"), and when I reached him, he was hiding out from this new pandemic in the north Georgia woods, leaving his house only once a week to buy the Sunday *New York Times*. At eighty-four his voice was shaky. Foege had watched with growing unease the way his old agency, and science itself, had been sidelined. He knew that the people who worked at the CDC had prepared their whole careers for just such a moment, and he was now seeing them rendered powerless. It took him a long time, he said, to accept just how bad it was and to try to do something. He didn't want to intervene. But Foege had been active on his own email chains and LISTSERVs throughout 2020, listening to and joining in with former and current CDC scientists who, like those on Red Dawn, were alternately dismayed and desperate to find solutions. It was the existence of these channels that gave him confidence, he said, to do something he never thought he would.

Foege wrote an emotional, forceful email to the then head of the agency, Robert Redfield, imploring him to get himself fired. He was sympathetic to the challenges Redfield faced and told me also that he's not sure what he would have done in the director's shoes, but he was unsparing about what had happened since the spring. "The biggest challenge in a century and we let the country down," he wrote. "The public health texts of the future will use this as an example of how not to handle an infectious disease pandemic." The reasons were by then well known: the total absence of a national plan, an administration in denial. "The prime lesson of 'Know the Truth' has been so obscured by the White House that the people and the media go to the academic community for truth, rather than the CDC." Foege was acknowledging those who had done the work the CDC was prevented from doing. The only solution, as he saw it, was for Redfield to plainly lay out what had gone wrong and apologize for his own part in it. "The White

House will, of course, respond with fury," Foege concluded. "But you will have right on your side. Like Martin Luther, you can say, 'Here I stand. I cannot do otherwise.'"

Foege never meant to raise his voice above a whisper—the only person who knew about the letter was his wife—but somehow it leaked and began circulating among the CDC scientists as a manifesto that gave voice to their collective frustration. "I was so surprised when it became public," he said. "That's just how naïve I am." But he felt no shame in his accusation, because as far as he was concerned, he was simply channeling the sentiment of the email chains. "I was able to say in my letter to him that his own people were questioning his leadership," Foege said. "And that he should apologize, but let them know the pressures he was under. The private email conversations allowed me to know that that was true, that that's the way the CDC employees were feeling, that they were not trusting their leadership." Those messages meant a lot to Foege. He saw in them the glue for putting the CDC's shattered credibility back together again in the future. "We'd always prided ourselves on this idea of truth and science, and resistance to politics," he said about his beloved agency. The fact that its workers, even as dissidents, had stayed true to that mission, if only among themselves, gave him hope.

Chapter 10

THE NAMES

MINNEAPOLIS, 2020

MISKI NOOR DIDN'T NEED to watch all nine minutes and twenty-nine seconds of torture. Just a glimpse at the video of George Floyd's murder—the man lying prone and handcuffed and being slowly asphyxiated by a police officer's knee pressing down on his neck—persuaded Miski to leave her friends at the local Dairy Queen and join the gathering protest. The life of a Black Lives Matter activist was conditioned by these moments of recorded brutality and death. They served to reignite a movement built on a terrible accumulation of names—Eric Garner, Sandra Bland, Freddie Gray, Tamir Rice, Walter Scott. Each was an added page in a brief against America and its system of policing. George Floyd was yet another, the sequence of events that led from being stopped for buying cigarettes with a counterfeit twenty-dollar bill to lying dead in the street, sadly, no surprise to Miski.

But this time was different. It had been a few years since the movement, born of a hashtag, had grabbed any wider attention. Since 2016, it seemed to be overtaken, along with the rest of social media, by the ceaseless spectacle of Donald Trump's presidency. By early 2020, Black

Lives Matter was talked about in the past tense, when it was talked about at all.

This new video, its unambiguous cruelty, an injustice evident to even a stone-cold skeptic, got the pendulum swinging again. And it did so during the restless, cooped-up summer of 2020—the coronavirus had by then shut down most of the country—when people were sufficiently free from work and school routines to take action and already agitated by a public health disaster that was disproportionately tearing through the lives of the poor, who bore the brunt of both sickness and joblessness.

Something was shaken loose. The protest began, with its greatest fury, in Minneapolis, a few blocks from Miski's home, on May 26, the day after Floyd's death, and led to a police precinct being set ablaze and the National Guard's intervention two days later. But it was the breadth of indignation and mourning that was really shocking. There was a demonstration in every major American city, from Los Angeles to Nashville to Louisville, Kentucky, where the name of Breonna Taylor, a twenty-six-year-old EMT who had been shot in her bedroom during a police raid a few months earlier, was added to the incantation. On June 6 alone—just one day—half a million people turned out in nearly 550 cities and towns across the United States. Within a month, it was estimated that as many as twenty-six million people had taken part in a protest. An analysis by *The New York Times* counted 4,700 demonstrations, or an average of 140 per day, and, shockingly, nearly 95 percent of the counties where people put on masks and carried signs and chanted the names were majority white. You could drive through rural parts of America or wealthy all-white suburbs and see signs with #BlackLivesMatter staked in lawns and plastered on people's windows, sometimes written with crayon in a child's hand. By July 3, *The New York Times* was declaring, with little equivocation, that this was "the largest movement in U.S. history."

Standing at the epicenter, Miski saw it all rippling further and further out. And rather than exhilaration—though there was that as well—there was an anxiety: How to grab hold of this moment, this great burst of visibility, and direct it in a way that would bring about something more than the sugar rush of symbolic wins? Every day that June and July gave reason to feel this strange blend of pride and wariness. What to make of a company like Lululemon, which sold $168 leggings, trumpeting that it was supporting an effort to "unveil historical erasure and resist capitalism"? Or the decision to take Aunt Jemima off a syrup bottle, remove the Confederate bars and cross from the Mississippi flag, or cancel the show *Cops* after thirty-two seasons? Or the vision of Jamie Dimon, CEO of JPMorgan Chase, solemnly taking a knee in front of a giant bank vault at a local Chase branch? How to see past the performance, the yard signs and kente cloth, and focus on what was actually going to change people's lives, and maybe even stop the killing?

Miski, who uses they/them pronouns, was not a newcomer to the feeling of being lifted up and then dropped. And they were determined to create leverage out of this national catharsis—a Pew Research Center survey in early June found that two-thirds of Americans said they supported the movement, including 60 percent of white people. But the work would have to happen locally and, most critically, Miski knew, in a way that avoided the sort of oscillations that had become a distraction in the past. There was nothing symbolic about what Miski and many of the other activists wanted. They believed that American policing, born as an institution in the nineteenth century in part—at least in the South—to catch runaway slaves, could never overcome this original sin simply through reform. Policing, in their eyes, was a tool of social control meant to route Black people into prison. Full stop. And yet in city after city, the police received the biggest share of the budget, without question and with disregard for the disproportionate harm they inflicted on Black and brown people. The maximal position on the question of what to do about this reality was called abolition, eliminating police departments completely and replacing them with a new model for public safety guided by the community's needs. A tactic on the way to abolition was defund, which meant moving money away from the police and toward other social services. These were real demands. Activists wanted to shift the thoughtless and automatic way that funds were doled out to the eighteen thousand police departments in the country. But first, they needed power, and as the democracy seekers in Tahrir Square learned all too well a decade before, attaining it was harder than protest.

MISKI NOOR WAS originally from Somalia but had lived in Minneapolis from the age of fourteen. They had moved through life with that immigrant's capacity to inhabit different worlds at once. "I'm Muslim. I'm queer, I identify as a gender-nonconforming person. I'm just somebody who lives at the intersection of a lot of marginalized identities," Miski told me. Their appearance was always self-confident and always tinged with some flair. Enormous green circular earrings would dangle off Miski's ears, or aviator glasses would take up half their face. And they had an easy laugh, which proved useful once they became the spokesperson for the city's Black Lives Matter chapter.

After majoring in political science and African American studies at the University of Minnesota, Miski had worked with a nonprofit to help resettle immigrants before ending up in the offices of Keith Ellison, the progressive representative who was also the first congressman to be sworn in with his hand on a Koran. Miski dealt with constituents, handling casework, and pretty quickly began to feel the limits of what was possible in their role as the proxy for a legislator. So in 2012, Miski quit the political realm altogether and became a pharmacy technician, happy to have a day job while they thought about a better way to make an impact—including by running for their neighborhood association. It was an election, Miski proudly told me, that they won. It was then, in the summer of 2014, that the news erupted about Michael Brown, an eighteen-year-old in the St. Louis suburb of Ferguson who was killed by the police, his barely covered body left in the street for hours. And as Miski put it, it was "like somebody had pressed the go button on Black liberation."

Miski's roommate turned their kitchen into the headquarters of the Black Lives Matter Minneapolis chapter, and for the next two years it was a hub of frenetic activity. Each new death pushed them out into the streets, a rhythm that mirrored the frequency of the hashtag that shot up out of the tear gas of Ferguson. In fact the dynamic of the movement in those years can best be understood by looking at the quantitative traces left by that slogan.

Patrisse Cullors, a Los Angeles–based activist, first used #Black LivesMatter on July 13, 2013. She had seen a Facebook post written by Alicia Garza, a friend and fellow community organizer from San Francisco, that ended with the words "Black people. I love you. I love us. We matter. Our lives matter." The idea was to promote it as a rallying cry, and they pulled in a third activist friend, Opal Tometi, who helped them set up Facebook and Twitter accounts encouraging people to share stories of why #BlackLivesMatter. It didn't work. No one paid much attention to the hashtag for at least another year— despite some high-profile killings, like that of Eric Garner, who was put in a choke hold by a police officer on Staten Island, repeating the words "I can't breathe" eleven times until he lost consciousness. That month, July 2014, #BlackLivesMatter appeared in only 398 tweets. Less than a month later, Michael Brown was shot in Ferguson. Still, the hashtag barely registered, even as #Ferguson and #MikeBrown helped draw attention to the clashes and helped protesters, who were in the streets facing down police in armored tanks, shape a narrative through videos and images and minute-by-minute tweets. (Egyptian revolutionaries, following along on Twitter, offered advice about how to handle tear gas: wash your eyes with milk or Coca-Cola, not water.)

It was only on November 25, 2014, as the tension in Ferguson subsided, and a full sixteen months after its coinage, that #BlackLives Matter became the unifying cry, online and off. That was the day after a grand jury declined to indict the officer who shot Michael Brown, and it was also three days after a Cleveland police officer killed Tamir Rice, a twelve-year-old who was playing with a toy gun. There were 172,772 mentions of the hashtag. And from there it took off. In the three previous months, the hashtag averaged fewer than 1,500 daily mentions; in the three months after, it averaged more than 30,000 a day. But the spikes were even more revealing. When a few days later the police officer whose choke hold led to Eric Garner's death went free, #BlackLivesMatter appeared 189,210 times on Twitter. It was mentioned 160,810 times the following day, too. Then the hashtag began showing up all over the country, on signs carried by over a hundred Black congressional aides who walked off the job in protest and in sports arenas where NBA players wore shirts underneath their jerseys that were printed with the words, "I can't breathe."

Looking at a graph of hashtag mentions over the next year and a half, you can see that the spikes were each correlated to a death—on April 19, 2015, Freddie Gray dies in Baltimore from injuries sustained in the back of a police van, more than 40,000 tweets; on June 17, a shooting in a Charleston, South Carolina, church by a white supremacist kills nine people, nearly 100,000; on July 13, Sandra Bland is found hanged in her prison cell three days after being stopped for a minor traffic violation, 125,000. On the day Philando Castile was killed in his car in a suburb of St. Paul, July 6, 2016, the hashtag was used 250,000 times and would soon reach a daily peak of 1.1 million.

Every movement needs such moments. They provoke and then produce action. We don't live our lives with constant awareness of these issues—even those most potentially affected by them avert their gaze. It's the moments that force a visceral reckoning with the violence. It was the shattered face of Emmett Till that helped launch the struggle for civil rights in 1955. But there was a danger, which the activists began to feel, in their dependence on these instances of sadness and rage to keep the movement aloft. "I think what people were witnessing was a community grieving," Patrisse Cullors told me. "And the response to the killing was like, at any moment, we could be next and it literally felt like we were trying to save our lives and we were the only ones trying to save our lives." But she also told me that her biggest regret in those years was not having "copyrighted" the hashtag that she had first used, by which I think she meant that it took on an unpredictable life of its own, driven by the desire for emotional release that had become social media's single and overwhelming mode.

An analysis of the #BlackLivesMatter tweets conducted in early 2016 by the Center for Media & Social Impact at American University confirmed this fear about the potential downside of the movement's virality. As an issue, police brutality—unlike, say, income inequality—was "extremely well-suited to internet-based activism," being "concrete, discrete in its manifestations, and above all, visual." The same dynamic worked to the benefit of the We Are All Khaled Said page. The report's conclusion, however, made the downside clear: "Activists may be somewhat limited in the extent to which they can generate large-scale online debate by themselves." One of the study's authors, Charlton McIlwain, an NYU professor, elaborated on this when I spoke to him. "If there was not a death, if there was not a catalyzing event, there was relatively little conversation on social media," McIlwain said. "And I think that for me that was a sign of the limitation."

In Minneapolis, Miski and the local Black Lives Matter chapter saw just how debilitating the need to ride these waves could be. In November 2015, the police killing of Jamar Clark, who some onlookers said was handcuffed and facedown when he was shot, led to Miski's group occupying the city's fourth police precinct for eighteen days. They camped out in freezing weather, attempting to sustain attention with their bodies. They demanded that the police release the dashcam and bodycam tapes of the incident, that the Department of Justice investigate, and that the police officers be charged with a crime. In the end they did manage to achieve two out of their three goals, Miski said: the tapes were made public, and an investigation was launched. But there were no wider repercussions, and the whole process had been depleting. It was obvious the conditions that had led to Clark's death hadn't changed. A lot of activists came to feel this way. Even Obama, at the end of his presidency, expressed his exasperation with the movement's limited tool kit, at one point telling protesters, "You can't just keep on yelling." By the fifth anniversary of Ferguson, though it was true that almost $100 million had been spent by police departments all over the country on body cameras, a report found that in Missouri, where it all began, Black people were being stopped by the police 5 percent more and white people were being stopped 11 percent less than they had been in 2013.

"We were tired of mobilizing over and over again in the face of Black death, and making either instrumental or symbolic demands that never got us the wind that would keep a mass of people engaged,"

Miski told me. And it all took a serious toll. Not long after the occupation, Miski was admitted to the hospital and ended up needing four blood transfusions. "A lot of us were suicidal or depressed," Miski said. "And we were like, okay, if we're actually doing work for Black liberation, we have to do this in ways that are sustainable. And that are not just responsive or reactive."

THERE WEREN'T MANY MODELS for stepping away from this reactiveness. But one group in Miami, the Dream Defenders, had tried, and Miski looked to them as an example of activism that wasn't strapped to the erratic ups and downs. The Dream Defenders, made up mostly of college students, gained national attention in 2013 when they staged an occupation, similar to the one Miski was involved in years later. They spent thirty-one days chanting outside the polished wood doors of the governor's office in Tallahassee, Florida, so that he might reconsider the state's Stand Your Ground law. This was the permissive set of gun regulations that allowed the courts to acquit the killer of Trayvon Martin, the teenager shot while walking home from a 7-Eleven holding nothing but a bag of Skittles and a can of iced tea. For all the publicity, the Dream Defenders weren't particularly successful, and by the summer of 2015, when Rachel Gilmer, a longtime organizer, became their chief of strategy, she found a group stripped of its vitality, tired of having to keep pace with the demands of social media and attempting to attract the bright lights that had, for a brief, exhilarating moment, shined on them. The activists felt as if their priorities, their very self-conception, had been molded by this chase, and they needed to just stop for a minute. So that fall, the Dream Defenders, led then by Phillip Agnew, who had co-founded the group as a recent graduate of Florida A&M University, agreed to stage what they called a Blackout.

In a post-Ferguson moment, when national magazines used follower counts on Twitter to create top ten lists of the most effective activists in the country, Rachel and Phillip chose to log off. It had been too easy "to mistake popularity for power," Rachel said. Anyone who worked for the organization would have to delete social media apps from their phone and stay off the platforms for what they decided would be a total of ten weeks, starting on September 21 and ending December 1. This would be a chance to see who they were off-line, to figure out what they called their "DNA." Avoiding the apps was essential to this process, Rachel wrote in a note to the group. "Social media is constantly fueling and draining our egos—making us feel hyper belittled and narcissistic at the same damn time." The damage was not just psychological. Social media was hurting their ability to connect in productive ways. "Movement relationships have eroded online, because we are competing for airtime," all because airtime itself had been made scarce, a commodity they were all vying for. "And I think the scariest part about all of this, is that we don't realize this dynamic exists or at the very least, believe that we are in control of it."

Taking a few steps away taught them so much during those weeks, Rachel and Phillip told me. At exactly the same time that Miski's group was throwing itself against the barricades in Minneapolis, the Dream Defenders were hunkering down in Miami. They saw, for one thing, just how dependent they had become on the violent images and videos that punctuated their activism. "It's created a landscape where our movement is more about death than about life," Rachel said. Even Darnell Moore, an activist who had organized Freedom Rides to Ferguson for social media influencers, hoping they might tweet and post widely about the protests, agreed with this assessment, telling me he worried that the movement was tapping into and profiting from a sick and preexisting phenomenon in American culture, a "trauma porn" that "spectacularizes Black death."

They also came to see more clearly that Twitter was not the democratizing platform it presented itself as. The model of a medium with a million entry points was attractive to the activist Left, which had been moving toward horizontalism long before social media. The trend could even be traced back to the 1930s as a response to the authoritarian tendencies of the Communist Party and Communist-led organizations. The newness of the 1960s New Left was in part a rejection of this top-down approach. And by the time the Occupy Wall

Street protests happened, in 2011, activists had practically made a fetish of their leaderlessness; they literally disdained microphones. For Cullors, Garza, and Tometi, any movement had to be as inclusive as possible, and particularly welcoming of the queer and transgender activists who had been marginalized in the past.

But if Twitter was supposed to foreground the collective, it frequently had the opposite effect, elevating certain individuals, and for all the wrong reasons. DeRay Mckesson was a case in point. When Mckesson, a protester turned media star, got to Ferguson, he had eight hundred followers on Twitter, and as I'm writing this, six years later, he has a million. Mckesson intuitively understood what Twitter wanted. He saw that it prized expressions of intimacy, and he offered a play-by-play of his thoughts and feelings as he made his way through the embattled city. He detailed everything he was observing, often with photos and videos. And he wrote in a direct and engaging style. When he wasn't tweeting out dramatic scenes of resistance, he would write messages meant to uplift ("Love is the Why") and jolt ("Justice is not an abstract concept. Justice is a living Mike Brown. Justice is Tamir playing outside again. Justice is Darren Wilson in jail"). And after weeks of being on the ground in Ferguson, working out of coffee shops and sleeping on couches, he had cultivated a huge following. He understood that on Twitter he was a character, and he began wearing a blue puffy Patagonia vest wherever he went. The blue vest worked better than the red shoes and red shirt he had initially tried, and it soon became part of his brand.

His celebrity drove the other activists nuts. Mckesson became the face of the movement, profiled in *The New York Times Magazine*, interviewed on cable television, and eventually invited to the Obama White House so often that he told a reporter it no longer made him nervous to be there. Many veiled and sometimes outwardly open attacks were directed against him. He was seen to be taking undue credit, especially by the three women who claimed to have founded the movement. Alicia Garza wrote a long screed called "A Herstory of the #Black LivesMatter Movement" lamenting "the charismatic Black men many are rallying around these days."

This was more than mere pettiness. Twitter, which the activists did not own or control, had created a system built on scarcity, and it didn't seem right that those who knew best how to game it should become the default leaders. What made matters worse is that Mckesson didn't just succeed at Twitter; he then valorized it as an unprecedented tool for making change. In this way he was a bit like the Wael Ghonim of Black Lives Matter. For Rachel and Phillip social media was draining; for Mckesson it was empowering. "I've always thought of Twitter as the friend that's always awake," he has written, and Twitter, as he experienced it, "has amplified the voice of the individual, always reminding each individual that she exists within a larger whole." There was no need for an organization "to begin protest," he asserted in a 2015 interview. Instead, "you are enough to start a movement. Individual people can come together around things that they know are unjust. And they can spark change. Your body can be part of the protest; you don't need a VIP pass to protest. And Twitter allowed that to happen." There would be time later to decide on a set of demands. For him, the platform had enabled "community." The problem was that the community being built had its own particular rules, and those rules gave him unequal standing, crowned him without any accountability. He might have felt as if it were "organic," but every utterance was skewed in one direction and with one overriding goal, even if subconscious: to acquire more followers.

Rachel thought the whole movement had a sort of DeRay derangement syndrome—they were all driven mad by his naked self-promotion—when really he was just the most visible symptom of a bigger problem. "We kind of used him as a piñata when other people were on Twitter in exactly the same way." All of it was a distraction, which she suddenly saw more clearly during the Blackout. "I think social media created a sense of false camaraderie among people," she told me. "I think we debated, but in a petty way. What is the short quippy thing you can say about somebody else's politics in 140 characters? But that isn't strategy. And we didn't get a space to do that."

When the Blackout opened up that space, the Dream Defenders began to really connect with their community. They started listening.

And what they heard surprised them. For one thing, as Rachel went door-to-door to talk to people in the poorer neighborhoods of Miami, she quickly found that the dream of defunding or abolishing the police was not a shared one.

"People were basically, like, we need *more* police," Rachel said. "And it was really jarring for me. I remember one conversation I had with a woman who had bullet holes in her car from when her son was killed, and who was I to convince her on police abolition? It's not like I have an alternative. So all of that was just very grounding for us as we thought about what the Dream Defenders' role was, who we were supposed to be in our relationship to communities, and social media definitely obfuscated how we were thinking about those things."

This upended their accepted wisdom. But, Rachel saw, it also pointed a way forward. If she truly felt abolition was the answer then the work would have to be local and would have to start with showing people there was another way. They had to actively collect and build a constituency, as opposed to waiting for a moment of outrage.

Phillip, the Dream Defenders founder, had a similar insight. For him, the experience of the Blackout had been a lesson in the varieties of power. Borrowing a concept from Joseph Nye, the political scientist, he now came to understand social media as a form of "soft power," a force that shapes culture through argument and story. But there was also "hard power," which Nye, in assessing the capacity of different nation-states, characterized as military and economic might. For movements, hard power was the ability to lobby for legislation, elect sympathetic political leaders, get resources allocated toward your cause. Social media, Phillip now saw more clearly, was good at building soft power. But when it came to hard power, it could do very little. And if for Nye every successful state needed a mix of the two, this was doubly true of social movements, which didn't start with a store of either.

The only way to build hard power was on the ground. As Rachel put it, "You just can't shortcut organizing." It made them want to drop the performance, the race for followers, even the reflex to always make their actions public—they would think carefully about if and when to use tactics like occupations and sit-ins. Phillip, once he emerged from the Blackout in early 2016, even saw the advantage of cultivating a more secluded space for conversation and planning. Social media was about "followship and diffusion of responsibility." Real leadership would come off-line. "We must re-embrace the great strategic value in everyone not knowing everything we do, when we do it, and whom we do it with."

IN MINNEAPOLIS, MISKI, physically wrecked, came to a similar conclusion. The two years of nonstop protesting had led to very little change. The pattern was the same in their city as elsewhere: activism would swell and then subside, and in spite of all this expended energy, their objectives would come to seem too small in the face of more foundational problems. Pinpointing what those challenges were and how exactly to attack them without ending up needing blood transfusions became the goal of Miski's group of friends. They were trying to solve a dilemma that Keeanga-Yamahtta Taylor, a professor at Princeton and close observer of Black Lives Matter, identified for me. It was undeniable, she said, that the movement had a salutary effect when it first appeared in the mid-2010s; concepts like institutional racism were shot into the American bloodstream like never before. But the progress would all be fleeting, empty words unless the activists found a way to "collectively assess, discuss, or ponder what the movement is or should be"—unless they did the work, that is, that couldn't be done on Twitter.

Miski and six friends decided to start a new sort of organization that would in every way reject the social media metabolism. They called it the Black Visions Collective, and eventually just Black Visions. They spent 2016 and 2017 exploring ideas that were sometimes large and abstract and other times micro-focused on how to pull the levers of power in their city. They began looking into transformative justice, which was also the alternative that Rachel had landed on in Miami, using counseling and mediation methods to defuse minor conflicts before they turned into altercations with the police. They brought in an expert on the subject to train them in how to break cycles of violence, and they started speaking honestly among themselves to determine what their principles should be as a group. "How do you practice punishment in your own personal life? If somebody does you wrong, what is your reaction?" The questions were intimate and intense, unhurried work among friends, but it helped them "get aligned," Miski said.

The seven core members also became more involved in local Minneapolis politics. Drawing attention at a national level had been the driving impetus of the earlier Black Lives Matter protests, which had relied on getting that hashtag to spike. Now it was clear that if their focal point was police funding, it would need to be a local effort, dependent on a partnership with the city council and the mayor's office, where these budgetary decisions were made. They would need to learn the mechanics and make some allies.

This was organizing as it had long been done, and they got good at it. It was also, in its way, what separated Minneapolis from Cairo. Whereas the Middle East lacked a democratic or grassroots political tradition—and had no way to even begin imagining how to create one—this wasn't the case in America. In Egypt the denizens of Tahrir Square were starting from the very beginning and with the wrong tools. But there was a long history of African American organizing that long predated Silicon Valley. Miski and their friends got to know city council members and their aides, inundated them with research material, visited their offices, and, maybe most important, brought people out to hearings when the budget was being discussed, arguing in forum after forum against the belief that all the police needed were a few more bodycams. All this happened without much fanfare and largely off-line.

In one of their earliest wins, in 2018, Black Visions managed to move more than a million dollars from the police budget to the health department to create what would be called the Office of Violence Prevention. It wasn't a lot of money, but it was a chance to build up an alternative and show the police that the stream of money directed at them unquestioningly every year could be siphoned off. The office would look for public health solutions as opposed to punitive ones—sending social workers, for example, when a homeless man started acting erratically, rather than dispatching the cops. This was accompanied by a change in the makeup of the city council itself. In 2017 they helped elect some new members who shared their progressive agenda, like Keith Ellison's son Jeremiah Ellison, who won one of the thirteen seats on the city council, and Andrea Jenkins, the first openly trans Black woman to be elected to public office in the United States. Black Visions was by no means a single-issue organization, but changing the system of policing was their priority. It was where they wanted to direct their energy the next time people began caring about Black lives. "We were always thinking about the next trigger moment," Miski said. "And making sure that when it happened, we'd have even more people ready to build towards abolition."

They also intuited what Rachel and Phillip had learned over the course of their Blackout: that Twitter was not a good place to develop ideas. They tended toward privacy among themselves. Some of them lived together in the same house. And they purposely kept the core group small, only very deliberately and slowly expanding their membership. If they came across a particularly engaged person at one of their events, they would have one-on-one sessions, working with them and building a relationship before bringing them into a wider membership pool that, even by the summer of 2020, numbered no more than a few dozen. They talked in person (or on Zoom once the pandemic hit), and when they couldn't, they used Signal, the encrypted chat app, to solve problems and plan. "It means sometimes writing whole paragraphs, but we have definitely made decisions, moved work, or come to some sort of consensus via Signal," Miski told me. If Black Lives Matter found itself contorted by social media's impulses, Black Visions set its own rhythm.

For this reason, in the days immediately following George Floyd's murder, Miski and the others spent little time on the large protests. Instead, they tried to build on their last three years of work. To use the terms Phillip Agnew borrowed from Joseph Nye, they were trying to harness the remarkable soft power generated by Floyd's death and turn it into the hard power needed to move the city council toward committing to something as inconceivable as abolition. This meant discipline. They turned to the city council members, especially the ones with whom they had developed relationships, and lobbied them. They called in the evenings once the protest started, sending over detailed plans to turn off the spigot of funds flowing to the police and instead make the Office of Violence Prevention a more substantial institution, capable of being a first responder and accountable to the community itself. And to reinforce these private actions, and make sure the city council was paying attention, Black Visions also staged a sit-in in front of the house of the young, progressive mayor, Jacob Frey, using shame as a strategic counterbalance.

And when their intentions were made clear—with the incredible blare of protests around the country still very audible—they let these city councillors know that they were planning a rally on June 8 at the city's Powderhorn Park. They were calling it the Path Forward, and what they hoped was to get local leaders then and there to pledge to end the Minneapolis Police Department. They gathered all the moral weight they could from that moment and lifted it onto the shoulders of those council members.

Soft and hard power came together under the park's giant ash trees. A thousand people showed up. Miski, wearing high-top sneakers and a jumpsuit in the bright yellow of the Black Lives Matter movement, read from their phone: "We have had citizen review boards, body cameras and a black chief, but we are still here, watching black people get murdered and teargassed in our streets." And there on a stage fronted by a giant sign that read "DEFUND POLICE" in block letters, less than two weeks after the killing of George Floyd, nine of the thirteen city council members (a veto-proof majority) did what would have been almost impossible for activists to imagine five years earlier: they promised to dismantle their city's law enforcement. Lisa Bender, the president of the city council, spoke words that startled even Miski: "Our commitment is to end our city's toxic relationship with the Minneapolis Police Department, to end policing as we know it, and to re-create systems of public safety that actually keep us safe."

———

THAT SUMMER, words and concepts once considered too radical crackled and burst out into the open all over the country. "Black Lives Matter means something very, very different now than it meant on May 25, 2020," Colin Wayne Leach, a psychologist and professor at Barnard College who has studied the protests, told me. He was referring, of course, to the date of George Floyd's killing, the turning point. "It's a meme now. And the question is whether the activists can use this to their benefit, or whether they'll suffer from it." A meme was an idea that could be endlessly replicated and repurposed, tossed from hand to hand. The beauty of it was that it touched everyone, and the danger was how ephemeral it could all be. This was a time when the air was suffused with questions that demanded immediate answers. The #MeToo movement in the fall of 2017 had a similar thrust, stories of sexual harassment shared on social media that set off exposure after exposure of men accused of everything from rape to making suggestive jokes at work. These powerful figures were taken down one by one. But once the fever broke, one could legitimately ask, what had changed? The meme had streaked through trailing fire, and perhaps left an aura of heightened sensitivity in the places it burned, but had it changed the situation for a woman working on a factory floor whose supervisor regularly whispered what he wanted from her in her ear?

The fever was the context for what happened in Miski's city. And Minneapolis was the clearest proof that perhaps this would be more than a moment, that the changes would last. There were other examples in June and July. The mayor of Atlanta moved forward with plans to close the Atlanta City Detention Center, the city's despised downtown jail, and turn the building into a "center for justice and equity." In New York, the state legislature repealed a fifty-year-old law that allowed police officers' records to be kept secret. Dozens of police departments pledged to ban choke holds. Two weeks after the protests started, Congress unveiled the Justice in Policing Act of 2020, which included a number of measures that would make it easier for police to be prosecuted for misconduct—Speaker of the House Nancy Pelosi and then Senate minority leader Chuck Schumer, kente cloth draped over their necks, took a knee and bowed their heads after announcing the bill.

But for Rachel, in Miami, the excitement of the summer only thinly covered a thrumming worry. A younger generation of protesters, who never experienced Ferguson or what came after—who missed the Blackout—suddenly entered the ranks of her organization with "burn-it-down energy," she said, and she was concerned that the "shortcuts and the purism" that had once derailed the movement would return. Rachel herself had evolved, as she saw it, from someone who in 2016 voted for Jill Stein, the spoiler Green Party candidate ("I get it now, I was young"), to a pragmatic supporter of Joe Biden. The Democratic candidate was a bitter pill, for sure, but she understood just how devastating the alternative would be—a Trump win would upend all her organizing work. The Dream Defenders were now tactical in their approach. Before Floyd's death, they had been busy working on the races of three Florida district attorneys, canvassing door-to-door for candidates like Monique Worrell in Orange County, who wanted to end mass incarceration, put more checks on the police, and rewrite bail policies. When the large protests began, Rachel tried to tune out the noise and keep the activists focused on these races, and they managed to help get Worrell elected.

The Dream Defenders also turned out hundreds of people to county commission meetings in the summer and fall to push the issue of policing, though here, too, there was an awareness of how far they had to go. "I think our communities aren't fully behind it. I don't think they understand it," Rachel said. "We sit down even with some of the most progressive county commissioners, and their response is like, okay, I get it, you don't want us to build this new jail. And what exactly are we supposed to be doing instead?" She wanted to workshop the language the activists used, emphasizing the investments that could be made with the money that would otherwise be spent on a police helicopter, as opposed to threatening to take something away. Defunding might not be the best articulation of this idea. "I'm honestly less committed to the words and more committed to the concept."

Rachel fretted about preserving this work and its gains, especially as the hashtag spiked again. Other activists worried as well. Allen Kwabena Frimpong, an experienced organizer and an artist who had worked with the Black Lives Matter chapter in New York City, told me that there were moments during the summer of 2020 that reminded him of what he'd heard about the mass protests and riots after Martin Luther King Jr.'s assassination, when for all the expressed pain the Black part of every city got an MLK Jr. Boulevard and not much else. That came to mind as he saw people thrill to the sight of the words Black Lives Matter printed on the wood of NBA basketball courts. "Those of us who have been organizing for quite some time could see this coming," he told me. "Those symbolic actions actually end up entrenching the status quo even further, because it creates the illusion that the work of addressing all these intractable issues is done." The symbols, he said, become pats on the head.

In the summer of 2020, Rachel claimed she saw only small pockets of activists who seemed aware of this and were thinking long term. One of them, she said, was in Minneapolis. "That was the result of years of strategy," Rachel said. "They stacked the county commission with people who were aligned with our movement. And that led to what happened when the protest erupted. But in general, overall, across the country, I think there's a leadership gap. The movement needs to take a lot more responsibility for being on the ground, identifying leaders in the protests that are coming up, thinking through their demands. And that's bigger than just writing 'defund the police' on social media."

She knew the way attention could rise and fall, and in the end she felt it was a good thing for the newer protesters, filled with revolution, to experience both the energy of the summer and the heartache of its limits. "They've now lived through a movement moment, seeing that it is necessary, not sufficient."

BY THE FALL, the placards were still up, but something had shifted. The thirty-five-foot-tall yellow letters, spelling out "Black

Lives Matter" in Washington, D.C., on a stretch of street in view of the White House and in front of the Trump Tower in Manhattan, still popped against the asphalt, though violent smears of black paint had defaced the words in New York many times over. The protests themselves had largely tapered off by the end of July, and where they did persist, they had taken on a more threatening tone, especially in cities like Portland and Seattle where mostly young white anarchists were running wild, marching menacingly through suburban streets. Even though an accounting of all the demonstrations from May 24 to August 22 by the Armed Conflict Location & Event Data Project found that 93 percent of them were free from any violence or property damage, the meme, uncontrollable as a meme can be, began to signify for some people danger and chaos. Activists themselves seemed uncomfortable with certain mutations of the meme, like the strange afterlife of the victims. Breonna Taylor's image appeared on T-shirts and mugs and the cover of glossy fashion magazines—there was even a "women's empowerment event" in Louisville called BreonnaCon, which included a "Bre-B-Q." But maybe most dispiriting of all was that when a Pew survey took the country's temperature on Black Lives Matter in September, the unprecedented support seen in June had dropped precipitously, from 67 percent to 55 percent (among white people it had plunged from 60 percent to 45 percent). Even production of the show *Cops* was back on in September, three months after it was very publicly canceled.

And in Minneapolis, Miski's story had taken a turn as well.

A few weeks after their pledge, the city council voted unanimously to draft a referendum that would decide the fate of the police department. But before the question could be put on November's ballot, a group of city volunteers appointed by the chief district judge weighed in. It was their task, as the Minneapolis Charter Commission, to assess any alteration to the charter, which was essentially the city's constitution. And they had problems with abolition. Crime was increasing in Minneapolis, and there were plenty of voices calling for more police on the street, not fewer. For the commissioners, it all felt too rushed. And then the Minneapolis *Star Tribune* released a poll that found strong support for the idea of shifting money away from the police budget and toward social services but clear opposition to dissolving the police—a position held by 50 percent of Black people. In early September, the commission voted to override the city council. There would be no referendum.

It was maddening to Miski that a handful of unelected, mostly white people who would seem to have a vested interest in maintaining the status quo had undermined their work. It felt like an undemocratic trump card played just as they were sure all their organizing was paying off, a system designed with a fail-safe to keep them from succeeding. But Miski also faced an uncomfortable reality as well, the same one Rachel had come to terms with in Miami: once the high of responding to George Floyd's murder subsided, most people did not understand or like the notion of abolishing the police. The commission was far from alone in its skepticism of a world without cops.

Miski was not deterred. They understood this as simply the next phase in a cycle that had now become very familiar. "There's a time after Ferguson, there's a time after Mike Brown, after Sandra Bland, after Jamar Clark, when attention starts to fade, and that's when organizers still have to dig in," Miski said. "This is when we still have to talk to the community; this is when we still have to work on our narrative strategy. We need to continue to organize. So I don't feel defeated." Black Visions meanwhile had raised an extraordinary thirty million dollars by the fall and was figuring out how to transform itself into a multimillion-dollar organization without losing its soul. Miski said the sudden lull was welcome. The group needed time to gather together and take a breath after the tumultuous summer, to assess their disappointments and achievements, to figure out how to best and most fairly use their new resources. They also understood what venues would work for this part—the corner conversations, their private Signal groups. Miski even fantasized about a Blackout of their own. "I've talked to Rachel about that," Miski said. "We've been thinking about what a Blackout looks like for us."

As far as the referendum on abolishing the police went, Miski was intent on getting it in front of the people of Minneapolis the following year, on the ballot in 2021. To this end, Black Visions built a campaign around what Miski called a "people's agenda, a people's budget, and a people's charter." The group planned to head out into the streets and get as many citizens as possible to sign a petition asking the city to give them a voice in the matter. And collecting signatures would serve another purpose. "We're going to talk to thousands and thousands of people in Minneapolis about what safety looks like," Miski said. "Because if we do that, and we get folks to give us their signatures and say they want this on the ballot next year, there's no way the charter commission or anybody else can stop it from being on the ballot." The canvassing would also try to shift the framing of the issue from "abolition" to what they were calling "community-led safety." When Miski told me about how they envisioned the petition not just reaching people and pulling the movement together but also creating small moments of communication that could build a constituency for a cause nobody could have imagined only ten years earlier, it brought to mind the working men and women in 1830s England who were pushing a people's charter of their own.

The more immediate fight Miski was gearing up for when we spoke at the end of 2020 was over the city's budget, how to funnel more money away from the police and toward the Office of Violence Prevention that the group had helped create in 2018. Ever since it was established, the city had offered no more than a million dollars every year toward its operation. But in early December, largely as a result of Black Visions and their growing political influence—members of the city council now felt they owed the group something—4.5 percent of the police budget, nearly eight million dollars, was diverted to the new office to pay for a team of mental health professionals who could respond to situations that had previously been left to the police. "That felt like a win," Miski said. The group had earned it—by applying pressure, making late-night phone calls, and always showing up in force to those community meetings. They were drawing on a different metabolism and, even if slow, it was working.

Epilogue

TABLES

———

IN *THE HUMAN CONDITION,* her 1958 philosophical treatise, Hannah Arendt fretted about the eventual disappearance of what she called "the common world." What exactly she meant by this phrase was always a little vague, but it seemed to signify for her all the concrete and stable elements—the institutions and artifacts, from schools to street signs—that constitute our shared reality. Her book was a response to what was the then-accelerating space race and push for automation that Arendt felt, presciently, would cause people to decouple from this common world (to, literally, escape the bounds of Earth) and move toward synthetic and virtual versions of reality in which the very definition of what it meant to be human would be utterly changed.

I am drawn to this idea that what saves us all from being atomized and adrift is a set of binding elements. For Arendt these elements were the prerequisite to politics, to maintaining society and culture, and, also, to living a meaningful life. At one point in the book she uses an extended metaphor to describe what it would be like if we lost them: "The weirdness of this situation resembles a spiritualistic séance where a number of people gathered around a table might suddenly, through some magic trick, see the table vanish from their midst, so that two persons sitting opposite each other were no longer separated but also would be entirely unrelated to each other by anything tangible."

You are all there together, sharing a table, eating lunch on it, getting angry, and slamming your fist down or seeing your spit fly over it or shaking hands over its grainy wood. And then it's gone, and you are nothing to one another, just people sitting around awkwardly. Arendt was saying that it was the existence of the table itself that connected us, that made a group, a community. And I think her use of a table as a metaphor was intentional: the context for this coming together was a human-made thing, something sawed and carved with thought, an object whose primary purpose was to draw individuals into deliberation, their faces turned toward one another.

This is what I've been searching for in our pre-digital past, these tables, and I found them in letters and samizdat and zines. For Arendt, the common world was more generally about what made humans human, but her thinking would also seem to apply to any group of people whose aspirations sit outside society's norms, who need a means to relate to each other, separate from everyone else. It's the tables that allow for new identities and possibilities to form.

When the internet began to colonize every corner of our lives, the promise was an infinitely vast room filled with such tables. But I didn't find very many of them when I began searching in the mid-2010s. Only destinations we all called "social." Much of the problem, I realized, was a semantic one. What had "social" become? We could join Facebook or Twitter and enter the rat's maze of rewards and punishment that made these sites' business models run and end up feeling quite alone, distracted, and confused. We've seen what this did to the activists of the Arab Spring and Black Lives Matter who had arrived with the best intentions, to pull up a chair, and found themselves knocked flat on their faces.

By the end of the decade, though, this misreading of what "social" signified was pretty well cleared up, and very few people had any illusions anymore about what it meant to interact on Facebook—including Mark Zuckerberg himself. In an extraordinary post in March 2019 in which he announced a new direction for his company, Zuckerberg acknowledged the category confusion. "Over the last 15 years," he wrote, his platform had helped people "connect with friends, communities, and interests in the digital equivalent of a town square." But it turns out that Facebook's users, woken up to the bustle and noise of the street vendors, the town criers, and the endless gossip, wanted a different sort of social sphere. "People increasingly also want to connect privately in the digital equivalent of the living room."

This "living room" sounds a lot like our table. As Zuckerberg described it, "People should have simple, intimate places where they have clear control over who can communicate with them and confidence that no one else can access what they share." In their seclusion and focus, these living rooms would be a break from what he said his site's objective had always been, to "accumulate friends or followers." It goes without saying that Arendt would be appalled by the notion of accumulation as the raison d'être of any social environment. And it's certainly not the way to nurture radical ideas.

In recent years, both degenerates and dissidents have come to this conclusion on their own, finding ways to repurpose new platforms like Discord, or older technologies like email chains, to provide them with what they needed. The desire for tables is human and has never gone away, and it's particularly strong when you wake up and realize that your own interests and concerns might skew sideways. For those early digital pioneers, this is what the internet was all about. They imagined they were building communes, off the grid and among their own, a pixelated reconstitution of the tribe. We have strayed from this original vision, and in truth it was always essentially a fantasy, a mescaline trip in the desert. But if we now understand just how necessary tables are, where can we find them today, and where might they be located in the future? Radical change can't wait for Zuckerberg to start constructing living rooms.

WHAT IF WE CONCEIVE of social media more broadly, as any digital platform that allows people to communicate with each other? This was what Ethan Zuckerman did as a visiting research scholar at the Knight First Amendment Institute in 2020 when he began a project to map the full breadth of social media. Zuckerman was intent on capturing not just the large landmasses, like Facebook, but also the tiny islands and peninsulas that jutted off the mainland. The former head of the MIT Center for Civic Media, Zuckerman has become something of a Buddha of digital activism, responsible early in his career for creating the pop-up ad, that bane of our online existence, for which he seems to have been atoning ever since. His tendency as a thinker is not to look outside the box necessarily, but to rummage around in it to make sure there aren't any unused tools. That was the impetus for this project. Rather than dream about regulations that might break up Facebook, critics need to look further afield, "identifying platforms that depart from the status quo." As he put it, "There is a diverse space of social media outside of the shadow of the major platforms and we believe it's there where the key to a different future lies."

To begin this search, he pinpointed the elements that make up any social network's character, among them its governance model (what speech is acceptable and who decides), its ideology as a platform (Facebook's, he said, was "connect everyone and maximize shareholder value"), and, most interestingly, what he called its "affordances," what it enables a user to do (share a post, "upvote" a comment, show off a number of "likes"). He believed these were the features that shaped a conversation, and he started using them to build his map, first dividing the full range of social media into broad regions, separate continents, each driven by a different "logic."

He found, for example, a group of platforms that were "local" in their orientation, meaning they hosted chatter around the doings in a neighborhood, like someone searching for a lost cat or pointing out a hawk spotted in a tree or advertising a garage sale. Even among these, using his gauges, he found some differentiation. A site like Nextdoor, for example, functions much like Facebook in its affordances. Anyone can post anything, it instantaneously appears on the site, and then others comment. And, like Facebook, this can sometimes devolve into rants about whether it was racist to assume a Black man was prowling around or whether a new zoning ordinance should pass. There are other sites with this local logic but different governance and affordances, like Front Porch Forum, which was started by a Vermont couple who were looking for support from their neighbors after their son developed cerebral palsy. The site now serves every town in Vermont and a few in New York, Massachusetts, and New Hampshire. Unlike Nextdoor, Front Porch Forum has a team of moderators that check out each post to make sure it adheres to the site's "community-building mission." Also, posts and comments don't appear right away but come bundled once a day, like a local newspaper, with the built-in slowness often leading to more thoughtfulness and fewer fights.

I liked the way Zuckerman was thinking about the architecture of a social network, how it can encourage certain kinds of talk and shut down others. When I asked him to point me toward his map's samizdat archipelago, though, Zuckerman was more circumspect. Mostly, he said, these kinds of private, intense, intimate group conversations happen when people are forced off the larger platforms. "These are groups essentially saying we can't have sufficient free speech in these environments, so we're going to carve out our own spaces," Zuckerman said. His examples of communities doing this were fairly horrifying. He mentioned Mastodon, a Twitter clone that has one critical difference: it is decentralized, meaning that anyone can host their own server node in the network (Mastodon users call these nodes "instances"), freeing groups up to create their own smaller, self-policed versions of Twitter.

At one point in 2017, curious about Mastodon, Zuckerman looked into it and discovered that it had mostly taken off in Japan, and when he dug deeper, he realized this was because one of the largest nodes was made of people interested in lolicon. Lolicon (brace yourself) is an offshoot of manga that consists of sexualized drawings of young girls. Twitter had knocked lolicon adherents off, classifying their hobby as child porn, so they found their way to a different, less restrictive place. The United States saw a similar trend with white supremacists: after Discord kicked them off, many of them went to Gab, another Mastodon node. This pattern was repeated after the storming of the Capitol in the last days of Trump's presidency, with his die-hard band of be-lievers leapfrogging from Parler to Rumble to MeWe to DLive.

I told Zuckerman I needed something a little more pro-social, a place on the map where, say, Black Lives Matter organizers could strategize among themselves about the best way to influence a local city council. "Taiwan," he said. "Look at Taiwan." It turns out Taiwan has been conducting an experiment with just the kinds of platforms I'd been looking for. It all started in 2014 with the Sunflower Movement, when a group of students occupied the parliament building in Taipei for three weeks to protest a trade bill that was about to be signed with China and that they feared would give the menacing superpower too much leverage over their country. As part of the government's attempt to resolve the tensions created by the standoff, it invited Sunflower activists to design a platform that would facilitate communication with Taiwan's youth. A group of civic-minded hackers known as g0v (pronounced "Gov Zero") soon produced vTaiwan, a social media tool for bringing a wider swath of the population into the legislative pro-cess. And powering this tool was a platform called Pol.is, which seemed to flip social media on its head by both incentivizing the ex-pression of a wider range of views and helping to create consensus.

In one of the earliest uses of Pol.is, in 2015, the Taiwanese govern-ment was faced with the question of how to regulate Uber. Young people liked the service, while local taxi drivers resented the competi-tion. Anyone who cared about this issue and wanted to weigh in was invited to join the debate on Pol.is. There, they were presented with a series of statements that ranged across the spectrum of opinion, some proposing Uber be banned altogether, others insisting the market de-cide, and others somewhere in the middle ("I think that Uber is a business model that can create flexible jobs"). Participants could also add their own statements, but they couldn't reply to other people's. To those, they could only indicate "Agree," "Disagree," or "Pass." Pol.is then used the accumulating data to build a real-time map of opinion. At first, this just broke down into large pro- and anti-Uber factions, but as each group looked to bring others along, people started produc-ing less polarizing statements such as "The government should set up a fair regulatory regime" or "It should be permissible for a for-hire driver to join multiple fleets and platforms." The map then began to break up, moving from two parts to seven clusters, each of which represented an opinion that most people thought reasonable and which became the starting point for actual regulation.

Even though Pol.is has been used almost exclusively in these sorts of large-scale democratic debates, what inspired the platform's creation was actually a social movement. Pol.is was dreamed up by a handful of Seattle-based poli-sci geeks, led by Colin Megill, who came to the project not with the skills of a programmer but as someone with a degree in international relations. Megill was motivated to develop it after seeing what was happening to activists: "I was watching a whole bunch of people in the Occupy Wall Street movement all try to talk simultaneously and no one had any idea whether they were speaking for everyone, but everyone thought they were. And that movement did pull itself right apart." His next data point was Tahrir Square. Twitter and Facebook were basically a place for "pillow fights," he said. "But when it came to saying, 'Let's write a constitution,' it was like, that's not really what this tool was built for. This is for pillow fights."

So Megill and his friends thought carefully about how to design a platform that allowed people to visualize their points of difference and areas of agreement. The decision not to permit users to reply to each other's opinion statements was purposeful and had its intended effect. "Think about social media as a soccer stadium. If everyone is just talking across the stadium to everyone else, you've got fistfights," Megill said. "But if a comment has to go onto the field, and everyone has to walk past it single file and add a tick mark, now there's some order imposed." There is still interaction, "but the interactions are producing a lot of helpful data." He said the largest group to test Pol.is has been a leftist German political movement, Aufstehen, in which thirty thousand people worked out their platform.

Megill sees social movements—the drivers of change—as limited in their actions and their ability to evolve and adapt because they rely on tools that only deal in binaries. When you can discern shades of difference, new strategies and alliances open up. "We live along one political dimension because our categories for expressing ourselves and our tools for thinking about ourselves and others are one-dimensional," he said.

POL.IS IS CERTAINLY a kind of social media, and one that Egyptian revolutionaries or Black Lives Matter activists could have made much use of—it could have aided even the emergency room doctors who were trying to harmonize the guidance they were presenting to a confused and fearful public during the pandemic. But it is also essentially a survey app equipped with some helpful data visualization. What people need is to be able to talk.

I saw more promise in another of Zuckerman's broad territories: chat apps like WhatsApp, Discord, iMessage, Snapchat, Slack, Telegram, and Signal. Zuckerman categorized their defining features as "privacy, ephemerality, and community governance," some of the exact qualities that made the pre-digital forms of interactive media so useful. By the end of the 2010s the top four messaging apps had surpassed the top four social networking apps in their number of monthly active users. It's probably the reason Mark Zuckerberg wants to turn Facebook in this direction (and why his purchase of WhatsApp in 2014 now looks so smart).

These chat apps, as we've already seen, can be quite useful for replicating in digital form the sorts of small communities that letter or samizdat or zine writers created among themselves. It's a point often forgotten because we tend to concentrate on their darker aspects—how they evade surveillance or provide a home to pedophiles or hate groups. But they also allow for a certain productive intensity and creativity. The creator of Signal, an elusive anarchist who goes by the name of Moxie Marlinspike, described his platform's role in a *New Yorker* profile in 2020. Because an app like Signal is infamous for its airtight end-to-end encryption, it's easy to forget what all this secrecy is for and to imagine the worst. But Marlinspike sees privacy as a necessary ingredient for the kind of experimentation that makes social change possible. "If I'm dissatisfied with this world—and I think that

I might be—a problem is that you can only desire based on what you know," Marlinspike said. "You have certain experiences in this world, they produce certain desires, those desires reproduce the world. Our reality today just keeps reproducing itself. If you can create different experiences that manifest different desires, then it's possible that those will lead to the production of different worlds."

Marlinspike's app allows people to control the size of their rooms and who can get in. It ensures that the walls are soundproof. For a group of dissidents, this is a wonderful thing. But it's also useful for any group of people who need to figure out how they are going to challenge a status quo, or even just convince themselves that they can.

I recently read about Alyssa Nakken becoming the first woman in the history of Major League Baseball to coach on the field. It turns out that she is part of a semisecret WhatsApp group among women who work in the sport. Starting with ten women, it grew to forty-nine in just a year and has become a place to commiserate, share stories, and offer support. It is their way of surviving and even possibly thriving in a heavily male-dominated culture (it's easier to imagine a female president than a female pitcher in the major leagues). The group, started by a life skills coordinator with the Cleveland Indians, has built solidarity among the women and has functioned as a launching pad from which to infiltrate this closed world. "This is like another type of family," said Nakken. "If there's something going on, I can share it with them and they'll get it. They just get it."

Could a larger platform, like Facebook, create these opportunities? A few people pointed me to China and its enormously popular WeChat as a glimpse into the future. WeChat began as a messaging app in 2011 and eventually took on a range of other functions, including an e-commerce platform adopted by practically everyone in the country. Part of its success has to do with the way it defines social networks: they are purposefully small-scale and mirror a person's actual contacts in the real world. If two people comment on the same post who aren't themselves connected on the app, they will never see what the other wrote. Because WeChat does not make most of its money from advertising, it has never had an incentive to maximize engagement. In other words, it's not meant to introduce human beings to each other (despite there being more than a billion human beings who use it). This was appealing to the Chinese who seem to prefer it now to Weibo, China's answer to Twitter. An Xiao Mina, a writer who has studied the Chinese internet, explained to me that after all the trolling and misinformation and contentiousness of Weibo (sound familiar?), there was a "shift to private, where it's just like, okay, at least I have my own little oasis."

WeChat is, of course, a fraught example because the privacy that its users experience is an illusion. WeChat users are being watched at all times, thanks to a surveillance system called Skynet that scans for politically sensitive phrases, links, and images, sophisticated enough to catch a joke at the leader Xi Jinping's expense. In the early months of the coronavirus, a watchdog group called the Citizen Lab found that more than two thousand keywords related to the pandemic were suppressed on WeChat. This included the name of Li Wenliang, the Wuhan doctor who, Red Dawn–like, tried to warn colleagues about the emergence of a possible new infectious disease, was reprimanded, and then died of the virus a few weeks later.

I could wander around Zuckerman's social media map for a long time. There are promising platforms, or corners of platforms, even as social media as a whole seems ever more dependent on capitalism and its familiar dialectic: when a surefire way of making a profit bumps up against what people actually want and need, there's a readjustment so that the money keeps flowing. Will Facebook really remake itself into a series of living rooms? Not unless it comes up with a business model that makes those rooms as lucrative as the town square. Can an app for secluded chatting like Signal remain a nonprofit? Maybe, but if it doesn't scale up—which will take money—how can it reach the people who could use the islands it provides?

Perhaps pining in this way, for a perfect, magic medium for social and political change, is in itself misguided. Hope for the future might come instead from a changed mindset, cutting through the dreaminess that has colored so much of our thinking about online communication for so long and finally ingesting this fact, that the platforms are not neutral. The internet is a world of hammers and screwdrivers, saws and pliers, each with its own particular function, useful for some tasks and utterly futile for others. For the vanguards of the present—Rachel Gilmer or Miski Noor—this is the essential insight: that the shape and extent of the change they seek depends as much on these tools as it does on their own will and hunger. They know now that they need to be thoughtful about which one they pick up.

WHEN WE LOOK BACK, what were the rewards of that quiet intensity when it was achieved? I wish history could offer us a resounding answer, one with chiming bells, but that's not how change works, even in the best of circumstances. To discern what followed from the stories of early incubation and what the future might look like, we need to get comfortable with progress that takes the form of a relay race.

When Mina Loy left Florence for New York in 1916 in the middle of World War I, she then moved through a series of bohemian enclaves for the next few decades, back and forth between Paris and Manhattan in the company of writers and artists like Ezra Pound and Marcel Duchamp, enjoying a counterculture where she felt freer. Still, she never dared to publish her "Feminist Manifesto." Her last years were spent working on assemblages of found objects, and she died in Aspen, Colorado, in 1966, three years after Betty Friedan published *The Feminine Mystique.* Mina's own manifesto was finally included in a posthumous collection of her writing in 1982, and ten years later a group of young women, who would become Riot Grrrls, fulfilled in their zines her directive to stop looking to men for self-definition and to "seek within yourselves what you *are.*" This is how it moves, a radical idea incubated in one place and time revealed nearly a hundred years later. For that matter the Manichaean, reactionary worldview of the Futurists, which had inspired Mina's own break with convention, bears not a small resemblance to the concepts that ignited the passions of a different group of young men in their internet forums, also a century later, when Pepe the Frog became their Mussolini.

In some cases, the movements that seemed promising are then undermined over time, obscuring the breakthroughs they once represented. After becoming the first president of independent Nigeria, Nnamdi Azikiwe was removed from office in a military coup in 1966 and barely avoided the fate of many others in his cohort: assassination. He died in 1996, honored as one of his country's founding fathers, but he also lived to see Nigeria undone by the tribal conflicts among Yoruba, Igbo, and Hausa—precisely the sort of sectarian violence that Zik had worried would hold Africans back from full self-realization. Natasha Gorbanevskaya was finally released from the Special Psychiatric Hospital in Kazan in 1972, a little more than a year after she was admitted. She left the Soviet Union for good in 1975, moving to Paris, where she would live for the rest of her life. But she did return to Moscow in 2013, more than a decade into Putin's rule, to re-create the 1968 protest in Red Square on its forty-fifth anniversary. Natasha and a group of nine friends unfurled a banner with the same slogan, "For Your Freedom and Ours," and stood at the same spot by the stone slab of Lobnoye Mesto. They were instantly arrested by the police, and Natasha died a few months later.

More often than not, though, the fights of the past just keep resurfacing in slightly different forms, but still call on the same methods for seeding a resistance. Over a century and a half after Feargus O'Connor traveled around the English countryside with his petition, demanding a government more representative of its people, Stacey Abrams did the same in the state of Georgia. Starting in 2011, when she became minority leader of the Georgia House of Representatives, Abrams set out to register more people of color to vote so that their concerns and demands might find fuller voice. Her first step, though, came from manuals that had helped her parents, United Methodist ministers, when they were looking to build up the church. They recommended intimate and frequent conversation. And that's what Abrams did. Her organizers set up dozens of listening tours centered on registering new voters, moving them past their sense of powerlessness, and letting them talk about their needs. Without much attention and with a projected time frame of a decade, Abrams's team did their slow, steady work, which culminated in turning Georgia, which had been a solidly red state for more than two decades, into a blue one in 2020—with the addition of a million new voters since the previous election.

Abrams's approach rhymes with O'Connor's because it embodies certain mechanics of how we've seen new ideas, like enfranchisement for all, make their way into actuality. Radical change—change that strips off the stucco and gets to the girders, that offers a chance to see ourselves and our relationship to nature or to others in new ways— doesn't start with yelling. It starts with deliberation, a tempo that increases, a volume set first at a whisper. How else can you begin to picture what doesn't yet exist?

Whatever new ways we find to carve a path beyond our current cacophony will have to take this into account—and it's safe to assume that we haven't even begun to imagine what uncharted territories of social media are still out there, existing now only in a programmer's mind. We can rage against it, dream as I do occasionally of pens and typewriters, but the internet, this network of networks, is where we live our lives in the twenty-first century. It has almost completely annihilated all those other modes of communication. So we need to ensure the possibility of those spaces apart, especially in a flattened, too-loud world that perceives dark corners only as dangerous. They are where the first inflections of progress can—and almost always do— occur.

Change seems hard to conceive of otherwise. Because it is the act of entering into those closed or semi-closed circles that alters identity in a fundamental way. Facing that gray unending slab of reality seems less lonely, and chipping away at it less foolish. You become something else: a person at a table.

Acknowledgments

—————

I'M SO GRATEFUL to be writing books. Don't get me wrong: there is anguish along the way, endless frustration—at one point, my wife said she felt this book was a third person in our marriage, which is not something you ever want to hear. It's a bruising marathon, day in and day out, through self-doubt and distraction. And yet, living in a moment in which time itself feels scarce, what greater luxury and privilege could there be than working on a creative endeavor that requires years? As often as I'd wished it were done already, I have also surrendered myself to the idea that the intense commitment books demand is their strength. With apologies to my wife, you need to marry a book in order to grow with it, to improve it. And I'm thankful beyond words that I get to do this, that a childhood dream of total immersion in a project of the mind is a part of my adult reality.

This book was built out of research and interviews. It stands supported by other books and other thinkers. The historical chapters benefited enormously from secondary sources. Some of these experts generously gave me their time—like Malcolm Chase on Chartism and Sara Marcus on the Riot Grrrls. In the case of other scholars, after months of being in the company of their research, I felt I knew them—

Peter Miller on Peiresc, Carolyn Burke on Mina Loy, and Stephanie Newell on newspapers in colonial West Africa. For the more contemporary chapters, I spoke with a great deal of helpful people who talked to me for hours, even knowing they might not see the finished book for years. Many, though not all, are in the notes, but I wanted to call out in particular John Coate, Wael Ghonim, Eva Lee, and Rachel Gilmer.

My editor, Amanda Cook, has believed in this project from when it was just airy thoughts over coffee, and she has never stopped pushing for it and dreaming about it with me—even when I most doubted, she could still see it. I owe so much to her. She is an editor like no other—meticulous, thoughtful, and unfailingly honest. I count it as the luckiest event in my life as a writer that I landed with her. There is no way this book would exist or be what it is without her guidance, and there is no one I would have rather been on this journey with than Amanda.

At Crown, I also profited from the incredible eye of Katie Berry, who read multiple versions of the manuscript and saved me from myself many times over. I'm thankful as well for two excellent fact-checkers, Gabe Levine-Drizin and Jordan Reed, who meticulously and expeditiously combed through the book.

Andrew Blauner, my agent, has been a steadfast friend over many years now, always available for a morale boost.

In order to write this book, I completed a PhD, crazy as that might sound, and I've had enormous support over the years from the faculty and my fellow students at Columbia University, who were quite patient and understanding that a father of two who was working a day job was rushing in and out of classes. From the early years of this project until it took on more shape, Todd Gitlin and Michael Schudson have been my rabbis, always pushing me toward greater rigor and offering me their intelligence and incisiveness. Richard John and Andie Tucher also helped me make my way through the program. I appreciate in particular my cohort—Burcu Baykurt, Max Foxman, and Joscelyn Jurich—who had to listen to many iterations of this idea as I inched toward a clearer understanding.

A special thanks to my first readers, who are also some of my dearest friends. It's my great fortune to know such brilliant people, but I was happy to take full advantage of their generosity and wisdom: Emily Eakin, Jennifer Szalai, and Brent Cunningham.

The same month that I signed on to write this book, I got a call offering me a job at *The New York Times Book Review*. I will forever be thankful to Pamela Paul for giving me that home. My colleagues there mean so much to me, and the mission we share, our unabashed geekiness about books, has made me feel like the awkward kid in the cafeteria who has finally found a table to sit at: these are my people.

Many friends have provided critical encouragement and support along the way, listening to me through my moments of excitement and dejection, and always telling me not to worry, that there will be an end: Jacob Levenson, Jason Zinoman, Kavitha Rajagopalan, Daniela Gerson, Lisa Goldman, Agata Lisiak, Adrian Tomine, Sarah Brennan, Alex Mindlin, Danielle Mindlin, Julian Kreimer, Allan Jalon, Nathaniel Popper, and Elissa Strauss. I was able to lean on some of my oldest friends, Helen Frazier and Deanna Kakassy, and some of my newest—Taffy Brodesser-Akner, master of the wonderfully endless text exchange.

Creating the conditions needed for writing a book when it's not your full-time job—if only!—is always a matter of jerry-rigging. But nothing could compare or could allow me to anticipate 2020. The most intense phase of the writing happened over a year and a half when, on the heels of the pandemic, I left together with my wife and daughters from our home in Brooklyn to join a family bubble in Los Angeles. I soon found myself turning an RV parked in the driveway into a makeshift writing studio. We all grew very close in that year of isolation. And they saw me work every day and got to experience the joys of me finishing. My always warm and loving family were involved in my tortured creative life as never before, and I'm grateful it allowed them to see me more fully. The bubble deserves full recognition: my incredibly supportive parents, Ami and Batia, along with Natalie, Dave, Maya, Yareeve, Elle, Ben, and Aviv. Also always there for us were the Kolbens: Alex and Nancy, Kevin and Michal, Avigayil and Yotam.

My daughters, Mika and Romi, saw the writing process especially up close. It's hard to talk about the advantages of the pandemic, which caused such suffering, but the chance to spend so much time with these girls, to eat every meal together, read together, and explore together every day, was an unexpected and treasured gift. They are growing up to be solid human beings who have in abundance that quality that counts most: kindness. I feel so lucky.

And finally, my wife, Deborah Kolben, who holds us all together. I'm not sure she knew exactly what was in store for her when she decided to make a life with me, but even when it felt impossible to balance everything, and I swallowed up so much time, she never stopped wanting me to pursue my own fulfillment. Her quickness and her sense of humor and her beauty sustain me. I've been dreaming since the day we met of dedicating a book to her, and it's the most gratifying thing in the world to finally be able to do so.

Notes

INTRODUCTION

4 "THE FIRST ACT" Saul Alinsky, *Rules for Radicals* (New York: Random House, 1971), xx.

5 "A FULL-BLOWN MOMENT" Zeynep Tufekci, *Twitter and Tear Gas: The Power and Fragility of Networked Protests* (New Haven, Conn.: Yale University Press, 2017), 75.

8 MARSHALL McLUHAN'S GREAT INSIGHT Marshall McLuhan, *The Gutenberg Galaxy: The Making of Typographic Man* (Toronto: University of Toronto Press, 1962).

8 "ITS FORM EXCLUDES THE CONTENT" Neil Postman, *Amusing Ourselves to Death: Public Discourse in the Age of Show Business* (New York: Viking, 1985), 7.

9 "THE MARVELS OF COMMUNICATION" Robert Darnton, *Poetry and the Police: Communication Networks in Eighteenth-Century Paris* (Cambridge, Mass.: Belknap Press of Harvard University Press, 2010), 1.

CHAPTER 1: PATIENCE—AIX-EN-PROVENCE, 1635

13   PEIRESC IS NOT SOMEONE Peter N. Miller, *Peiresc's Europe: Learning and Virtue in the Seventeenth Century* (New Haven, Conn.: Yale University Press, 2000), 38. Biographical information on Peiresc throughout from Miller, *Peiresc's Europe;* Peter N. Miller, *Peiresc's Orient: Antiquarianism as Cultural History in the Seventeenth Century* (Farnham, U.K.: Ashgate, 2012); Peter N. Miller, *Peiresc's Mediterranean World* (Cambridge, Mass.: Harvard University Press, 2015).

14   "LOOKED AT THE WRONG SIDE" Peiresc to Gassendi, Aug. 29, 1635, in *Lettres de Peiresc,* ed. Philippe Tamizey de Larroque (Paris, 1893), 4:534–35. A large selection from Peiresc's correspondence was published in seven volumes by Philippe Tamizey de Larroque as *Lettres de Peiresc* (Paris, 1888–98). Another series prepared by the same editor, *Les correspondants de Peiresc: Lettres inédites,* was issued in twenty-one parts (Paris, 1879–97; reprinted in 2 vols., Geneva, 1972).

14   "THE RAIN CAME" Peiresc to Mersenne, Sept. 1, 1635, in *Correspondance du P. Marin Mersenne,* ed. Paul Tannery, Cornelis de Waard, and Armand Beaulieu (Paris, 1932), 5:374.

15   "ALL THE PREPARATION" Peiresc to Gassendi, Aug. 29, 1635, in *Lettres de Peiresc,* 4:535.

15   100,000 PIECES OF PAPER Miller, *Peiresc's Europe,* 2.

15   LIKE GIORDANO BRUNO David Freedberg, *The Eye of the Lynx: Galileo, His Friends, and the Beginnings of Modern Natural History* (Chicago: University of Chicago Press, 2003), 83.

16   "THE BREVITY OF HUMAN LIFE" Peiresc to Campanella, July 3, 1635, in *Fra Tommaso Campanella ne'castelli di Napoli, in Roma ed in Parigi,* 2 vols. (Naples, 1887), 2:256.

16   MANY LIFELONG PROJECTS Miller, *Peiresc's Mediterranean World,* 28.

17   FOR ACCURACY, LONGITUDE WAS NEEDED Seymour L. Chapin, "The Astronomical Activities of Nicolas Claude Fabri de Peiresc," *Isis* 48, no. 1 (March 1957): 15.

17   "WAS EQUAL TO" Letter from Peiresc, Sept. 20, 1611, quoted in

Pierre Humbert, "Le probleme des longitudes entre 1610 et 1666," *Archives Internationales d'Histoire des Sciences* 2 (1948): 383–84.

18 "EXACTLY WHERE OUR CALCULATIONS" Peiresc to Pace, Jan. 10, 1611, Bibliothèque Inguimbertine, Carpentras, MS 1875, fols. 105–6. Most of Peiresc's surviving letters are housed at this library and have been digitized and made available online on the Early Modern Letters website: emlo-portal.bodleian.ox.ac .uk/collections/?catalogue=nicolas-claude-fabri-de-peiresc #partners.

18 "IF GOD GRACES ME" Lombard to Peiresc, Jan. 8, 1612, Bibliothèque Inguimbertine, MS 1803, fol. 254, quoted in Miller, *Peiresc's Mediterranean World,* 244.

18 WHERE HE MET GALILEO John Lewis, *Galileo in France: French Reactions to the Theories and Trial of Galileo* (Bern: Peter Lang, 2006), 142.

19 "A LABORATORY IN WHICH IDEAS" Miller, *Peiresc's Europe,* 50.

19 "A SUBSTITUTE FOR GENTLEMANLY" Ian F. McNeely and Lisa Wolverton, *Reinventing Knowledge: From Alexandria to the Internet* (New York: W. W. Norton, 2008), 129.

19 "WITH THE LATER PERSONS" From the peroration to Descartes's *Discourse on Method* (1637), quoted in Marc Fumaroli, "The Republic of Letters," *Diogenes* 143 (1988): 135–36.

20 "IF IT WERE USEFUL" Quoted in Arnaldo Momigliano, *Classical Foundations of Modern Historiography* (Berkeley: University of California Press, 1990), 55.

20 HIS INTERESTS EXTENDED Miller, *Peiresc's Europe,* 3.

20 SIGHTINGS OF MONSTROUS Ibid., 26.

21 "TO NEGLECT NOTHING" Peiresc to Mersenne, July 23, 1635, in *Correspondance du Mersenne,* 5:332.

21 "COULD NOT CARE FOR A WIFE" Pierre Gassendi, *The Mirrour of True Nobility and Gentility,* trans. William Rand (London, 1657), 162–63.

21 "PAR LE PARISIEN" Miller, *Peiresc's Europe,* 82.

21 "I OPENED A LETTER" Peiresc to Gassendi, April 19, 1635, in *Lettres de Peiresc,* 4:477.

22   "THE BARBARISM AND UNCOUTHNESS" Peiresc to P. Dupuy,
      March 4, 1628, in *Lettres de Peiresc,* 1:548.

22   WHEN TWO PORTUGUESE TRADERS Peter N. Miller, "Mapping
      Peiresc's Mediterranean: Geography and Astronomy, 1610–
      1636," in *Communicating Observations in Early Modern Letters,
      1500–1575: Epistolography and Epistemology in the Age of the
      Scientific Revolution,* ed. Dirk van Miert (Oxford: Warburg
      Institute Colloquia, 2012), 16.

23   "ALL THE INSTRUCTIONS" Peiresc to Hazard, July 10, 1635, in
      Bibliothèque Inguimbertine, MS 1874, fol. 374r.

23   "IF YOU WOULD ENCOUNTER" Peiresc to Celestin, Nov. 14,
      1635, Bibliothèque Inguimbertine, MS 1874, fols. 396v–397r.

24   "IT IS NOT NECESSARY TO PROBE" From Saint Augustine, *The
      Enchiridion on Faith, Hope, and Love,* chap. 9, quoted in Joyce
      Appleby, *Shores of Knowledge: New World Discoveries and the
      Scientific Imagination* (New York: W. W. Norton, 2013), 3.

24   "SUPPRESS" THE PUBLICATION Descartes to Mersenne, Feb.
      1634, in *Correspondance du Mersenne,* 4:27.

24   "POOR GALILEO HAD TO DECLARE" Peiresc to P. Dupuy,
      Aug. 16, 1633, in *Lettres de Peiresc,* 2:582.

25   "CAREFULLY AND OVER TIME" Peiresc to P. Dupuy, Feb. 6,
      1634, in *Lettres de Peiresc,* 3:28.

25   TO STRENGTHEN THEIR BOND D'Arcos to Peiresc, June 30,
      1634, in "Suite des lettres inédites de Peiresc, communique par
      M. Millen," ed. Alexandre-Jules-Antoine Fauris de Saint-
      Vincens, *Magasin Encyclopédique* 5 (1806): 143–44, quoted in
      Jane T. Tolbert, "Ambiguity and Conversion in the
      Correspondence of Nicolas-Claude Fabri de Peiresc and
      Thomas d'Arcos, 1630–1637," *Journal of Modern History* 13
      (2009): 19.

25   "FRAGILITY IS SOMETIMES WORTHY" Peiresc to Barberini,
      Dec. 5, 1634, quoted in Maurice A. Finocchiaro, *Retrying
      Galileo, 1633–1992* (Berkeley: University of California Press,
      2005), 54.

25   "SO MUCH REPROACHED" Peiresc to Barberini, Jan. 31, 1635,
      quoted in Finocchiaro, *Retrying Galileo,* 55.

26	"UNDERTAKING WHERE SO MANY OTHERS" Galileo to Peiresc, Feb. 22, 1635, in Galileo, *Dialogues, lettres choisies,* ed. Paul-Henri Michel (Paris, 1966), 422.
26	"THE BOOK OF NATURE" Peiresc to Celestin, April 29, 1635, in *Lettres de Peiresc,* 7:856–57.
26	"NOT BE INJURIOUS" Peiresc to Michelange de Nantes, Aug. 1, 1634, in *Correspondance de Peiresc avec plusieurs missionaires et religieux de l'ordre des Capucins, 1631–1637,* ed. Apollinaire de Valence (Paris, 1891), 82.
26	FOR THOSE WHO PASSED THROUGH AIX Peiresc to P. Dupuy, March 4, 1628, in *Lettres de Peiresc,* 1:549.
27	"YOU MUST TRY TO VIEW" Peiresc to Vendôme, May 17, 1635, in Valence, *Correspondance de Peiresc,* 137.
27	HIS ANNOYANCE JUST BARELY Peiresc to Vendôme, Sept. 29, 1635, in Valence, *Correspondance de Peiresc,* 188.
27	PEIRESC'S ATTENTION Tolbert, "Ambiguity and Conversion in the Correspondence of Nicolas-Claude Fabri de Peiresc and Thomas d'Arcos," 6–7.
28	"AROUND 2:30 AFTER MIDNIGHT" Peiresc to d'Arcos, April 29, 1635, in *Lettres de Peiresc,* 7:150.
28	"SINCE THE LAST LETTER" Peiresc to d'Arcos, May 11, 1635, in *Lettres de Peiresc,* 7:152–53.
29	"ABSENT THE INSTRUMENTS" Peiresc to M. de Nantes, Aug. 21, 1636, in Valence, *Correspondance de Peiresc,* 257.
29	"A BIT TOO GRAND FOR ME" Peiresc to Fabre, May 21, 1636, Bibliothèque Nationale, Paris, MS Nouvelles acquisitions françaises, 5172, fol. 72v, quoted in Miller, *Peiresc's Mediterranean World,* 136.
29	"ONE MUST ABSTAIN" Peiresc to Constans, Nov. 22, 1635, Bibliothèque Inguimbertine, MS 1874, fol. 402v.
29	TWO OTHERS THAT NIGHT Miller, *Peiresc's Mediterranean World,* 351.
30	"PREFER TO BELIEVE" Peiresc to M. de Nantes, Aug. 21, 1635, in Valence, *Correspondance de Peiresc,* 257.
30	"KNOCKING SOME SENSE" Peiresc to Contour, Nov. 22, 1635, Bibliothèque Inguimbertine, MS 1874, fol. 401v.

30   "ASTONISHING AND WORTHY" Gassendi to Peiresc, n.d., Bibliothèque Inguimbertine, MS 1832, fol. 34v, quoted in Miller, "Mapping Peiresc's Mediterranean," 26.

31   "FOR WHICH THEY COULD NEVER UNDERSTAND" Peiresc to J. Dupuy, Aug. 12, 1636, in *Lettres de Peiresc,* 7:182.

31   "VERY MOST EXPERT MARINERS" Peiresc to d'Arcos, July 20, 1636, in *Lettres de Peiresc,* 7:182.

31   IN THE LAST PORTRAIT Miller, *Peiresc's Mediterranean World,* 1.

32   CARDINAL BARBERINI ORGANIZED Momigliano, *Classical Foundations of Modern Historiography,* 54.

32   PEIRESC COMMISSIONED HIM Jane T. Tolbert, "Fabri de Peiresc's Quest for a Method to Calculate Terrestrial Longitude," *Historian* 61, no. 4 (Summer 1999): 818.

CHAPTER 2: COHERENCE—MANCHESTER, 1839

34   ALTOGETHER THE NAMES Malcolm Chase, *Chartism: A New History* (Manchester, U.K.: Manchester University Press, 2007), 73.

34   "THAT RIDICULOUS PIECE OF MACHINERY" *The Parliamentary Debates from the Year 1803 to the Present Time* (London: Hansard, 1839), 115:226.

34   "THAT IT MIGHT PLEASE" Ibid., 227.

35   "THE ONLY PEACEABLE AND CONSTITUTIONAL" *Correspondence of the Right Honourable Edmund Burke,* ed. Charles William, Earl Fitzwilliam, and Richard Burke (London: Francis & John Rivington, 1844), 2:61.

36   IN THE YEAR BEFORE THE PETITION Frank McLynn, *The Road Not Taken: How Britain Narrowly Missed a Revolution* (London: Bodley Head, 2012), 292.

36   "BRAWNY MUSCULAR FIGURE" Quoted in James Epstein, *The Lion of Freedom: Feargus O'Connor and the Chartist Movement, 1832–1842* (Kent, U.K.: Croom Helm, 1982), 10.

36   AT A MASS MEETING William Lovett, *The Life and Struggles of William Lovett* (New York: Alfred A. Knopf, 1920).

37   "YOU CARRY YOUR FAME" Quoted in Chase, *Chartism,* 10.

37   "A SORT OF UNCROWNED KING" Ramsden Balmforth, *Some Social and Political Pioneers of the Nineteenth Century* (London: Swan Sonnenschein, 1900), 189.

37   "SO GENERALLY POPULAR" Feargus O'Connor, *A Series of Letters from Feargus O'Connor to Daniel O'Connell* (London: H. Heatherington, 1836), v.

37   IN AN INFAMOUS CASE McLynn, *Road Not Taken*, 284.

38   IN HIS STUDY OF MANCHESTER Friedrich Engels, *The Condition of the Working Class in England*, trans. W. O. Henderson and W. H. Chaloner (Stanford, Calif.: Stanford University Press, 1958), 111.

38   THE CAUSE GREW Chase, *Chartism*, 32.

38   "FUSTIAN JACKETS" Quoted in Epstein, *Lion of Freedom*, 76.

38   "BY TWELVE O'CLOCK" "News of the Week," *The Spectator*, Sept. 29, 1835, 912.

39   "MAKING THE HEAVENS ECHO" R. G. Gammage, *History of the Chartist Movement, 1837–54* (Newcastle-on-Tyne: Browne & Browne, 1894), 94–95.

39   "TO SILENCE THEM" *Northern Star*, Feb. 23, 1839, 4.

39   MORE THAN SIX HUNDRED ASSOCIATIONS Dorothy Thompson, *The Chartists: Popular Politics in the Industrial Revolution* (1984; repr., London: Breviary Stuff Publications, 2013), 60.

40   "THERE WERE ASSOCIATIONS" John Bates, *John Bates of Queensbury, Veteran Reformer* (Queensbury, 1895), 1, quoted in Thompson, *Chartists*, 60.

40   "A UNION BASED" *Northern Star*, April 21, 1838.

41   THERE WERE ONLY SO MANY HOURS Chase, *Chartism*, 64.

41   "SUCH IS THE ENSLAVED STATE" Letters to the convention quoted in ibid., 64.

41   "WHEREVER THERE IS A HALFPENNY" *Sheffield Iris*, March 3, 1840.

42   "EDUCATIONAL PROCESS" Malcolm Chase, "What Did Chartism Petition For? Mass Petitions in the British Movement for Democracy," *Social Science History* 47, no. 3 (Fall 2019): 533.

42   "PETITIONS PARADE CHARTISM" *Northern Star*, May 7, 1842.

42   I<small>N A TOWN LIKE</small> K<small>IDDERMINSTER</small> Chase, "What Did Chartism Petition For?," 535.

42   "W<small>HEREVER</small> I <small>HAVE BEEN</small>" *Leicestershire Mercury*, Nov. 10, 1838.

43   O<small>F THE</small> 1.2 <small>MILLION NAMES</small> Paul A. Pickering, "'And Your Petitioners, &c.': Chartist Petitions in Popular Politics, 1838–48," *English Historical Review* 116, no. 466 (April 2001): 382.

43   B<small>Y THE SPRING</small> Chase, "What Did Chartism Petition For?," 538.

43   "T<small>HERE IS NOW MORE</small>" *Western Vindicator*, March 30, 1839.

43   "A<small>S THE OBJECT</small>" Lord Broughton, *Recollections of a Long Life*, vol. 5, *1834–1840*, ed. Lady Dorchester (Cambridge, U.K.: Cambridge University Press, 2011), 240.

44   A <small>SHIPMENT FROM THE</small> R<small>OYAL</small> A<small>RMOURIES</small> Chase, *Chartism*, 78.

44   T<small>HERE WERE BANNERS AND FLAGS</small> "Riots at Birmingham," *The Scotsman*, July 10, 1839.

44   "<small>THERE IS NO SECURITY</small>" *The Trial of W. Lovett for a Seditious Libel* (London: Hetherington, 1839), 4.

45   "<small>IF NOT DOWNRIGHT INSANE</small>" *The Scotsman*, May 22, 1839.

45   "O<small>NCE LET THEM BE DEFEATED</small>" *Northern Star*, July 25, 1839.

45   "<small>AS A THING IN THE CLOUDS</small>" *Northern Star*, Sept. 14, 1839.

45   T<small>HERE WERE A FEW THOUSAND</small> Thompson, *Chartists*, 79.

46   "O<small>N THEY CAME</small>" Chase, *Chartism*, 113.

46   T<small>HEY BEGAN FIRING THEIR MUSKETS</small> Ibid., 116.

47   "T<small>HERE WAS A DREADFUL SCENE</small>" Quotation from Chartist Trials, 6, letter from J. Wafins, Dec. 6, 1839, in the case of Joseph Davies, quoted in David J. V. Jones, *The Last Rising: The Newport Chartist Insurrection of 1839* (Oxford: Clarendon Press, 1985), 153.

47   "N<small>O.</small> 5 <small>OF</small> H D<small>IVISION</small>" Chase, *Chartism*, 116.

47   "<small>A CLEAR INTERPRETATION</small>" Thomas Carlyle, *Chartism* (London: James Fraser, 1840), 6.

47   "T<small>HEY CALL THEMSELVES</small>" *London Examiner*, Nov. 10, 1839.

48   "<small>THAN THE MAN IN THE MOON</small>" *Northern Star*, Nov. 23, 1839.

48   A<small>ND SO</small> J<small>ONES</small>, W<small>ILLIAMS</small>, <small>AND</small> F<small>ROST</small> Chase, *Chartism*, 127.

49   "ill-advised in the extreme" *Northern Star,* Jan. 4, 1840.

49   "It was then, for the first time" *The Observer,* Jan. 12, 1840.

49   "You, John Frost" *The Chartist Riots at Newport* (Newport, U.K.: W. N. Johns, 1889), 64.

50   "were indispensable to prevent" Lord Broughton, *Recollections of a Long Life,* 240.

50   Whereas it had taken weeks Chase, *Chartism,* 139.

50   There were Chartist songs Ibid.

51   The fanatically committed *Northern Star,* July 17, 1841; A. Briggs, "Industry and Politics in Early Nineteenth-Century Keighley," *Bradford Antiquary,* n.s., 9 (1952): 314, quoted in Chase, *Chartism,* 145.

51   In a letter to Parliament *The Life and Correspondence of Thomas Slingsby Duncombe,* ed. Thomas H. Duncombe (London: Hurst and Blackett, 1868), 293.

52   "wan and haggard" *Barclay Fox's Journal,* ed. R. L. Brett (London: Bell & Hyman, 1979), 181.

52   "the result of peaceful" Dorothy Thompson, *The Dignity of Chartism,* ed. Stephen Roberts (New York: Verso, 2015), 4.

52   nearly 1.5 million signatures McLynn, *Road Not Taken,* 305.

52   "I shall console myself" *Northern Star,* March 7, 1840.

53   "This is my last letter" *Northern Star,* April 25, 1840.

53   "His meals are" *York Gazette,* June 6, 1840.

54   The door frame had to be taken apart Chase, "What Did Chartism Petition For?," 22.

54   From 1838 to 1848 Pickering, "'And Your Petitioners, &c.,'" 371.

Chapter 3: Imagination—Florence, 1913

55   "anchovies in a tin" *Corriere della Sera,* Dec. 13, 1913.

55   Her career as a painter Biographical material on Mina Loy from Carolyn Burke, *Becoming Modern: The Life of Mina Loy* (New York: Farrar, Straus and Giroux, 1996).

56   "OF SHILLY-SHALLYING SHYNESS" Biographical sketch (ca. 1915) for Carl Van Vechten's article "Some 'Literary Ladies' I Have Known," quoted in Burke, *Becoming Modern*, 119.

56   "RISORGIMENTO" Loy to Mabel Dodge Luhan, Feb. 1914, Mabel Dodge Luhan Papers, box 24, folder 664, YCL MSS 196, Yale University Library. I consulted the digitized version of the collections at the Yale University Library.

56   "CAFFEINE OF EUROPE" Günter Berghaus, *Futurism and Politics: Between Anarchist Rebellion and Fascist Politics, 1909–1944* (Providence: Berghahn Books, 1996), 23.

56   "UGLIEST MAN IN ITALY" M. de Filippis, "Giovanni Papini," *Modern Language Journal* 28, no. 4 (April 1944): 352.

56   "AN INFERNO" Ardengo Soffici, *Fine di un mondo: Autoritratto d'artista italiano nel quadro del suo tempo* (Florence: Vallecchi, 1955), 4:328.

57   "THROW AN IDEA" Günter Berghaus, *Italian Futurist Theatre, 1909–1944* (Oxford: Clarendon Press, 1997), 37.

57   THE EVENING ENDED Francis Simpson Stevens, "Today and the Futurists," *Florence Herald,* Dec. 27, 1913.

57   "I'VE HAD ENOUGH" From the manifesto "Le declamazione dinamica e sinottica," March 11, 1916, included in F. T. Marinetti, *Teoria e invenzione futurista* (Milan: Mondadori, 1968), 105–6.

57   "PERSONALLY I AM" Loy to Carl Van Vechten, 1914, Carl Van Vechten Papers, box 76, YCL MSS 1050, Yale University Library.

58   "WE HAD STAYED UP" F. T. Marinetti, *Marinetti: Selected Writings* (New York: Farrar, Straus and Giroux, 1972), 14–15.

59   "WE MUST BREATHE" Lawrence Rainey, Christine Poggi, and Laura Wittman, eds., *Futurism: An Anthology* (New Haven, Conn.: Yale University Press, 2009), 62.

59   "WE DEMAND, FOR TEN YEARS" "Futurist Painting: Technical Manifesto," in Rainey, Poggi, and Wittman, *Futurism*, 64.

59   "THE SIDEWALK CAN CLIMB" "Futurist Sculpture," in Rainey, Poggi, and Wittman, *Futurism*, 113.

60   LATER, AS A STUDENT Ernest Ialongo, *Filippo Tommaso*

Marinetti: The Artist and His Politics (Teaneck, N.J.: Fairleigh Dickinson University Press, 2015), 19.

60   "STIRS UP THE DELIRIOUS" Berghaus, *Futurism and Politics*, 18.

60   "NOT ALL OF THE NUTS" Press reactions to *La donna è mobile* in Giovanni Antonucci, *Cronache del teatro futurista* (Rome: Abete, 1975), 35–41; Berghaus, *Italian Futurist Theatre*, 32–35.

61   "WE WILL GLORIFY WAR" Marinetti, *Marinetti: Selected Writings*, 17.

61   "MANIFESTOS FREQUENTLY OVERCOMPENSATE" Martin Puchner, *Poetry of the Revolution: Marx, Manifestos, and the Avant-Gardes* (Princeton, N.J.: Princeton University Press, 2006), 5.

61   "LET US HASTEN" "Against Passéist Venice," in Rainey, Poggi, and Wittman, *Futurism*, 67.

62   "YOU SHOULD THROW" F. T. Marinetti, *Critical Writings*, ed. Günter Berghaus (New York: Farrar, Straus and Giroux, 2006), 168.

62   OFFERING SOME ADVICE Marjorie Perloff, *The Futurist Moment: Avant-Garde, Avant-Guerre, and the Language of Rupture* (Chicago: University of Chicago Press, 1986), 81.

62   "AS THE DIVINE RESERVOIR" F. T. Marinetti, *Let's Murder the Moonshine: Selected Writing*, ed. R. W. Flint (Los Angeles: Sun & Moon Press, 1991), 80.

63   "I AM IN THE THROES" Loy to Mabel Dodge Luhan, Feb. 1914, Dodge Luhan Papers, box 24, folder 664, YCL MSS 196.

63   "HIS TACTILE ADROITNESS" Mina Loy, "First Costa Visit," in "Brontolivido," Mina Loy Papers, box 1, folder 2, YCAL MSS 6, Yale University Library.

63   "SOME TERRIBLE GOLEM" "Esau Penfeld," Loy Papers, box 5, folder 134, YCAL MSS 6.

64   WHAT IMMEDIATELY STANDS OUT Mina Loy, "Aphorisms on Futurism," in *The Lost Lunar Baedeker: Poems of Mina Loy*, ed. Roger L. Conover (New York: Farrar, Straus and Giroux, 1996), 149.

66 "Humanity is mediocre" "Manifesto of the Futurist Woman," in Rainey, Poggi, and Wittman, *Futurism,* 109.

66 "What happens to all" Marshall Berman, *All That Is Solid Melts into Air: The Experience of Modernity* (New York: Verso, 1982), 25.

67 "His mass of curly" Mina Loy, "Notes on Johannes and Geronimo," in "Brontolivido," Loy Papers, box 1, folder 6, YCAL MSS 6.

67 Papini's memoir Giovanni Papini, *The Failure (Un uomo finito),* trans. Virginia Pope (New York: Harcourt, Brace, 1924).

67 "the sketch over the composition" Quoted in Walter L. Adamson, *Avant-Garde Florence: From Modernism to Fascism* (Cambridge, Mass.: Harvard University Press, 1993), 168.

68 In a poem Mina Loy, "Songs to Joannes," in *Lost Lunar Baedeker,* 53–70.

68 "His proximity was" Loy, "First Costa Visit."

68 "Women must disappear" Giovanni Papini, "Il massacro delle donne," *Lacerba,* April 1, 1914, quoted in Adamson, *Avant-Garde Florence,* 178.

68 "it is a physical commotion" Mina Loy, "Rome," in "Brontolivido," Loy Papers, box 1, folder 7, YCAL MSS 6.

69 "He had said" Ibid.

69 "dancing and singing" Marinetti, *Critical Writings,* 208.

69 "apocalyptic transition" Robert Wohl, *The Generation of 1914* (Cambridge, Mass.: Harvard University Press, 1979), 169.

69 "blood is the wine" Giovanni Papini, "La vita non è sacra," *Lacerba,* Oct. 15, 1913.

69 "Only war knows" F. T. Marinetti, *Futurismo e fascismo* (Foligno: Campitelli, 1924), 96–97, quoted in Wohl, *Generation of 1914,* 169.

70 "invigorating wine" Giovanni Papini, "Il dovere dell'Italia," *Lacerba,* Aug. 15, 1914.

70 In a new sort of manifesto "Futurist Synthesis of War," in Rainey, Poggi, and Wittman, *Futurism,* 363.

71   "While round the hotel" Mina Loy, "Italian Pictures," in
       Lost Lunar Baedeker, 9.

71   "These weights thicknesses" F. T. Marinetti, *Zang Tumb
       Tuuum* (Milan: Edizione Futuriste de "Poesia," 1914), 5.

71   "As a volunteer" Marinetti to Soffici, n.d., in *Archivi del
       futurismo*, ed. Maria Drudi Gambillo and Teresa Fiori (Rome:
       De Luca, 1962), 2:344–45, quoted in Selena Daly, *Italian
       Futurism and the First World War* (Toronto: University of
       Toronto Press, 2016), 18.

72   "You've got a wonderful brain" Mina Loy, "Vallombrosa,"
       in "Brontolivido," Loy Papers, box 1, folder 9, YCAL MSS 6.

72   "A manifesto writing painter" G. C. Cook, *The Chicago
       Evening Post*, Sept. 25, 1914, 7.

73   "Has interested herself" Carl Van Vechten, *The Trend*,
       Nov. 1914, 101.

73   "In no way considered" Loy to Carl Van Vechten, n.d., Van
       Vechten Papers, box 76, YCL MSS 1050.

73   "Tight-fitting, colourless" "Futurist Men's Clothing:
       A Manifesto," in Rainey, Poggi, and Wittman, *Futurism*, 194.

73   He got more specific "The Antineutral Suit: A Manifesto,"
       in Rainey, Poggi, and Wittman, *Futurism*, 202.

73   "To influence the Italian" "The Futurist Synthetic
       Theater," in Rainey, Poggi, and Wittman, *Futurism*, 204.

74   "Futurist Reconstruction of the Universe," ibid., 209.

74   "The Brute" Loy to Mabel Dodge Luhan, 1914, Dodge
       Luhan Papers, box 24, folder 664, YCL MSS 196.

74   "His recent actions" Ialongo, *Filippo Tommaso Marinetti*, 55.

74   "We want to act" Wohl, *Generation of 1914*, 172.

75   "He's getting fat" Loy to Mabel Dodge Luhan, 1914,
       Dodge Luhan Papers, box 24, folder 664, YCL MSS 196.

75   "As a mother" Marinetti, *Let's Murder the Moonshine*, 80.

75   "The Feminist movement" Mina Loy, "Feminist Manifesto,"
       in *Lost Lunar Baedeker*, 153–56.

77   "Juvenile, crowd-pleasing" Aldo Palazzeschi, Giovanni
       Papini, and Ardengo Soffici, "Futurismo e Marinettismo,"
       Lacerba, Feb. 14, 1915.

77 "DON'T EVER LIVE" Loy to Mabel Dodge Luhan, ca. 1914, Dodge Luhan Papers, box 24, folder 664, YCL MSS 196.

77 "THE FUTURE HAS CEASED" Loy to Carl Van Vechten, n.d., Van Vechten Papers, box 76, YCL MSS 1050.

77 "YOU HAVE NO IDEA" Ibid.

78 "WHAT I FEEL NOW" Ibid.

CHAPTER 4: DEBATE—ACCRA, 1935

79 "ON GENERAL PRINCIPLE" Public Record Office, Colonial Office 96/714/6, Bills for Newspapers, Books, and Printing Presses Ordinance, Criminal Code (Amendment) Ordinance, Control of Imported Books, "Memo Signed Arthur Grey Hazlerigg," Feb. 26, 1934, quoted in Stephanie Newell, *The Power to Name: A History of Anonymity in Colonial West Africa* (Athens: Ohio University Press, 2013), 65.

80 AN ISSUE LIKE POLYGAMY L. H. Ofuso-Appiah, *The Life and Times of J. B. Danquah* (Accra: Waterville Publishing House, 1974).

81 "A GREATER MEASURE" "Memo Signed Arthur Grey Hazlerigg," Feb. 26, 1934, quoted in Newell, *Power to Name*, 11.

81 "THERE IS NOT A SINGLE EDITOR" Public Record Office, Colonial Office 96/716/15, Control of the Press of the Gold Coast: Newspapers, Books, and Printing Presses Ordinance, 1934 (closed until 1985), "Memorandum by the Inspector General of Police [Henry W. M. Bamford] Regarding the Draft Bill (44a) Cited as the Newspapers, Books, and Printing Presses Ordinance, 1934," n.d., quoted in Newell, *Power to Name*, 12.

81 "IT IS THE ILLITERATES" Public Record Office, Colonial Office 96/714/6, Bills for Newspapers, Books, and Printing Presses Ordinance, Criminal Code (Amendment) Ordinance, Control of Imported Books, "Message from Shenton Thomas to Alex Fiddian," Feb. 2, 1934, quoted in Newell, *Power to Name*, 67.

81   "COULD HARDLY BE DESCRIBED" Public Record Office, Colonial Office 96/716/15, Control of the Press of the Gold Coast: Newspapers, Books, and Printing Presses Ordinance, 1934 (closed until 1985), "Extract from a Note of a Meeting at the Colonial Office," June 14, 1934, quoted in Newell, *Power to Name*, 77.

81   "A HARMLESS ORGAN" The text of a petition opposing the law, Public Record Office, Colonial Office 96/714/6, 16, Bills for Newspapers, Books, and Printing Presses Ordinance, Criminal Code (Amendment) Ordinance, Control of Imported Books, "Letter from James A. Busum to the Secretary of State for the Colonies," Feb. 16, 1934, quoted in Newell, *Power to Name*, 32.

81   "A DANGEROUS MAN" Stanley Shaloff, "Press Controls and Sedition Proceedings in the Gold Coast, 1933–39," *African Affairs* 71, no. 284 (July 1972): 250.

82   THE DELEGATION WAS TREATED J. B. Danquah, "The Gold Coast and Ashanti Delegation: A Gesture and a Lesson," *Keys: The Official Organ of the League of Colored People*, Oct.– Dec. 1934, 23–26.

83   "I SHALL DEDICATE MY LIFE" Nnamdi Azikiwe, *My Odyssey: An Autobiography* (New York: Praeger, 1970), 174.

83   IT TOLD THE STORY Ibid., 40.

84   "FRIENDLESS, DEJECTED" Ibid., 100.

85   "I AM RETURNING" Ibid., 162.

85   "I WHISPERED TO MYSELF" Ibid., 217.

86   "MASTERS" Ibid.

86   "INDEPENDENT IN ALL THINGS" Vincent C. Ikeotuonye, *Zik of New Africa* (New York: P. R. Macmillan, 1961), 121.

86   "TINY AND CLUTTERED" Richard Wright, *Black Power* (New York: Harper, 1954), 186.

87   "WE SHALL BE HAPPY" *The African Morning Post*, July 7, 1938, 3.

87   "BE YOURSELF" *The Gold Coast Leader*, July 5, 1902, 4.

88   "MUST CONSIST OF AFRICANS" J.A.B. Jones-Quartey, *A Life of Azikiwe* (New York: Penguin, 1965), 116–24.

89   "LET DOWN THE AFRICAN" *The African Morning Post,* Oct. 4, 1937.

89   "I MUST SAY" *The African Morning Post,* Oct. 5, 1937.

89   "INDEFINITELY STRETCHABLE NETS OF KINSHIP" Benedict Anderson, *Imagined Communities: Reflections on the Origin and Spread of Nationalism* (New York: Verso, 1983), 6.

89   "THESE FELLOW-READERS" Ibid., 44.

89   A TYPICAL ISSUE *The African Morning Post,* June 4, 1935.

91   HER ELITIST SENSIBILITIES Mabel Dove, *Selected Writings of a Pioneer West African Feminist,* ed. Stephanie Newell and Audrey Gadzekpo (Nottingham, U.K.: Trent, 2004).

91   "IF AN INDIAN LADY" Marjorie Mensah, "Ladies' Corner," *The Times of West Africa,* Nov. 3, 1934, 2.

91   THE INITIAL VOTE WAS NO *The Times of West Africa,* April 24, 1931, 1.

92   "THE DICTION AND FIRM GRIP" Asuana Quartey, letter to the editor, *The Times of West Africa,* April 21, 1931.

92   "WHAT DO YOU THINK" Marjorie Mensah, "Ladies' Corner," *The Times of West Africa,* April 27, 1931.

92   THE CONTROVERSY WAS SO INTRIGUING Jinny Kathleen Prais, "Imperial Travelers: The Formation of West African Urban Culture, Identity, and Citizenship in London and Accra, 1925–1935" (PhD diss., University of Michigan, 2008), 291.

92   "IS THE GOLD COAST A NATION?" *The African Morning Post,* Jan. 29, 1938.

93   "ILL AT EASE" Jones-Quartey, *Life of Azikiwe,* 129.

94   "MUST BE DESTROYED" Ikeotuonye, *Zik of New Africa,* 134.

94   "WE HAVE HEARD" Nnamdi Azikiwe, *Renascent Africa* (Accra: the author, 1937), 21.

95   IT LEFT WIDE OPEN *Legislative Council Debates,* March 21, 1934, quoted in Shaloff, "Press Controls and Sedition Proceedings in the Gold Coast," 246.

95   "IT IS WELL KNOWN" Public Record Office, Colonial Office 96/716/15, Control of the Press of the Gold Coast: Newspapers, Books, and Printing Presses Ordinance, 1934 (closed until 1985), "Memo from Arnold Hodson,

Government House, Accra, to the Rt. Hon. Sir Philip
Cunliffe-Lister, Secretary of State for the Colonies," Nov. 29,
1934, quoted in Newell, *Power to Name*, 65.

95 THE GOVERNOR HANDED HIM Azikiwe, *My Odyssey*, 282.

96 "DO THE EUROPEANS" *The African Morning Post*, May 15, 1936.

96 "IN THE ART OF SUBVERSIVE" Shaloff, "Press Controls and
Sedition Proceedings in the Gold Coast," 245.

97 "INTELLECTUAL REVOLUTION" Azikiwe, *My Odyssey*, 219.

97 "ABSOLUTE POWER TO SUPPRESS" Public Record Office,
Colonial Office 96/729/31205/1936, Hodson to Cunliffe-
Lister, Feb. 12, 1936, quoted in Shaloff, "Press Controls and
Sedition Proceedings in the Gold Coast," 255.

98 "THE FRENCH WOULD NOT TOLERATE" Public Record Office,
Colonial Office 96/731/31230/1937, Extract of Hodson to
Bottomley, Jan. 14, 1936, quoted in Shaloff, "Press Controls
and Sedition Proceedings in the Gold Coast," 256.

98 "ARE YOU MR. NNAMDI AZIKIWE?" Azikiwe, *My Odyssey*, 267.

99 "IT IS A VERY SERIOUS OFFENSE" Ibid., 270.

99 "FOR THE INEVITABLE" Ibid.

99 "LIVING SPIRIT OF AN IDEA" *Zik: A Selection from the Speeches of
Nnamdi Azikiwe* (Cambridge, U.K.: Cambridge University
Press, 1961), 57.

100 "MEANT NOTHING" Shaloff, "Press Controls and Sedition
Proceedings in the Gold Coast," 258.

100 "EVEN BREATHING" Jones-Quartey, *Life of Azikiwe*, 134.

101 "HILARIOUS UPROAR" Azikiwe, *My Odyssey*, 272.

101 "REVIVED AT ABOUT THAT TIME" *The Autobiography of Kwame
Nkrumah* (New York: T. Nelson, 1957), 22.

101 AS DID LANGSTON HUGHES Hughes's poem about Azikiwe's
arrest and trial was called "Azikiwe in Jail" and included the
lines "The British said to Azikiwe, / We're tired of you running
around loose. / We're going to grab you— / And cook your
goose. / Azikiwe said to the British, / That may be— / But
you'll have a tough goose / If you cook me!"

101 "THE FIRST WARNING PUFF" *Autobiography of Kwame Nkrumah*,
18–19.

CHAPTER 5: FOCUS—MOSCOW, 1968

104   OTHER STUDENTS ATTACKED HER Natalya Gorbanevskaya, "Writing for 'Samizdat,'" interview with Michael Scammell, *Index on Censorship,* Jan. 1, 1977.

104   NEVER FORGAVE HERSELF Additional biographical information on Gorbanevskaya came from an oral history that was posted on YouTube and translated for me by Lillian Feldman: www .youtube.com/watch?v=8J0Nl52s8Ac.

104   AFTER SHE PURCHASED Mark Hopkins, *Russia's Underground Press: "The Chronicle of Current Events"* (New York: Praeger, 1983), 16.

105   "I ENTER MY BEING" "Something's with Me . . ." and "And You . . . ," in *Making for the Open: The Chatto Book of Post-feminist Poetry,* ed. Carol Rumens (London: Chatto & Windus, 1985), 57–58.

106   "RESPECT THE CONSTITUTION" Hopkins, *Russia's Underground Press,* 23.

106   "PROCESS OF THE CHAIN REACTION" Mentioned by Gorbanevskaya in oral history.

107   "AS LONG AS ARBITRARY ACTION" Natalya Gorbanevskaya, *Selected Poems* (Oxford, U.K.: Carcanet Press, 1972), 75.

107   "WHY ARE THEY KEEPING ME HERE?" Natalya Gorbanevskaya, "Free Health Service," in ibid., 75–105.

109   AT THE TOP OF ISSUE NO. 1 Hopkins, *Russia's Underground Press,* 17.

110   "WITHOUT ANY WARNING" Issues of the *Chronicle of Current Events* were translated and published in Peter Reddaway, *Uncensored Russia: Protest and Dissent in the Soviet Union* (New York: American Heritage, 1972), 81.

110   "IT WOULD OFFER NO COMMENTARY" Ludmilla Alexeyeva and Paul Goldberg, *The Thaw Generation: Coming of Age in the Post-Stalin Era* (Pittsburgh: University of Pittsburgh Press, 1993), 206.

111   SHE FINISHED RETYPING Hopkins, *Russia's Underground Press,* 17.

111 THE MOST IMPORTANT In addition to Reddaway, *Uncensored Russia,* 456, all issues of the *Chronicle of Current Events* were digitized and made available online: chronicle-of-current -events.com/.

113 "PEOPLE HAD HARDLY BEGUN" Natalia Gorbanevskaya, *Red Square at Noon* (New York: Holt, Rinehart & Winston, 1970), 33.

113 "WE WERE ABLE EVEN IF BRIEFLY" The text of her 1968 letter was reprinted in "The Sludge of Unbridled Lies," *The New York Times,* July 15, 1970.

114 "NON-RESPONSIBLE FOR HER ACTIONS" Gorbanevskaya, *Selected Poems,* 10.

114 "FROM THE FIVE ISSUES" Reddaway, *Uncensored Russia,* 53.

115 IN THAT SAME ISSUE Ibid., 54.

115 IN LENIN'S VIEW Vladimir Ilyich Lenin, *Where to Begin? Party Organization and Party Literature* (1901; repr., Moscow: Progress Publishers, 1966).

116 "THE EFFECT OF THE *CHRONICLE*" Hopkins, *Russia's Underground Press,* xx.

116 "IN THOSE INSTANCES" Reddaway, *Uncensored Russia,* 58.

117 THE INITIAL ITEMS Ibid., 165.

118 "ALL THOSE CHOSEN TO REPRESENT" Ibid., 116.

119 THEN SHE PULLED OUT Gorbanevskaya, *Selected Poems,* 140.

120 HER FIRST SUCCESSOR Hopkins, *Russia's Underground Press,* 40.

121 "GO THROUGH THE DESK" Ibid., 42–43.

121 "SLUGGISH SCHIZOPHRENIA" Sidney Bloch and Peter Reddaway, *Psychiatric Terror: How Soviet Psychiatry Is Used to Suppress Dissent* (New York: Basic Books, 1977).

121 "DOES NOT RENOUNCE HER ACTIONS" Gorbanevskaya, *Selected Poems,* 108.

122 "IF MY DAUGHTER HAS COMMITTED" Ibid., 145.

122 "UNSOUND MIND" Ibid., 11.

122 "I'LL TRY TO SAY" Ibid., 123.

123 "IF THE PATIENTS COMMIT" Bloch and Reddaway, *Psychiatric Terror,* 12, from *Chronicle of Current Events,* no. 10.

123 "In the madhouse" Gorbanevskaya, *Selected Poems,* 99.

123 "process of justice" Alexeyeva and Goldberg, *Thaw Generation,* 109.

124 In Issue No. 18 *Chronicle of Current Events,* no. 18 (March 1971), text found on *Chronicle of Current Events* website: chronicle-of-current-events.com/2015/09/22/18-1-political -prisoners-in-psychiatric-hospitals-a-survey-of-documents/.

Chapter 6: Control—Washington, 1992

125 "JIGSAW IS NOT" Tobi Vail, *Jigsaw,* no. 2 (Feb. 1990). Vail has posted images and transcriptions of early issues of her zine: jigsawscrapbook.blogspot.com/2009/09/jigsaw-2-theres -no-ideas-in-time.html.

126 "to kill one another" Paul Tough, "Into the Pit," *The New York Times,* Nov. 7, 1993.

126 Young women were shoved *Don't Need You: The Herstory of Riot Grrrl,* directed by Kerri Koch (Urban Cowgirl Productions, 2005).

126 "from the GEEKS" Donna Dresch, *Chainsaw,* no. 2 (ca. 1990), excerpted in *The Riot Grrrl Collection,* ed. Lisa Darms (New York: Feminist Press at CUNY, 2014), 23.

127 "I am making" Vail, *Jigsaw,* no. 3.

127 "It's really inspiring" Vail to Neuman, May 9, 1990, printed in Darms, *Riot Grrrl Collection,* 28–29.

128 For Allison Wolfe, interview with author, Feb. 23, 2018.

128 Molly was more intense Sara Marcus, *Girls to the Front: The True Story of the Riot Grrrl Revolution* (New York: HarperPerennial, 2010), 57.

128 As soon as they read Molly Neuman and Allison Wolfe, *Girl Germs,* no. 3 (ca. 1992), reprinted in full in Darms, *Riot Grrrl Collection,* 51–93.

129 "I felt like we are" Marcus, *Girls to the Front,* 46.

129 She had recently stood *The Punk Singer,* directed by Sini Anderson (Sundance Selects, 2013).

129 "I'm really interested" Mark Andersen and Mark Jenkins,

Dance of Days: Two Decades of Punk in the Nation's Capital
(New York: Akashic Books, 2003), 310.

130 WHEN A STORM HIT Marcus, *Girls to the Front*, 59–60.

131 "MY BROTHER WHO IS TWO" Molly Neuman and Allison
Wolfe, *Girl Germs*, no. 1 (Dec. 1990), quoted in Andersen and
Jenkins, *Dance of Days*, 311.

132 "I THINK IT'S REALLY GOOD" Marcus, *Girls to the Front*, 82–83.

133 "THERE HAS BEEN A PROLIFERATION" *Riot Grrrl*, no. 1 (July
1991), reprinted in Darms, *Riot Grrrl Collection*, 31.

133 "CREATED ITS AUDIENCE OF GIRLS" Marcus, *Girls to the
Front*, 81.

133 "BE AS VULNERABLE" *Riot Grrrl*, no. 2 (1991), quoted in
Marcus, *Girls to the Front*, 86.

134 "ZINES ARE PROFOUNDLY PERSONAL" Stephen Duncombe,
*Notes from the Underground: Zines and the Politics of Alternative
Culture* (New York: Verso, 1997), 70.

135 "I SERIOUSLY BELIEVE" Marcus, *Girls to the Front*, 91.

135 "WELL I'M A RIOT GRRRL" Joanna writing in *Fantastic Fanzine*,
no. 3, in Zan Gibbs Riot Grrrl Collection, MSS.364, box 2,
folder 20, New York University.

135 "BECAUSE WE GIRLS" Erika Reinstein, *Fantastic Fanzine*,
no. 2 (1992), quoted in Kevin Dunn and May Summer
Farnsworth, "We ARE the Revolution: Riot Grrrl Press,
Empowerment, and DIY Self-Publishing," *Women's Studies* 41
(2012): 141.

136 "WE ARE TURNING CURSIVE LETTERS" Darms, *Riot Grrrl
Collection*, 13.

136 "RIOT GRRRL IS SO MUCH" Neuman and Wolfe, *Girl Germs*,
no. 3.

137 "I KNOW I'M NEVER GONNA BE THIN" Nomy Lamm, *I'm So
Fucking Beautiful*, no. 2 (1994), reprinted in Darms, *Riot Grrrl
Collection*, 243–61.

137 "I THINK I WAS ONE" Ramdasha Bikceem, *Gunk*, no. 4
(ca. 1993), reprinted in Darms, *Riot Grrrl Collection*, 158.

138 "GIRL'S NIGHT WILL ALWAYS" Molly Neuman and Allison
Wolfe, *Girl Germs*, no. 4 (ca. 1993).

138 "PUNK ROCK DREAM" Emily White, "Revolution Girl-Style Now!," *LA Weekly*, July 10–16, 1992.

139 THE RESULTING ARTICLE Ibid.

140 IT WAS A WEEKEND Dunn and Farnsworth, "We ARE the Revolution," 139.

141 ANOTHER WAS RESEARCHING Marcus, *Girls to the Front*, 166.

141 "BETTER WATCH OUT" Elizabeth Snead, "Feminist Riot Grrrls Don't Just Wanna Have Fun," *USA Today*, Aug. 7, 1992.

142 "INTERVIEW MAGAZINE CALLED" Kathleen Hanna and Melissa Klein, "Riot Grrrl! Meet the Teen Feminist Movement Storming the States," *Off Our Backs* 23, no. 2 (Feb. 1993): 10.

142 "I FEEL LIKE I HAVE SO LITTLE" Erika Reinstein, *Fantastic Fanzine*, no. 3 (1993), quoted in Kevin Dunn, *Global Punk: Resistance and Rebellion in Everyday Life* (New York: Bloomsbury, 2016), 52.

143 "ONE THING I AM PARTICULARLY UPSET ABOUT" Marcus, *Girls to the Front*, 198–99.

143 THE ARTICLE APPEARING IN *SPIN* Dana Nasrallah, "Teenage Riot," *Spin*, Nov. 1992.

144 ALLISON AND MOLLY TOURED Molly Neuman Riot Grrrl Collection, New York University, box 3, folder 10.

144 "HOW SOMETHING THAT WAS ONCE MINE" Tobi Vail, *Jigsaw*, no. 5 (ca. 1993).

145 "IF YOU WANT TO START" Marcus, *Girls to the Front*, 244.

145 IT WAS A CONVERSATION *What Is Riot Grrrl, Anyway?*, partly reprinted in Darms, *Riot Grrrl Collection*, 184.

145 "THE MEDIA HAS MADE US" From *What Is Riot Grrrl, Anyway?*, quoted in Marcus, *Girls to the Front*, 225.

145 "MEAN, MAD" Steve Hochman, "Mean, Mad, and Defiantly Underground," *Los Angeles Times*, Nov. 8, 1992.

145 "FEMINIST FURY" Linda Keene, "Feminist Fury: 'Burn Down the Walls That Say You Can't,'" *The Seattle Times*, March 21, 1993.

145 EVEN *COSMO* Louise Bernikow, "The New Activists: Fearless, Funny, Fighting Mad," *Cosmopolitan*, April 1993.

146   SEVENTEEN MAGAZINE Nina Malkin, "It's a Grrrl Thing," *Seventeen*, May 1993.

146   THE ARTICLE, OF COURSE Marcus, *Girls to the Front*, 237.

146   A DISTRIBUTION SERVICE Dunn and Farnsworth, "We ARE the Revolution."

146   IN THE INITIAL CALL Marcus, *Girls to the Front*, 232.

147   "WE STILL SAY IF YOU ARE" Ibid., 252.

147   "HERE IS A LIST" Catalog with Hanna's handwriting reprinted in Darms, *Riot Grrrl Collection*, 161.

147   "TO PUSH BEYOND" Rebecca Walker, "Becoming the Third Wave," *Ms.*, Jan.–Feb. 1992, 39.

148   "WE'RE FRESHENING UP FEMINISM" "Spice and All Things: In Their Own Words," *The Guardian*, March 11, 1997, A3.

INTERLUDE: CYBERSPACE

149   "VIRTUAL COMMUNITY" Howard Rheingold, *The Virtual Community: Homesteading on the Virtual Frontier* (Reading, Mass.: Addison-Wesley, 1993).

150   A MINUTE WITH COATE Coate, interview with author, Sept. 24, 2019.

151   "SPANNED THE WORLDS" Fred Turner, *From Counterculture to Cyberculture: Stewart Brand, the Whole Earth Network, and the Rise of Digital Utopianism* (Chicago: University of Chicago Press, 2006), 5.

152   BRILLIANT WOULD SUPPLY Katie Hafner, *The Well: A Story of Love, Death, and Real Life in the Seminal Online Community* (New York: Carroll & Graf, 2001), 9–10.

153   THEY WERE BUILDING A NEW Jim Windolf, "Sex, Drugs, and Soybeans," *Vanity Fair*, May 2007.

154   PICOSPAN, THE CONFERENCING SOFTWARE Hafner, *Well*, 16.

154   HE HAD SET THE SUBSCRIPTION FEE Ibid., 13.

154   "YOU OWN YOUR OWN WORDS" Turner, *From Counterculture to Cyberculture*, 145.

155   "TO WELCOME NEWCOMERS" Rheingold, *Virtual Community*, 26.

156   "A GROUP MIND" Howard Rheingold, "A Slice of My Life in My Virtual Community," in *High Noon on the Electronic Frontier: Conceptual Issues in Cyberspace,* ed. Peter Ludlow (Cambridge, Mass.: MIT Press, 1996), 422; Rheingold, interview with author, Sept. 20, 2019.

156   "THE COMMUNITY JUST DUG ITSELF" Gans, interview with author, Oct. 3, 2019.

156   TOPIC #103 FROM BACKSTAGE "Temperatures Are Rising," Backstage, Topic #103, Feb. 22, 1988.

157   "THE THEORY GOING IN" Hafner, *Well,* 85.

157   MARK ETHAN SMITH Ibid., 34–40. In her book, Hafner used female pronouns for Smith, but in a blog post following the publication of *The Well,* Smith, writing before the days of gender-neutral pronouns, objected to being identified in this way: "Although my sex is female, something I have never denied, I stopped being a woman in 1981, several years before I discovered The Well, and I never became a man, nor do I wish to be known as a man, or, for that matter, as a woman" (www.angelfire.com/bc3/dissident/).

158   "MOSTLY EVERYONE TRIED TO GET" John Seabrook, *Deeper: Adventures on the Net* (New York: Simon & Schuster, 1997), 153.

158   BY THE LATE 1980s Turner, *From Counterculture to Cyberculture,* 152.

159   SHE LOVED HER FORUM Horn, interview with author, Oct. 4, 2019.

159   "WASN'T GOING TO BRING PEACE" Stacy Horn, *Cyberville: Clicks, Culture, and the Creation of an Online Town* (New York: Warner Books, 1998), 247.

159   "REAR-VIEW MIRROR THINKING" Marshall McLuhan and Quentin Fiore, *The Medium Is the Massage* (New York: Bantam Books, 1967), 74.

159   TEX POINTED TO A NUMBER OF DIFFERENT WAYS John Coate, "A Village Called the WELL," *Whole Earth Review* (Fall 1988): 84–87.

160   "TRANSACTIONS, RELATIONSHIPS, AND THOUGHT ITSELF" John
Perry Barlow, "A Declaration of the Independence of
Cyberspace," Davos, Switzerland, Feb. 8, 1996, www.eff.org
/cyberspace-independence.

161   "HAS BEEN REALIZED" Eric E. Schmidt, "Eric Schmidt on
How to Build a Better Web," *The New York Times,* Dec. 7,
2015, www.nytimes.com/2015/12/07/opinion/eric-schmidt
-on-how-to-build-a-better-web.html.

161   "LIKE SWITCHING FROM A SCHWINN" Rheingold, *Virtual
Community,* 24.

161   ITS FOUNDER, STEVE CASE Howard Rheingold, "What the
WELL's Rise and Fall Tells Us About Online Community,"
The Atlantic, July 6, 2012, www.theatlantic.com/technology
/archive/2012/07/what-the-wells-rise-and-fall-tell-us-about
-online-community/259504/.

162   "THE ODDS ARE ALWAYS GOOD" Rheingold, *Virtual
Community,* 6.

CHAPTER 7: THE SQUARE—CAIRO, 2011

163   "HIS LOWER LIP" Wael Ghonim, *Revolution 2.0: The Power of
the People Is Greater Than the People in Power* (Boston:
Houghton Mifflin Harcourt, 2013), 54.

164   "AN INVITATION TO PAY ATTENTION" Susan Sontag, *Regarding
the Pain of Others* (New York: Farrar, Straus and Giroux, 2003),
104.

164   FAMILIAR WITH THE SITE'S FUNCTIONALITY Ghonim,
Revolution 2.0, 43.

164   "TODAY THEY KILLED KHALED" Ibid., 60.

164   GHONIM NEVER SET OUT Biographical information from
Ghonim, interview with author, April 10, 2016.

165   "EMBODIED WHO I WAS" Ghonim, *Revolution 2.0,* 25.

165   "I FIND VIRTUAL LIFE" Ibid., 24.

165   IN JUST THE FIRST DAY Ibid., 62.

165   "A LANGUAGE CLOSER TO MY HEART" Ibid., 91.

166   "My name is Khaled" Ibid., 69.

166   Abdelrahman Ayyash Ayyash, interview with author, Nov. 18, 2019.

166   "Would you marry a girl" Linda Herrera, *Revolution in the Age of Social Media: The Egyptian Popular Insurrection and the Internet* (New York: Verso, 2014), 15.

168   It wouldn't be too different Ghonim, *Revolution 2.0*, 67.

169   "its own culture" Ibid., 84.

169   "These people are not zombies" Wael Ghonim interview, "The Facebook Dilemma," *Frontline*, May 16, 2018, transcript posted online: www.pbs.org/wgbh/frontline/interview/wael -ghonim/.

170   Ghonim's anonymity was something Ghonim, *Revolution 2.0*, 102.

170   "Down, down with Hosni Mubarak" Ibid., 104.

171   "If Bouazizi had burned himself" Ibid., 133.

171   "I Wish" Ibid., 150.

173   He had made the mistake Ibid., 204.

173   "I was just a loudspeaker" Wael Ghonim interview, Dream TV, Feb. 7, 2011, video cached as part of "Wael Ghonim Anointed Voice of the Revolution by Tahrir Square Faithful," *The Guardian*, Feb. 8, 2011, www.theguardian.com /world/2011/feb/08/wael-ghonim-tahrir-square.

174   A Facebook page Ghonim, *Revolution 2.0*, 301.

174   "the Google guy" Mark Landler, "Obama Seeks Reset in Arab World," *The New York Times*, May 12, 2011. Obama is quoted as saying, "What I want is for the kids on the street to win and for the Google guy to become president."

175   "Tahrir's pulse" Ghonim, *Revolution 2.0*, 269.

176   "favor declaration" Siva Vaidhyanathan, *Antisocial Media: How Facebook Disconnects Us and Undermines Democracy* (Oxford: Oxford University Press, 2018), 144.

177   "Are we representing society" Mansour, interview with author, Nov. 20, 2019.

177   "like teenage boyfriends with noble intentions" Thanassis Cambanis, *Once upon a Revolution: An Egyptian*

Story (New York: Simon & Schuster, 2015), 106; Cambanis, interview with author, Nov. 14, 2019.

178 "THE BLOODTHIRSTY HEARTS OF THE BOLSHEVIKS" Cambanis, *Once upon a Revolution,* 5.

178 GHONIM RECEIVED A REPORTED $2.5 MILLION "Wael Ghonim's New Book 'Revolution 2.0' Will Benefit Charity Work in Egypt," *MTV News,* May 12, 2011, web.archive.org /web/20120103163040/http://act.mtv.com/posts/wael -ghonims-new-book-revolution-2-0-will-benefit-charity -work-in-egypt/.

178 I WAS WORKING ON AN ARTICLE Gal Beckerman, "The New Arab Conversation," *Columbia Journalism Review,* Jan./Feb. 2007.

179 "RUNNING FOR OFFICE MEANT YOU" Mahmoud Salem, "You Can't Stop the Signal," *World Policy Journal* (Fall 2014).

180 SALEM RAN, HE TOLD ME Salem, interview with author, Nov. 12, 2019.

180 "EVEN THOUGH IT IS NOT STANDARD" Cambanis, *Once upon a Revolution,* 200.

181 A FILM PROGRAM Ibid., 164.

182 "WHAT TAHRIR IGNITED, RABAA EXTINGUISHED" David D. Kirkpatrick, *Into the Hands of the Soldiers: Freedom and Chaos in Egypt and the Middle East* (New York: Viking, 2018), 286.

182 "I WAS WRONG" Wael Ghonim, "Let's Design Social Media That Drives Real Change," TED Talk, Geneva, Switzerland, Dec. 2015, www.ted.com/talks/wael_ghonim_let_s_design _social_media_that_drives_real_change#t-12847.

182 WHEN HE FINALLY DID From Ghonim, *Frontline* interview, May 16, 2018: "Actually, I remember it was funny at the time, because I asked to take a photo with him, and I don't put online photos with people I meet. I find that—I don't do that. Let me not judge others who do it; I just don't do that. But I think Mark was not comfortable with the idea, and he said, 'Oh, we'll take the photo and mail it to you.' And I said, 'Sure.' I knew they were never going to mail it to me, and he never did."

183   FELL INTO A DEPRESSION Wael Ghonim, "Egypt's Revolution,
       My Life, and My Broken Soul," Medium, March 20, 2018,
       ghonim.medium.com/egypts-revolution-my-life-and-my
       -broken-soul-91fae189d778.

184   "DO YOU THINK I'M AN ATTENTION WHORE" Signal voice
       message to author, Dec. 2, 2019.

185   THE CONVERSATION TURNED TO FACEBOOK "Alaa Abd El
       Fattah: There's No Solution—We Need to Talk," *Mada*,
       May 11, 2019, www.madamasr.com/en/2019/05/11/feature
       /politics/video-alaa-abd-el-fattahs-interview-with-mada
       -masr-part-1/.

CHAPTER 8: THE TORCHES—CHARLOTTESVILLE, 2017

186   "THEY ARE TRYING" Events of May 13, 2017, captured on
       Richard Spencer's Periscope account in uploaded video: www
       .pscp.tv/RichardBSpencer/1mnGeEwMvdaGX?t=653.

187   THE STATUE OF ROBERT E. LEE On July 9, 2021, both the
       Robert E. Lee statue and the monument to Stonewall Jackson
       were removed; Hawes Spencer and Michael Levenson,
       "Charlottesville Removes Statue at Center of 2017 White
       Nationalist Rally, *The New York Times*, July 11, 2021.

187   IT DIDN'T LAST VERY LONG Jonah Engel Bromwich, "White
       Nationalists Wield Torches at Confederate Statue Rally," *The
       New York Times*, May 14, 2017.

187   SPENCER WAS BEING INTERVIEWED YouTube video of Spencer
       being punched: www.youtube.com/watch?v=aFh08JEKDYk.

188   SLAMMED HIS FIST Shane Bauer, "A Punch in the Face
       Was Just the Start of the Alt-Right's Attack on a Berkeley
       Protester," *Mother Jones*, April 27, 2017, www.motherjones
       .com/politics/2017/04/berkeley-rally-alt-right-antifa-punch/.

189   "WE DON'T WANT TO BE SEEN" John Sepulvado and Bert
       Johnson, "Californian Who Helped Lead Charlottesville
       Protests Used Berkeley as a Test Run," KQED, Aug. 14, 2017,
       www.kqed.org/news/11611600/californian-who-helped
       -organize-charlottesville-protests-used-berkeley-as-a-test-run.

189   "FUN TO ENGAGE IN TROLL STORMS" "Unite the Right: Towards Alt-Right Activism," *Occidental Dissent,* July 10, 2017.

190   "EVERY GENERATION HAS A FIGHT" Dean Seal, "GOP's Stewart Rallies Against Lee Statue Removal," *Daily Progress,* Feb. 21, 2017.

190   WHITE SUPREMACIST SERVERS The leaks obtained by Unicorn Riot are on their website and its searchable index of hundreds of Discord servers: unicornriot.ninja/2017/charlottesville -violence-planned-discord-servers-unicorn-riot-reports/.

191   THE SITE HAD ABOUT 45 MILLION USERS Abram Brown, "Discord Was Once the Alt-Right's Favorite Chat App. Now It's Gone Mainstream and Scored a New $3.5 Billion Valuation," *Forbes,* June 30, 2020.

191   KEEGAN HANKES Hankes, interview with author, March 23, 2020.

192   "PLEASE STOP THE FIGHTING" All Discord posts from the #general_01 channel of the Charlottesville 2.0 server, which can be found on the Unicorn Riot website: discordleaks .unicornriot.ninja/discord/channel/33.

193   "THE ALT-LIGHT IS DEFINED" Greg Johnson, "White Nationalism, the Alt Right, and the Alt Light," *Counter-Currents,* Jan. 4, 2017, counter-currents.com/2017/01/white -nationalism-the-alt-right-and-the-alt-light/.

195   TALKED ABOUT THE JOYS Chris Schiano, "LEAKED: The Planning Meeting That Led Up to Neo-Nazi Terrorism in Charlottesville," Unicorn Riot, Aug. 16, 2017, unicornriot .ninja/2017/leaked-planning-meetings-led-neo-nazi -terrorism-charlottesville/.

198   PROUD BOYS INITIATION RITUAL Anti-Defamation League entry for "Proud Boys," includes a description of the initiation process: www.adl.org/proudboys.

199   THE ANTAGONISM BETWEEN THE ALT-RIGHT "Feuding Rallies in DC Reveal Far-Right Group's Different Priorities," Anti-Defamation League, June 27, 2017, www.adl.org/blog/feuding -rallies-in-dc-reveal-far-right-groups-different-priorities.

200   "I AM NOT AFRAID" "New Alt-Right 'Fight Club' Ready for

Street Violence," Southern Poverty Law Center, Aug. 8, 2017, www.splcenter.org/fighting-hate/intelligence-report/2017 /new-alt-right-%E2%80%9Cfight-club%E2%80%9D-ready -street-violence.

200 ENOCH ALSO INFAMOUSLY CONFESSED Southern Poverty Law Center entry on Michael "Enoch" Peinovich, www.splcenter .org/fighting-hate/extremist-files/individual/michael-enoch -peinovich.

202 "EVERYTHING HAS TO BE BUILT" Condis, interview with author, Feb. 5, 2020.

203 ERIKA WAS EVENTUALLY REVEALED Glenna Gordon, "American Women of the Far Right," *The New York Review of Books,* Dec. 13, 2018.

204 "A NORMIE'S GUIDE" Andrew Anglin, "A Normie's Guide to the Alt-Right," The Daily Stormer, Aug. 31, 2016.

206 THAT MORNING, THE ALT-RIGHT The account of the day's events is from the independent report carried out by U.S. Attorney Timothy Heaphy, who delivered his 220-page findings in December 2017.

207 "MY RECOMMENDATION: DISPERSE" Richard Spencer (@RichardBSpencer), Twitter, Aug. 12, 2017, 12:38 p.m., twitter.com/RichardBSpencer/status/896410449654185984.

209 "I KNOW THAT SOME OF THE GROUPS" Feidt, interview with author, Feb. 7, 2020.

209 TWENTY-FOUR HOURS TO REGISTER Christine Hauser, "GoDaddy Severs Ties with Daily Stormer After Charlottesville Article," *The New York Times,* Aug. 15, 2017.

209 DELETED MORE THAN A HUNDRED Brown, "Discord Was Once the Alt-Right's Favorite Chat App."

209 JASON KESSLER EXPERIENCED Zack Beauchamp, "The Organizer of the Charlottesville Rally Just Got Humiliated by His Own Father," *Vox,* Aug. 15, 2018, www.vox.com/policy -and-politics/2018/8/15/17692552/charlottesville-unite-the -right-jason-kessler-father.

209 "I THINK THERE IS BLAME" "Full Text: Trump's Comments on White Supremacists, 'Alt-Left' in Charlottesville," *Politico,*

Aug. 15, 2017, www.politico.com/story/2017/08/15/full-text
-trump-comments-white-supremacists-alt-left-transcript
-241662.

CHAPTER 9: THE VIRUS—NEW YORK CITY, 2020

211 SHE LOVES ALGORITHMS Lee, interviews with author, Nov. 12
and Dec. 4, 2020.

212 "RED DAWN" Matthew Mosk, Kaitlyn Folmer, and Josh
Margolin, "As Coronavirus Threatened Invasion, a New 'Red
Dawn' Team Tried to Save America," ABC News, July 28,
2020.

213 "OPPORTUNITY TO PROVIDE THOUGHTS" Email from Caneva,
Feb. 16, 2020. The leaked text of the "Red Dawn" emails,
covering January 28 to March 17, 2020, was shared by *The
New York Times,* int.nyt.com/data/documenthelper/6879
-2020-covid-19-red-dawn-rising/66f590d5cd41e11bea0f
/optimized/full.pdf#page=1.

213 "A LARGE GROUP OF FRIENDS" Email from Gerald W. Parker
Jr., March 12, 2020.

213 "AM GOING THROUGH AN INTERESTING" Email from Richard
Hatchett, Jan. 28, 2020.

213 "A BAD FLU YEAR" Email from Matthew Hepburn, Jan. 28,
2020.

213 "CERTAINLY NO PUBLIC HEALTH EXPERT" Email from Mecher,
Jan. 28, 2020.

213 "I WISH THERE WAS" Email from Mecher, Jan. 29, 2020.

214 "A PROXY FOR A YOUNG" Email from Mecher, Feb. 20, 2020.

214 "THE WORST FORM OF SOCIAL GATHERING" Email from Lee,
Feb. 18, 2020.

215 "LOOKS LIKE BY APRIL" Shannon K. Crawford, "What
President Trump Said About the Coronavirus Versus What
Bob Woodward Reported in Interviews: Timeline," ABC
News, Sept. 10, 2020.

215 "SO SPREADING AND ITS WIDE SCOPE" Email from Lee,
Feb. 23, 2020.

215 "Eva is this true?!" Email from Kadlec, Feb. 23, 2020.

215 "We cannot prepare for the future" Email from Lee, Feb. 10, 2020.

216 in a briefing to journalists Transcript for the CDC Telebriefing Update on COVID-19, Feb. 25, 2020, www.cdc .gov/media/releases/2020/t0225-cdc-telebriefing-covid-19 .html.

216 "My feeling is that" Email from Lee, Feb. 7, 2020.

216 "It might be eye opening" Email from Mecher, March 3, 2020.

217 "The unknown is what" Email from Lee, Feb. 28, 2020.

217 "As a state public health official" Email from Gruber, March 10, 2020.

217 "Frustrating doesn't capture it" Email from McDonald, March 7, 2020.

217 "Maybe we should use" Email from Gerald W. Parker Jr., March 11, 2020.

217 "We should be treating" Email from Redacted, March 5, 2020.

217 "I think a tree" Email from Lee, March 5, 2020.

218 "I ran a few models" Email from Lee, March 3, 2020.

218 "I really learn a lot" Email from Lee, March 12, 2020.

218 "I notice a lot" Email from Redacted, March 11, 2020.

218 "I don't think it would be prudent" Email from Mecher, March 13, 2020.

219 "to take action before the storm" Email from Mecher, March 17, 2020.

219 "We all used to be" Lawler, interview with author, Nov. 15, 2020.

220 "I was like, I totally see" Choo, interview with author, Nov. 10, 2020.

220 "a hotbed of activity" Spencer, interview with author, Sept. 17, 2020.

221 "The bright fluorescent lights" Craig Spencer (@Craig_A_Spencer), Twitter, March 23, 2020, 12:09 a.m., twitter.com/craig_a_spencer/status/1242302403338219520.

221   IT BEGAN FOR HER Samantha Swindler, "Portland Doctor Esther Choo Responds to Racism in the Emergency Room," *The Oregonian* (Portland, Ore.), Aug. 15, 2017.

223   "ONE OF THE BIGGEST GAME CHANGERS" Libby Cathey, "Timeline: Tracking Trump Alongside Scientific Developments on Hydroxychloroquine," ABC News, Aug. 8, 2020.

223   ONE MAN IN ARIZONA Neil Vigdor, "Man Fatally Poisons Himself While Self-Medicating for Coronavirus, Doctor Says," *The New York Times,* March 24, 2020.

223   ONE SURVEY REVEALED Lisa Singh et al., "A First Look at COVID-19 Information and Misinformation Sharing on Twitter," arXiv, April 1, 2020.

223   ANOTHER ANALYSIS EXAMINED 200 MILLION Virginia Alvino Young, "Nearly Half of the Twitter Accounts Discussing 'Re-opening America' May Be Bots," Carnegie Mellon University, press release, May 20, 2020.

223   "A LONG-TERM PROJECT" Kass, interview with author, Nov. 17, 2020.

224   "IT'S A REMARKABLE MISMATCH" Bergstrom, interview with author, Sept. 11, 2020.

226   "THERE'S BEEN A TON" Rasmussen, interview with author, July 3, 2020.

226   AMERICANS STAYED HOME Kevin Schaul, Brittany Renee Mayes, and Bonnie Berkowitz, "Where Americans Are Still Staying Home the Most," *The Washington Post,* May 6, 2020.

226   WHEN A LARGE-SCALE SURVEY David Lazer et al., "The State of the Nation: A 50-State Covid-19 Survey," Northeastern University, April 20, 2020.

228   SHE HAD JUST BEEN CONVICTED Bill Rankin, "Georgia Tech Continues to Deny Professor Lee Access to Fight COVID-19," *The Atlanta Journal-Constitution,* April 23, 2020.

229   IN ONE ARTICLE Jeffrey Mervis, "Georgia Tech Researcher Pays a High Price for Mismanaging an NSF Grant," *Science,* April 29, 2020.

229   "DO YOU HAVE ANY ADDITIONAL" Email from Lee, March 23,

2020. This batch of Red Dawn emails was given to me by Lee, including selections of the group's communication from March 19 to July 24, 2020. Lee redacted many of the names of other participants.

230   "Eva makes a very good point" Email from RH, March 19, 2020.

230   "We also now have" Email from CMH, April 15, 2020.

230   "The 4-max model per table" Email from Lee, April 16, 2020.

230   "One question I have" Email from WL, April 17, 2020.

231   "I don't know what" Email from Lee, May 4, 2020.

231   "would never see the light of day" Jason Dearen and Mike Stobbe, "Trump Administration Buries Detailed CDC Advice on Reopening," Associated Press, May 6, 2020.

232   "Every time that the science" Noah Weiland, "How the C.D.C. Lost Its Voice Under Trump," *The New York Times*, Dec. 17, 2020.

232   "If asking for a national strategy" Email from Lee, July 18, 2020.

233   "a disgruntled employee" Morgan Chalfant, "Trump Attacks Whistleblower Bright as 'Disgruntled Employee,'" *The Hill*, May 14, 2020.

234   Lee pleaded with the judge Bill Rankin, "Judge Thanks and Sentences Acclaimed GA Tech Coronavirus Researcher," *The Atlanta Journal-Constitution*, Aug. 12, 2020.

234   "From what I've read" Ibid.

234   "an ad hoc consortium" Rankin, "Georgia Tech Continues to Deny Professor Lee Access to Fight COVID-19."

234   I had a conversation with William Foege Foege, interview with author, Nov. 12, 2020.

235   "The biggest challenge in a century" Brett Murphy and Letitia Stein, "'It Is a Slaughter': Public Health Champion Asks CDC Director to Expose White House, Orchestrate His Own Firing," *USA Today*, Oct. 6, 2020.

Chapter 10: The Names—Minneapolis, 2020

237   Miski Noor didn't need Noor, interview with author,
Oct. 22, 2020.

238   On June 6 alone Larry Buchanan, Quoctrung Bui, and
Jugal K. Patel, "Black Lives Matter May Be the Biggest
Movement in U.S. History," *The New York Times,* July 3, 2020,
www.nytimes.com/interactive/2020/07/03/us/george-floyd
-protests-crowd-size.html.

238   "the largest movement in U.S. history" Ibid.

239   a company like Lululemon Noah Manskar, "Lululemon
Slammed for Promoting Event to 'Resist Capitalism,'"
New York Post, Sept. 11, 2020.

239   Or the vision of Jamie Dimon Thornton McEnery, "Jamie
Dimon Drops into Mt. Kisco Chase Branch, Takes a Knee
with Staff," *New York Post,* June 5, 2020.

239   Americans said they supported Kim Parker, Juliana
Menasce Horowitz, and Monica Anderson, "Amid Protests,
Majorities Across Racial and Ethnic Groups Express Support
for the Black Lives Matter Movement," Pew Research Center,
June 2020.

241   Still, the hashtag barely registered Statistics on
Twitter usage from Monica Anderson and Paul Hitlin, "Social
Media Conversations About Race," Pew Research Center,
Aug. 2016, www.pewresearch.org/internet/2016/08/15/social
-media-conversations-about-race/; Niraj Chokshi, "How
Twitter Hashtag Came to Define Black Lives Matter
Movement," *The New York Times,* Aug. 23, 2016.

242   "I think what people" Cullors, interview with author,
Oct. 25, 2019.

242   not having "copyrighted" Cullors used this term in her
interview with me though I believe she was thinking of a
"trademark," which one would use to claim ownership over a
logo or phrase.

242   "extremely well-suited to internet-based" Deen
Freelon, Charlton D. McIlwain, and Meredith D. Clark,

"Beyond the Hashtag," Center for Media & Social Impact, School of Communications, American University, Washington, D.C., Feb. 2016, cmsimpact.org/wp-content /uploads/2016/03/beyond_the_hashtags_2016.pdf.

243 "IF THERE WAS NOT A DEATH" McIlwain, interview with author, Dec. 11, 2019.

243 EVEN OBAMA, AT THE END Michael D. Shear and Liam Stack, "Obama Urges Activists to Do More Than 'Yelling,'" *The New York Times,* April 24, 2016.

243 BY THE FIFTH ANNIVERSARY John Eligon, "There Were Changes, but for Black Drivers, Life Is Much the Same," *The New York Times,* Aug. 7, 2019.

244 SHE FOUND A GROUP Gilmer, interviews with author, Dec. 20, 2019, and Oct. 2, 2020.

245 "SOCIAL MEDIA IS CONSTANTLY" Kate Aronoff, "Inside the Dream Defenders' Social Media Blackout," *Waging Nonviolence,* Sept. 30, 2015, wagingnonviolence.org/2015/09 /inside-dream-defenders-social-media-blackout/.

245 EVEN DARNELL MOORE, AN ACTIVIST Moore, interview with author, Jan. 10, 2020.

246 DERAY MCKESSON WAS A CASE IN POINT Jay Caspian Kang, "'Our Demand Is Simple: Stop Killing Us,'" *The New York Times Magazine,* May 10, 2015.

246 THE BLUE VEST WORKED Ibid.

246 GARZA WROTE A LONG SCREED Alicia Garza, "A Herstory of the #BlackLivesMatter Movement," *The Feminist Wire,* Oct. 7, 2014, thefeministwire.com/2014/10/blacklivesmatter-2/.

247 "I'VE ALWAYS THOUGHT OF TWITTER" DeRay Mckesson, *On the Other Side of Freedom: The Case for Hope* (New York: Viking, 2018), 168.

247 THERE WAS NO NEED Noah Berlatsky, "Hashtag Activism Isn't a Copout," *The Atlantic,* Jan. 7, 2015, www.theatlantic.com /politics/archive/2015/01/not-just-hashtag-activism-why -social-media-matters-to-protestors/384215/.

249 "WE MUST RE-EMBRACE" Agnew spoke at a conference, "The Black Radical Tradition in Our Time," Jan. 7, 2016, Temple

University, blackcommentator.com/637/637_up_you_mighty
_race_selah_guest.html.

249   THEY WERE TRYING TO SOLVE Taylor, interview with author,
       Dec. 20, 2019.

249   MISKI AND SIX FRIENDS Jenna Worthem, "The Vision
       Forward," *The New York Times Magazine,* Aug. 30, 2020.

250   IN ONE OF THEIR EARLIEST WINS Jon Collins, "Mpls. Council
       Moves to Shift $1.1 Million from Police Department," MPR
       News, Dec. 1, 2018, www.mprnews.org/story/2018/11/30
       /mpls-budget-amendment-removes-million-dollars-police.

252   BLACK VISIONS ALSO STAGED A SIT-IN "Minneapolis Mayor
       Booed out of Rally," *The New York Times,* June 6, 2020, www
       .nytimes.com/video/us/politics/125225307178355
       /minneapolis-mayor-booed-out-of-rally.html.

252   "OUR COMMITMENT IS TO END" Brandt Williams, "Veto-Proof
       Majority of Minneapolis Council Members Supports
       Dismantling Police Department," MPR News, June 7, 2020,
       www.mprnews.org/story/2020/06/07/vetoproof-majority
       -minneapolis-council-members-gives-support-dismantling
       -police-department.

253   "BLACK LIVES MATTER MEANS SOMETHING" Leach, interview
       with author, Nov. 3, 2020.

253   THE MAYOR OF ATLANTA Adele Peters, "This Atlanta Jail Will
       Transform into a Center for Justice and Equity," *Fast
       Company,* June 15, 2020, www.fastcompany.com/90515296
       /this-atlanta-jail-will-transform-into-a-center-for-justice
       -and-equity.

253   IN NEW YORK, THE STATE LEGISLATURE Christopher Robbins,
       "New York State Legislature Votes to Repeal Law 50-A That
       Shields Police from Scrutiny," *Gothamist,* June 9, 2020,
       gothamist.com/news/new-york-state-legislature-votes-repeal
       -law-50-shields-police-scrunity.

255   "THOSE OF US WHO HAVE BEEN" Frimpong, interviews with
       author, Dec. 23, 2019, and Sept. 29, 2020.

256   AN ACCOUNTING OF ALL THE DEMONSTRATIONS
       "Demonstrations and Political Violence in America: New

Data for Summer 2020," ACLED, Sept. 2020, acleddata
.com/2020/09/03/demonstrations-political-violence-in
-america-new-data-for-summer-2020/.

256 MUTATIONS OF THE MEME Karen Attiah, "Breonna Taylor
Deserves Better Than Memes and Barbecues," *The Washington
Post,* Aug. 22, 2020.

256 BUT MAYBE MOST DISPIRITING Deja Thomas and Juliana
Menasce Horowitz, "Support for Black Lives Matter Has
Decreased Since June but Remains Strong Among Black
Americans," Pew Research Center, Sept. 16, 2020, www
.pewresearch.org/fact-tank/2020/09/16/support-for-black
-lives-matter-has-decreased-since-june-but-remains-strong
-among-black-americans/.

256 RELEASED A POLL Eric Roper, "Poll: Cuts to Minneapolis
Ranks Lack Majority Support," Minneapolis *Star Tribune,*
Aug. 15, 2020.

257 THE COMMISSION VOTED TO OVERRIDE Astead W. Herndon,
"A Quiet Retreat from 'Defund' in Minneapolis," *The New York
Times,* Sept. 27, 2020.

257 THE REFERENDUM ON ABOLISHING THE POLICE As of this
writing, a coalition of activist groups, including Black
Visions, appears to have gathered enough signatures to get
a referendum on the ballot in November 2021 that would
propose major changes to policing in the city, including
creating a new public safety department and making it
possible for the city council to eliminate the police department
as currently constituted; Liz Navratil, "Minneapolis Residents
Will Likely Vote in November on Future of City's Police
Department,"Minneapolis *Star Tribune,* May 14, 2021.

258 4.5 PERCENT OF THE POLICE BUDGET Jenny Gross and
John Eligon, "Minneapolis City Council Votes to Remove
$8 Million from Police Budget," *The New York Times,* Dec. 10,
2020.

Epilogue: Tables

259   HER BOOK WAS A RESPONSE Hannah Arendt, *The Human Condition* (Chicago: University of Chicago Press, 1958), 53.

261   "OVER THE LAST 15 YEARS" Mark Zuckerberg, "A Privacy-Focused Vision for Social Networking," Facebook, March 12, 2019, www.facebook.com/notes/mark-zuckerberg/a-privacy -focused-vision-for-social-networking/10156700570096634/.

262   "IDENTIFYING PLATFORMS THAT DEPART FROM" Ethan Zuckerman and Chand Rajendra-Nicolucci, "Beyond Facebook Logic: Help Us Map Alternative Social Media!," Knight First Amendment Institute at Columbia University, Oct. 8, 2020.

262   THE DOINGS IN A NEIGHBORHOOD Chand Rajendra-Nicolucci and Ethan Zuckerman, "Local Logic: It's Not Always a Beautiful Day in the Neighborhood," Knight First Amendment Institute at Columbia University, Nov. 30, 2020.

263   WHEN I ASKED HIM Zuckerman, interview with author, Dec. 3, 2020.

264   IN ONE OF THE EARLIEST USES Chris Horton, "The Simple but Ingenious System Taiwan Uses to Crowdsource Its Laws," *MIT Technology Review,* Aug. 21, 2018.

265   "I WAS WATCHING" Megill, interview with author, Jan. 8, 2021.

266   "IF I'M DISSATISFIED WITH THIS WORLD" Anna Wiener, "Taking Back Our Privacy," *The New Yorker,* Oct. 19, 2020.

267   "THIS IS LIKE ANOTHER TYPE OF FAMILY" James Wagner, "'They Just Get It': How Women in M.L.B. Found Support in a Group Text," *The New York Times,* Oct. 19, 2020.

268   "SHIFT TO PRIVATE, WHERE" Mina, interview with author, Dec. 23, 2020.

268   WECHAT USERS ARE BEING WATCHED Louise Matsakis, "How WeChat Censored the Coronavirus Pandemic," *Wired,* Aug. 27, 2020.

Index

Frimpong, Allen Kwabena, 255
Frost, John, 46, 48–49, 50–51
"Futurist Men's Clothing: A
    Manifesto" (Balla), 73
"Futurist Painting: Technical
    Manifesto" (Boccioni), 59
"The Futurist Reconstruction of
    the Universe" (anon.), 73–74
Futurists. *See also* manifestos by
    Futurists
  establishment of, 58
  feminism and, 64–66, 68,
    75–76, 269
  internal as well as external
    change, 65
  modernity and, 59
  in Russia, 64
  theater of contempt, 55, 56–57,
    62, 70
  Venice and, 61–62
  violence as way to change, 55,
    56, 60–61, 69, 70, 73
  World War I and, 69–70, 71–73
"Futurist Synthesis of War"
    (Papini), 70
"Futurist Synthetic Theater"
    (anon.), 73

G
Gabai, Galina, 120
Galaup de Chasteuil, François, 14
Galileo Galilei, 17, 24–26
Gans, David, 156
Garner, Eric, 241
Garza, Alicia, 241, 246
Gaskin, Ina May, 152

Gaskin, Stephen, 152, 153, 154
Gassendi, Pierre, 14, 32
Ghonim, Wael. *See also* "We Are
    All Khaled Said"
  after failure of revolution,
    182–184
  attacks on, 178
  basic facts about, 164–165
  death of Said and, 163–164
  protests and, 170–171
  Tahrir Square and, 173–174
Gibson, William, 160
Gilmer, Rachel, 244–245, 247,
    249, 254–255
girl bands, 130, 131–132, 138,
    144, 145
Girl Germs, 128, 130–131, 136
girls and 1990s feminism, 127,
    128
girl zines. *See also* specific titles
  compared to samizdat, 127
  creators of, 137–138
  as letters, 139
  as means of owning
    vulnerability, 135
  on media exploitation of, 142
  as outlets for concerns and
    rage, 126, 137, 147–148
  as participatory
    communication, 134, 135
  proliferation of, 133, 135–136,
    137, 146–147
  visual vocabulary of, 136
Gold Coast (British colony)
  British cocoa cartel, 89
  British rule, 80, 81
  class divisions in, 80, 85, 86

About the Author

——————

GAL BECKERMAN is a writer and editor at *The New York Times Book Review* and the author of the widely acclaimed *When They Come for Us, We'll Be Gone,* which won the National Jewish Book Award and the Sami Rohr Prize and was named a best book of the year by *The New Yorker* and *The Washington Post.* He has a PhD in media studies from Columbia University and writes for many publications, including *The New Republic* and *The Wall Street Journal.* He lives in Brooklyn with his wife and two daughters.

galbeckerman.com

Twitter: @galbeckerman

About the Type

This book was set in Caslon, a typeface first designed in 1722 by William Caslon (1692–1766). Its widespread use by most English printers in the early eighteenth century soon supplanted the Dutch typefaces that had formerly prevailed. The roman is considered a "workhorse" typeface due to its pleasant, open appearance, while the italic is exceedingly decorative.

21982320220027